STAR WARS®

❖ L E G A C Y ❖

❖ LEGACY ❖

(Forty years after the Battle of Yavin and beyond)

As this era began, Luke Skywalker had unified the Jedi Order into a cohesive group of powerful Jedi Knights. It was a time of relative peace, yet darkness approached on the horizon. Now, Skywalker's descendants face new and resurgent threats to the galaxy, and to the balance of the Force.

The events in this story begin approximately 137 years after the Battle of Yavin.

STAR WARS®
LEGACY

VOLUME FIVE
❧ THE HIDDEN TEMPLE ❧

STORY
John Ostrander and Jan Duursema

SCRIPT
John Ostrander

PENCILS
Jan Duursema

INKS
Dan Parsons

COLORS
Brad Anderson

LETTERS
Michael Heisler

COVER ART
Jan Duursema and Brad Anderson

DARK HORSE BOOKS®

PUBLISHER
Mike Richardson

COLLECTION DESIGNER
Scott Cook

ART DIRECTOR
Lia Ribacchi

ASSOCIATE EDITOR
Dave Marshall

ASSISTANT EDITOR
Freddye Lins

EDITOR
Randy Stradley

Special thanks to Elaine Mederer, Jann Moorhead, David Anderman, Leland Chee, Sue Rostoni, and Carol Roeder at Lucas Licensing.

STAR WARS: LEGACY VOLUME FIVE—THE HIDDEN TEMPLE

This volume collects issues twenty-three through twenty-six of the Dark Horse comic-book series *Star Wars: Legacy*.

Published by
Dark Horse Books
A division of Dark Horse Comics, Inc.
10956 SE Main Street
Milwaukie, OR 97222

darkhorse.com
starwars.com

To find a comics shop in your area, call the Comic Shop Locator Service toll-free at 1-888-266-4226

First edition: February 2009
ISBN 978-1-59582-224-6

3 5 7 9 10 8 6 4 2
Printed at Midas Printing International, Ltd., Huizhou, China

After a desperate escape from the clutches of Emperor Darth Krayt and his Sith minions, Cade Skywalker learns that he owes his freedom to the help of two of his bounty-hunter rivals, Chak and Kee, who had threatened his life just weeks before—and to his mother, Imperial spy Morrigan Corde, whom Cade has never met and has long thought dead.

But no mother-and-son reunion is in the offing—Corde has her own agenda, as well as a double life to lead. And so, with a Sith bounty on their heads, Cade, Jariah Syn, and Deliah Blue must put distance between themselves and Coruscant.

First, there are some scores to be settled before Cade returns to his much-loved obscurity as a member of the underworld. That is, if after breaking out of the Sith Temple and incurring the wrath of Darth Krayt, one can ever go home again or find any place to hide . . .

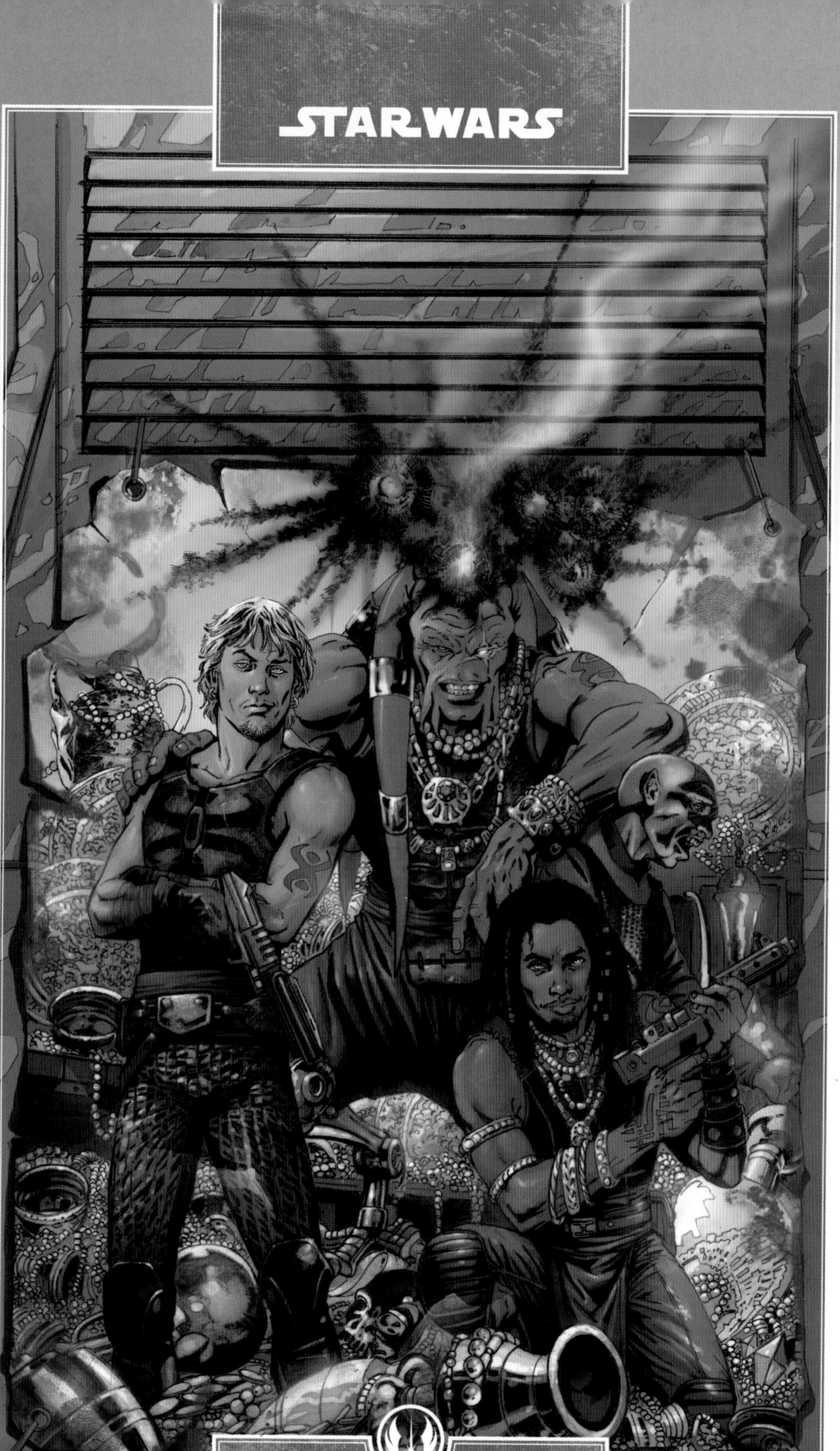
STAR WARS
JAN DUURSEMA AND
BRAD ANDERSON

LOYALTIES

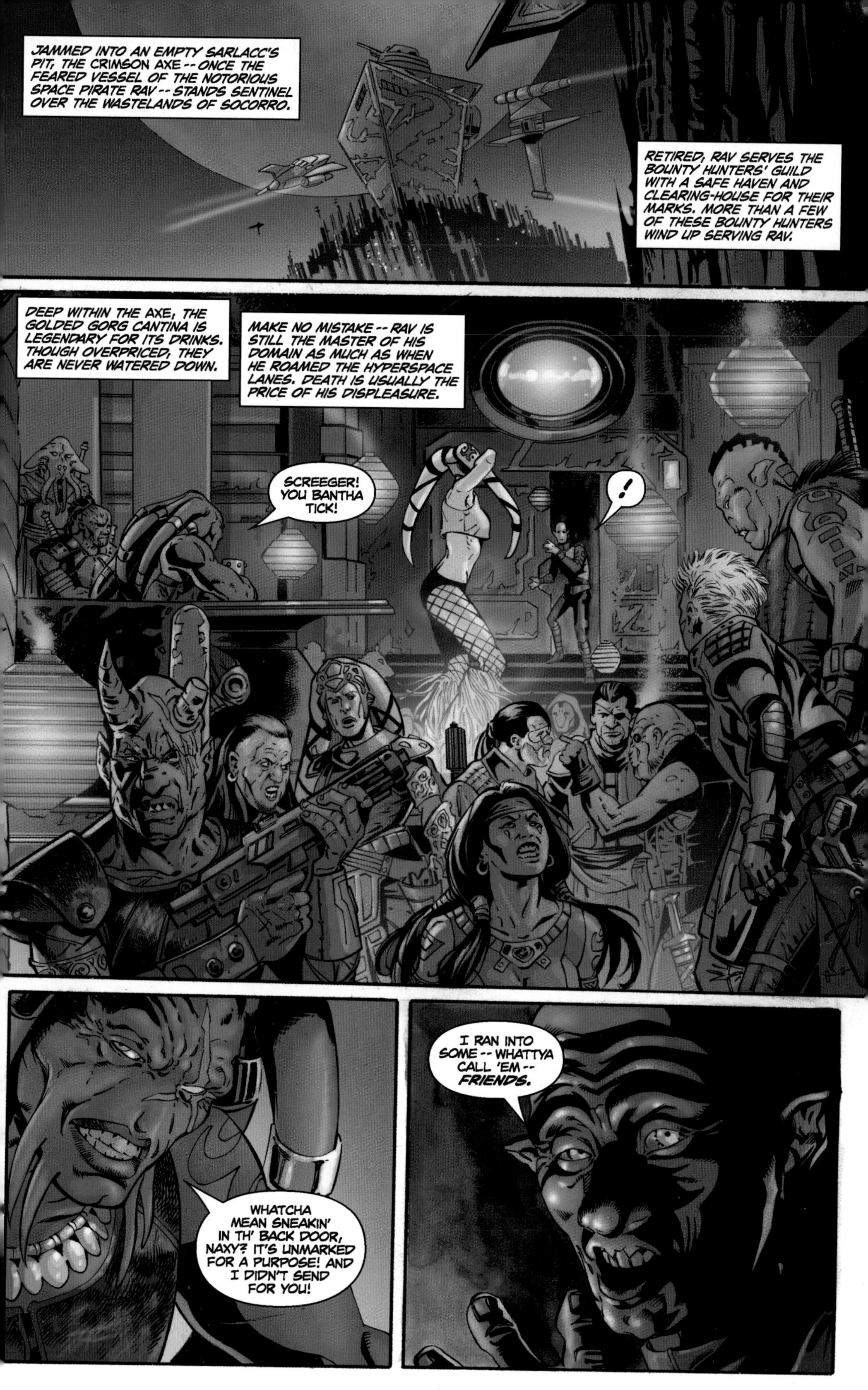
JAMMED INTO AN EMPTY SARLACC'S PIT, THE CRIMSON AXE -- ONCE THE FEARED VESSEL OF THE NOTORIOUS SPACE PIRATE RAV -- STANDS SENTINEL OVER THE WASTELANDS OF SOCORRO.
RETIRED, RAV SERVES THE BOUNTY HUNTERS' GUILD WITH A SAFE HAVEN AND CLEARING-HOUSE FOR THEIR MARKS. MORE THAN A FEW OF THESE BOUNTY HUNTERS WIND UP SERVING RAV.
DEEP WITHIN THE AXE, THE GOLDED GORG CANTINA IS LEGENDARY FOR ITS DRINKS. THOUGH OVERPRICED, THEY ARE NEVER WATERED DOWN.
MAKE NO MISTAKE -- RAV IS STILL THE MASTER OF HIS DOMAIN AS MUCH AS WHEN HE ROAMED THE HYPERSPACE LANES. DEATH IS USUALLY THE PRICE OF HIS DISPLEASURE.
SCREEGER! YOU BANTHA TICK!
!
WHATCHA MEAN SNEAKIN' IN TH' BACK DOOR, NAXY? IT'S UNMARKED FOR A PURPOSE! AND I DIDN'T SEND FOR YOU!
I RAN INTO SOME -- WHATTYA CALL 'EM -- FRIENDS.

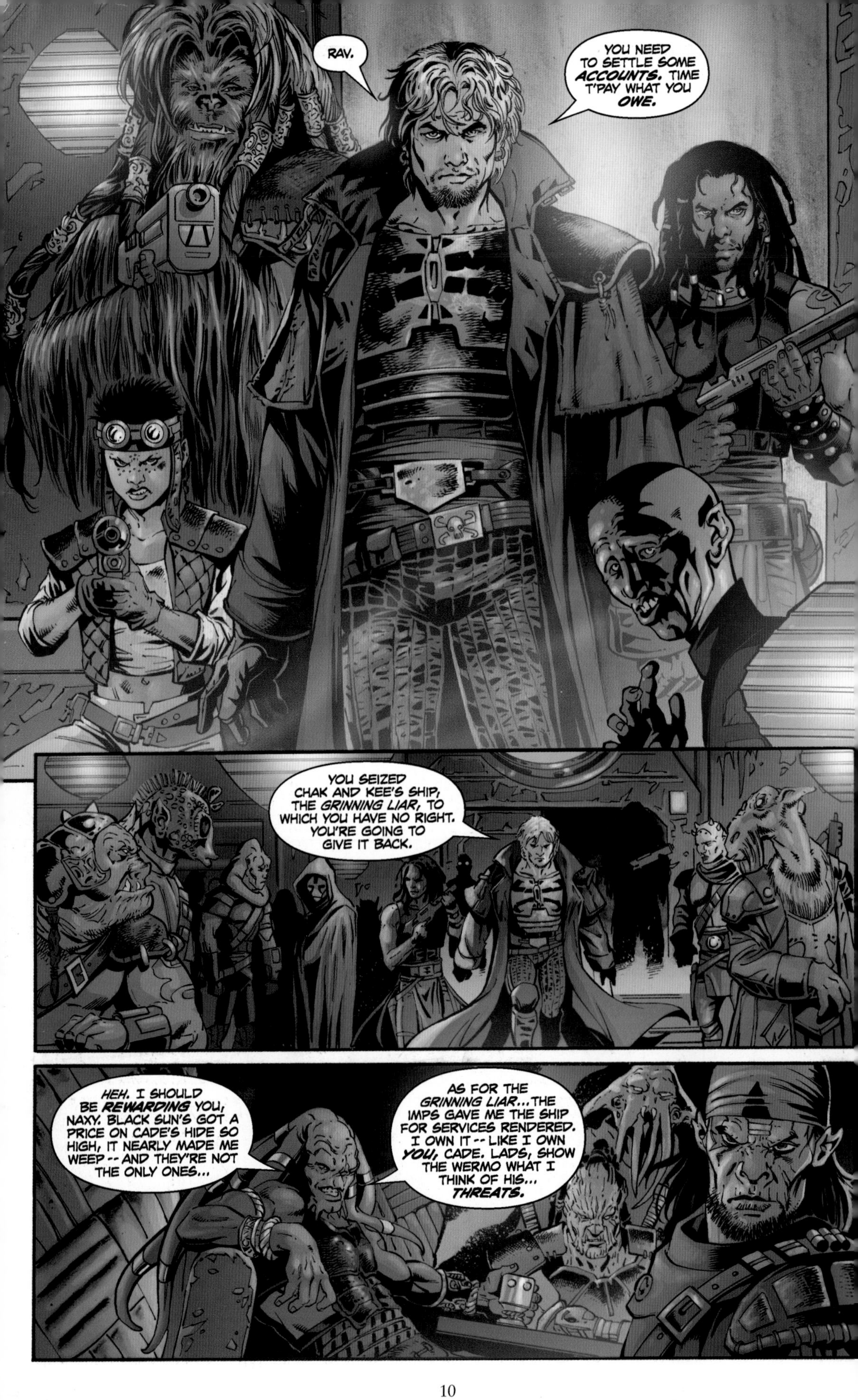
RAV.
YOU NEED TO SETTLE SOME ACCOUNTS. TIME T'PAY WHAT YOU OWE.
YOU SEIZED CHAK AND KEE'S SHIP, THE GRINNING LIAR, TO WHICH YOU HAVE NO RIGHT. YOU'RE GOING TO GIVE IT BACK.
HEH. I SHOULD BE REWARDING YOU, NAXY. BLACK SUN'S GOT A PRICE ON CADE'S HIDE SO HIGH, IT NEARLY MADE ME WEEP -- AND THEY'RE NOT THE ONLY ONES...
AS FOR THE GRINNING LIAR... THE IMPS GAVE ME THE SHIP FOR SERVICES RENDERED. I OWN IT -- LIKE I OWN YOU, CADE. LADS, SHOW THE WERMO WHAT I THINK OF HIS... THREATS.

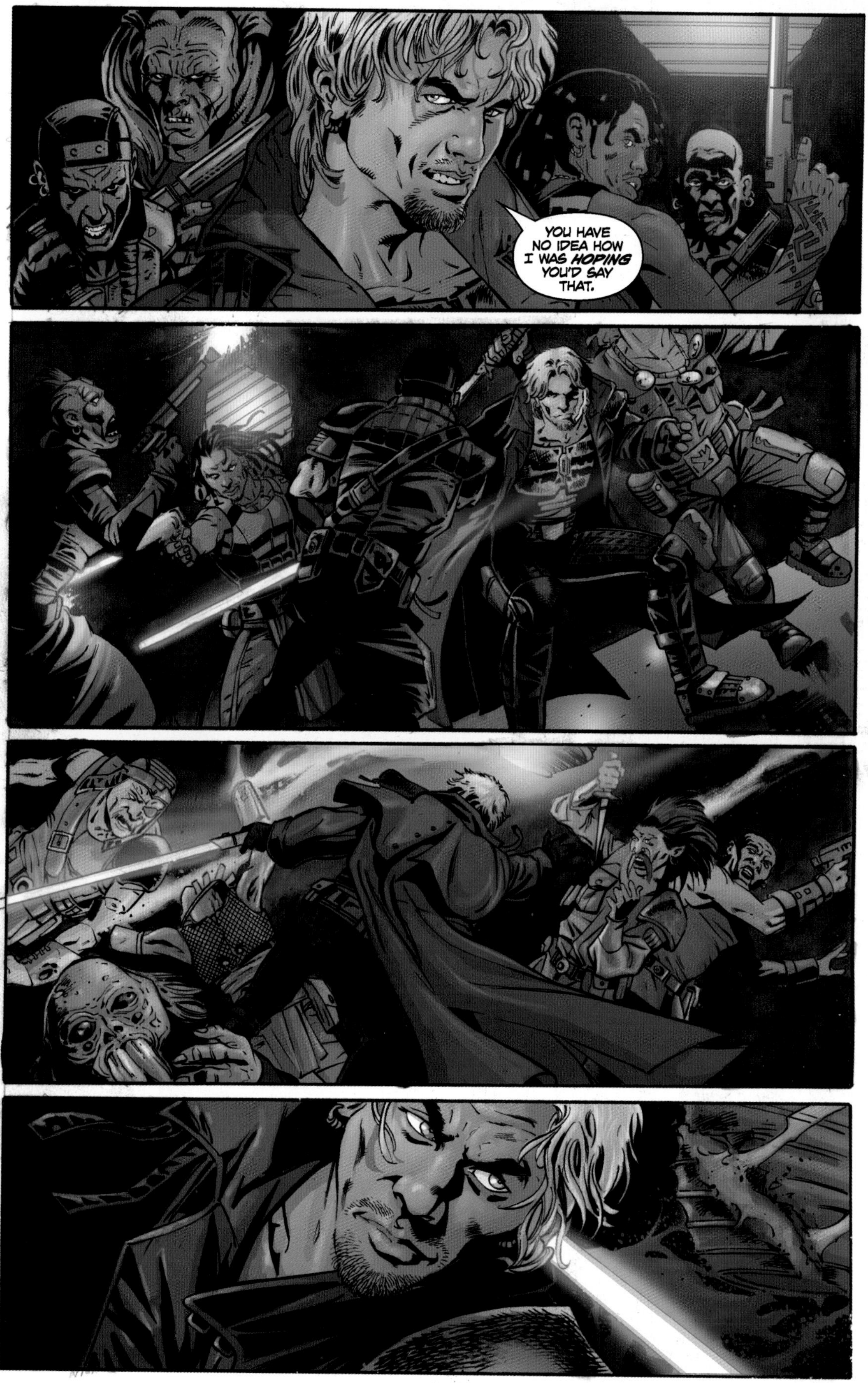
YOU HAVE NO IDEA HOW I WAS HOPING YOU'D SAY THAT.

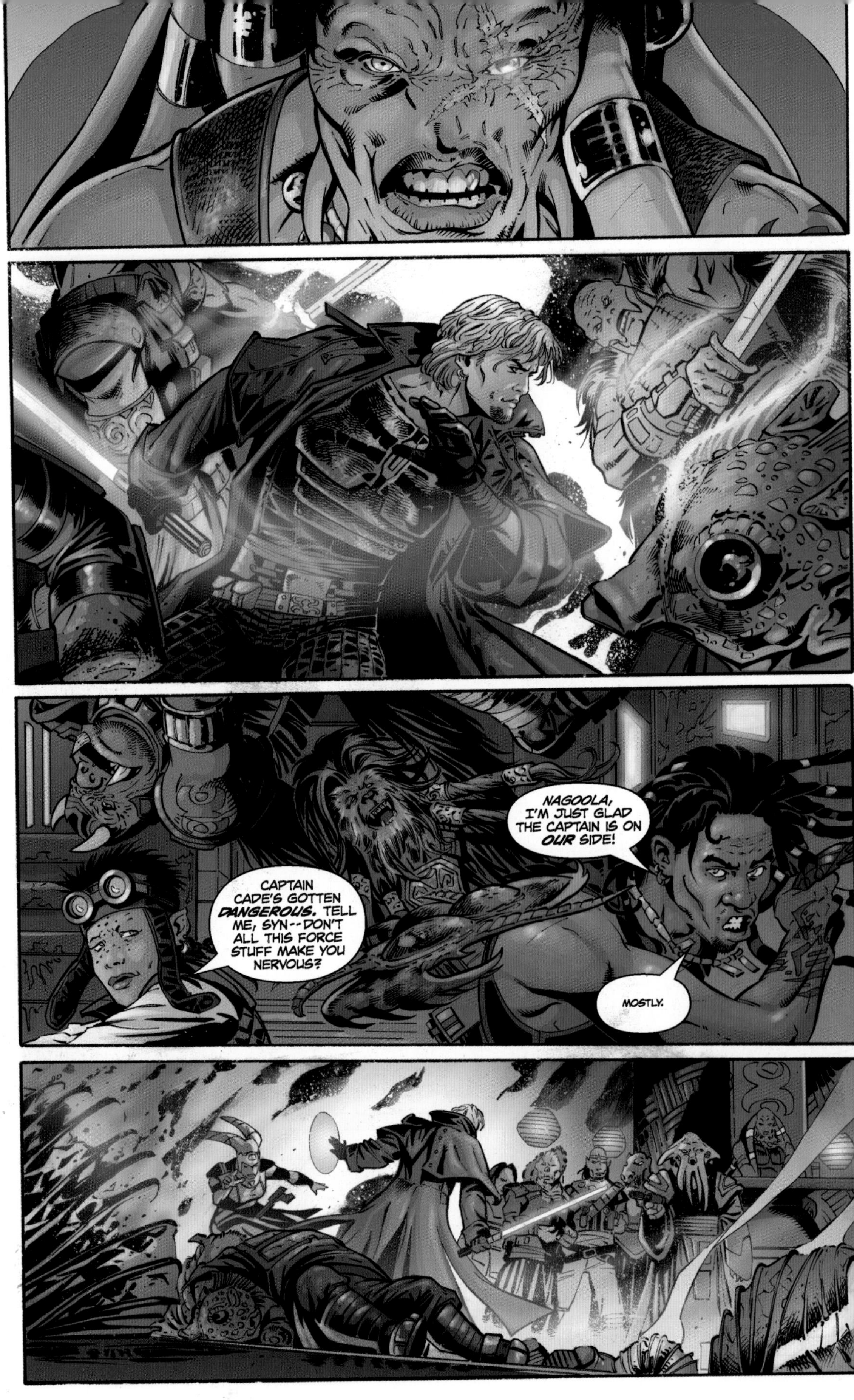

CAPTAIN CADE'S GOTTEN *DANGEROUS.* TELL ME, SYN--DON'T ALL THIS FORCE STUFF MAKE YOU NERVOUS?
NAGOOLA, I'M JUST GLAD THE CAPTAIN IS ON *OUR* SIDE!
MOSTLY.

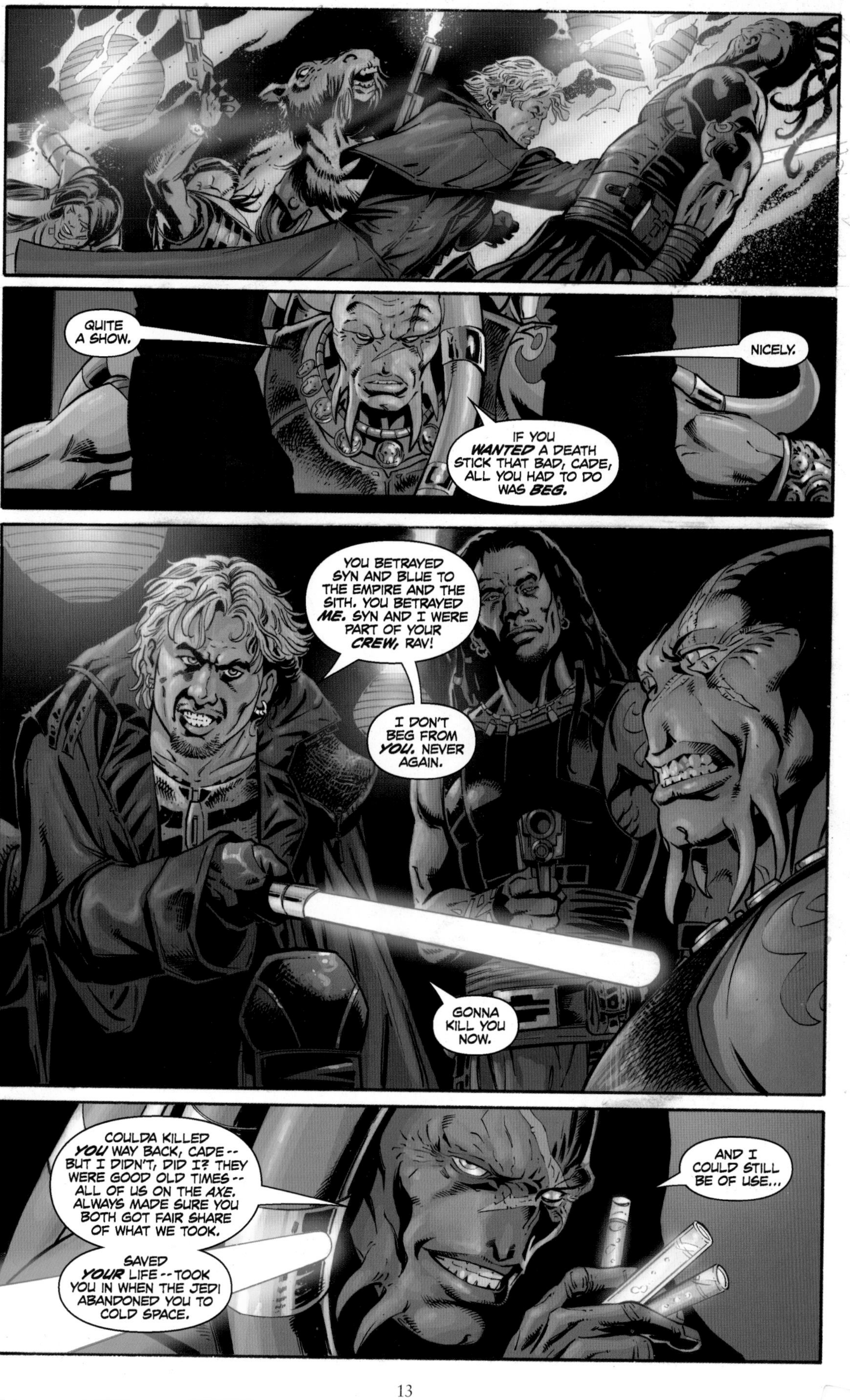
QUITE A SHOW.
NICELY.
IF YOU WANTED A DEATH STICK THAT BAD, CADE, ALL YOU HAD TO DO WAS BEG.
YOU BETRAYED SYN AND BLUE TO THE EMPIRE AND THE SITH. YOU BETRAYED ME. SYN AND I WERE PART OF YOUR CREW, RAV!
I DON'T BEG FROM YOU. NEVER AGAIN.
GONNA KILL YOU NOW.
COULDA KILLED YOU WAY BACK, CADE-- BUT I DIDN'T, DID I? THEY WERE GOOD OLD TIMES-- ALL OF US ON THE AXE. ALWAYS MADE SURE YOU BOTH GOT FAIR SHARE OF WHAT WE TOOK.
SAVED YOUR LIFE--TOOK YOU IN WHEN THE JEDI ABANDONED YOU TO COLD SPACE.
AND I COULD STILL BE OF USE...

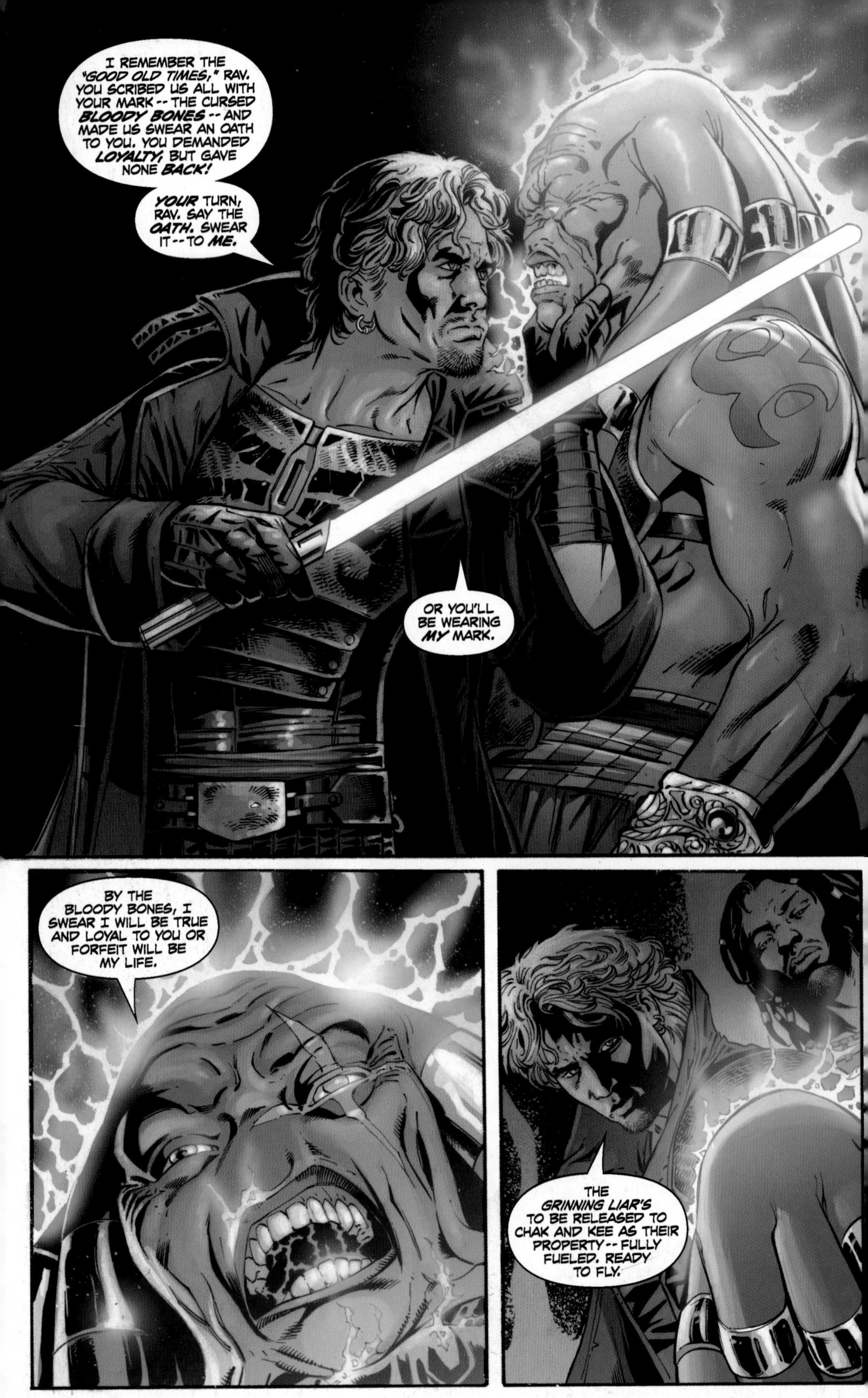
I REMEMBER THE "GOOD OLD TIMES," RAV. YOU SCRIBED US ALL WITH YOUR MARK -- THE CURSED BLOODY BONES -- AND MADE US SWEAR AN OATH TO YOU. YOU DEMANDED LOYALTY, BUT GAVE NONE BACK!
YOUR TURN, RAV. SAY THE OATH. SWEAR IT -- TO ME.
OR YOU'LL BE WEARING MY MARK.
BY THE BLOODY BONES, I SWEAR I WILL BE TRUE AND LOYAL TO YOU OR FORFEIT WILL BE MY LIFE.
THE GRINNING LIAR'S TO BE RELEASED TO CHAK AND KEE AS THEIR PROPERTY -- FULLY FUELED. READY TO FLY.

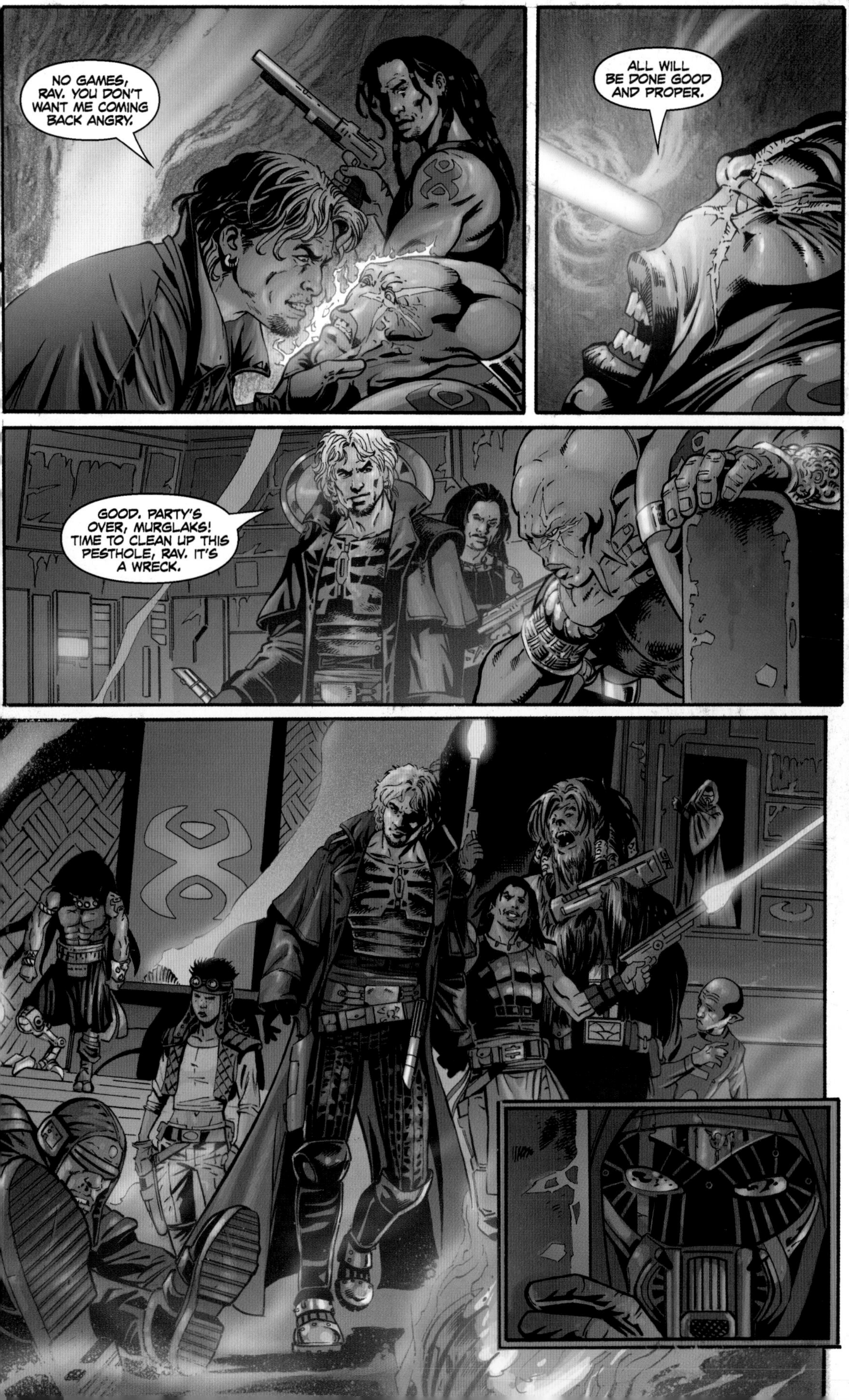
NO GAMES, RAV. YOU DON'T WANT ME COMING BACK ANGRY.
ALL WILL BE DONE GOOD AND PROPER.
GOOD. PARTY'S OVER, MURGLAKS! TIME TO CLEAN UP THIS PESTHOLE, RAV. IT'S A WRECK.

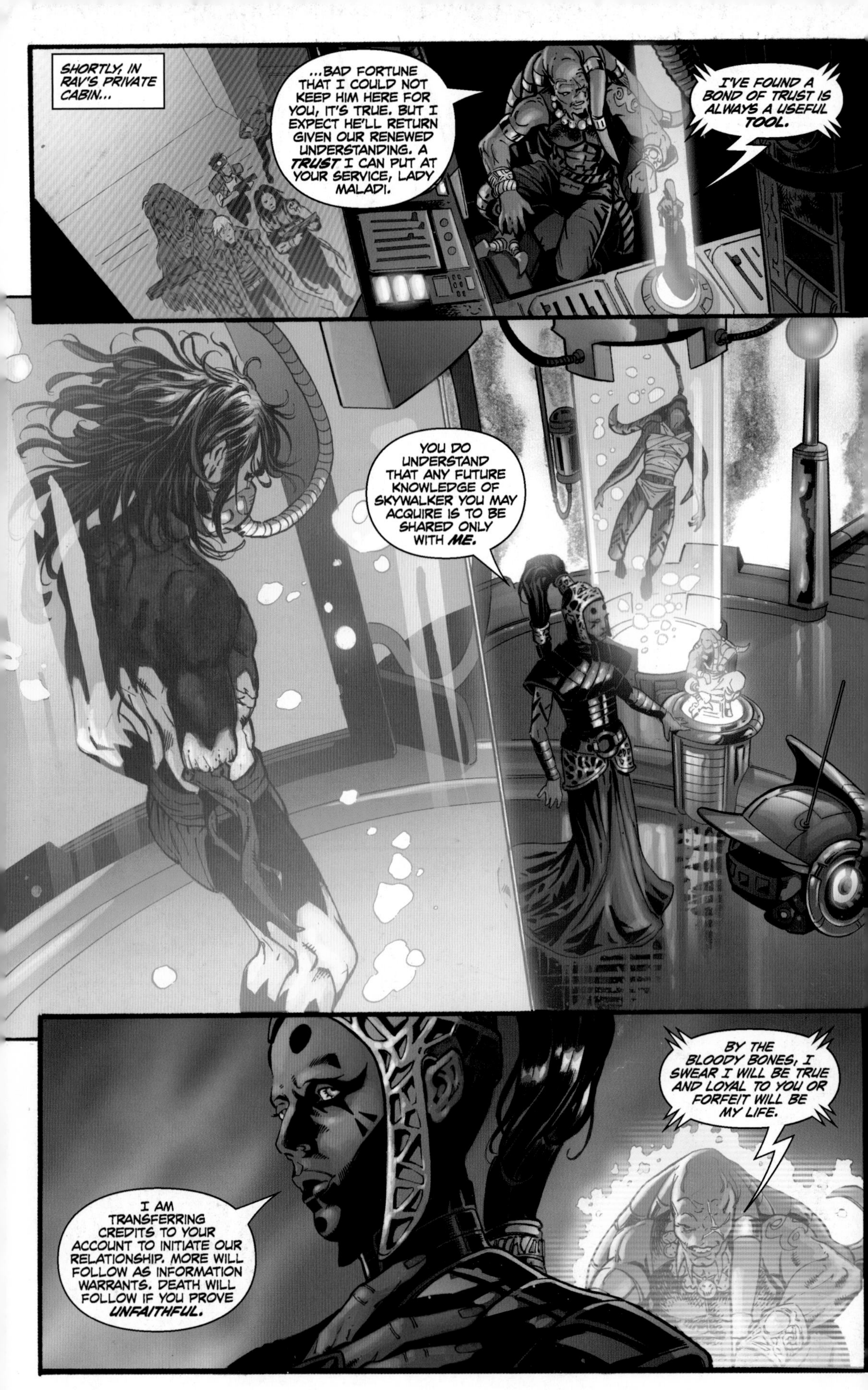
SHORTLY, IN RAV'S PRIVATE CABIN...
...BAD FORTUNE THAT I COULD NOT KEEP HIM HERE FOR YOU, IT'S TRUE. BUT I EXPECT HE'LL RETURN GIVEN OUR RENEWED UNDERSTANDING. A TRUST I CAN PUT AT YOUR SERVICE, LADY MALADI.
I'VE FOUND A BOND OF TRUST IS ALWAYS A USEFUL TOOL.
YOU DO UNDERSTAND THAT ANY FUTURE KNOWLEDGE OF SKYWALKER YOU MAY ACQUIRE IS TO BE SHARED ONLY WITH ME.
BY THE BLOODY BONES, I SWEAR I WILL BE TRUE AND LOYAL TO YOU OR FORFEIT WILL BE MY LIFE.
I AM TRANSFERRING CREDITS TO YOUR ACCOUNT TO INITIATE OUR RELATIONSHIP. MORE WILL FOLLOW AS INFORMATION WARRANTS. DEATH WILL FOLLOW IF YOU PROVE UNFAITHFUL.

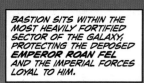

BASTION SITS WITHIN THE MOST HEAVILY FORTIFIED SECTOR OF THE GALAXY, PROTECTING THE DEPOSED *EMPEROR ROAN FEL* AND THE IMPERIAL FORCES LOYAL TO HIM.

YOU SUMMONED, SIRE?

MASTER KRIEG. I HAVE WORD FROM MY CONTACT ON CORUSCANT THAT CADE SKYWALKER HAS ESCAPED THE *SITH* AND HAS AGAIN MANAGED TO VANISH INTO THE UNDERSIDE OF THE GALAXY.

SITHSPAWN! I SHOULD NEVER HAVE LET MARASIAH TALK ME INTO PERMITTING SKYWALKER TO LEAVE BASTION IN THE FIRST PLACE!

SKYWALKER *DID* SAVE HER LIFE, SIRE. YOU WERE SIMPLY MAKING GOOD ON PRINCESS MARASIAH'S PROMISES.

PROMISES THAT SHE SHOULD NEVER HAVE *MADE!*

I AM THE RIGHTFUL EMPEROR. MY PRIMARY *RESPONSIBILITIES* LIE NOT WITH SOME SPACE JUNKIE, OR EVEN MY DAUGHTER, BUT WITH THE EMPIRE AND THE GALAXY.

NO DOUBT THE SITH TORTURED CADE SKYWALKER. HOW MANY OF OUR SECRETS HAS THAT WEAK-WILLED *SCAVENGER* DIVULGED?

I SHOULD HAVE HAD SKYWALKER ENLISTED, INCARCERATED, OR EMBALMED. HE'S TOO MUCH OF A WILDCARD. I WILL NOT MAKE THE SAME MISTAKE *TWICE.*

WHERE'S *ANTARES DRACO?*

DELAYED. I'M CERTAIN HE WILL ARRIVE SHORTLY, SIRE.

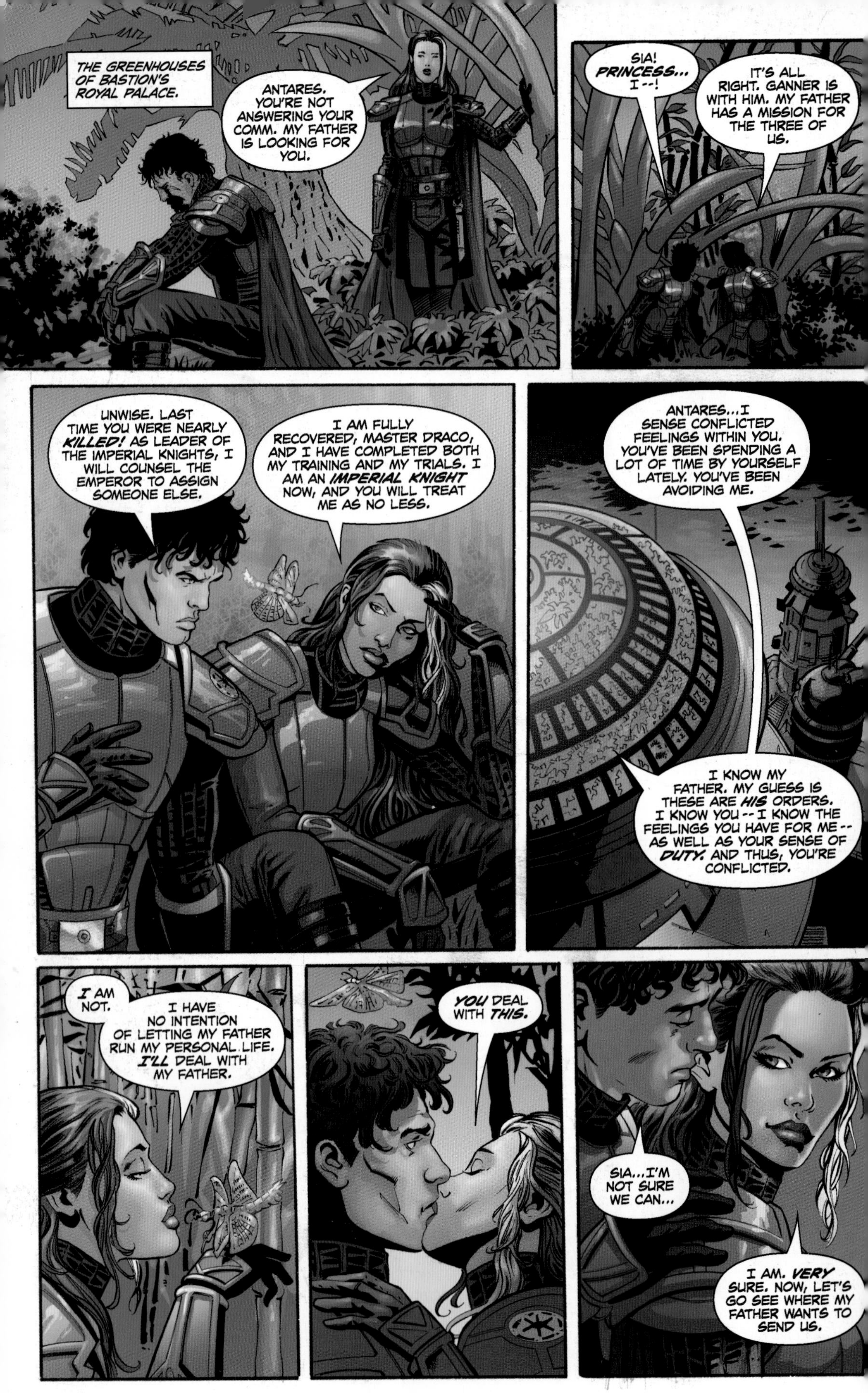
THE GREENHOUSES OF BASTION'S ROYAL PALACE.
ANTARES. YOU'RE NOT ANSWERING YOUR COMM. MY FATHER IS LOOKING FOR YOU.
SIA! PRINCESS... I --!
IT'S ALL RIGHT. GANNER IS WITH HIM. MY FATHER HAS A MISSION FOR THE THREE OF US.
UNWISE. LAST TIME YOU WERE NEARLY KILLED! AS LEADER OF THE IMPERIAL KNIGHTS, I WILL COUNSEL THE EMPEROR TO ASSIGN SOMEONE ELSE.
I AM FULLY RECOVERED, MASTER DRACO, AND I HAVE COMPLETED BOTH MY TRAINING AND MY TRIALS. I AM AN IMPERIAL KNIGHT NOW, AND YOU WILL TREAT ME AS NO LESS.
ANTARES...I SENSE CONFLICTED FEELINGS WITHIN YOU. YOU'VE BEEN SPENDING A LOT OF TIME BY YOURSELF LATELY. YOU'VE BEEN AVOIDING ME.
I KNOW MY FATHER. MY GUESS IS THESE ARE HIS ORDERS. I KNOW YOU -- I KNOW THE FEELINGS YOU HAVE FOR ME -- AS WELL AS YOUR SENSE OF DUTY. AND THUS, YOU'RE CONFLICTED.
I AM NOT.
I HAVE NO INTENTION OF LETTING MY FATHER RUN MY PERSONAL LIFE. I'LL DEAL WITH MY FATHER.
YOU DEAL WITH THIS.
SIA...I'M NOT SURE WE CAN...
I AM. VERY SURE. NOW, LET'S GO SEE WHERE MY FATHER WANTS TO SEND US.

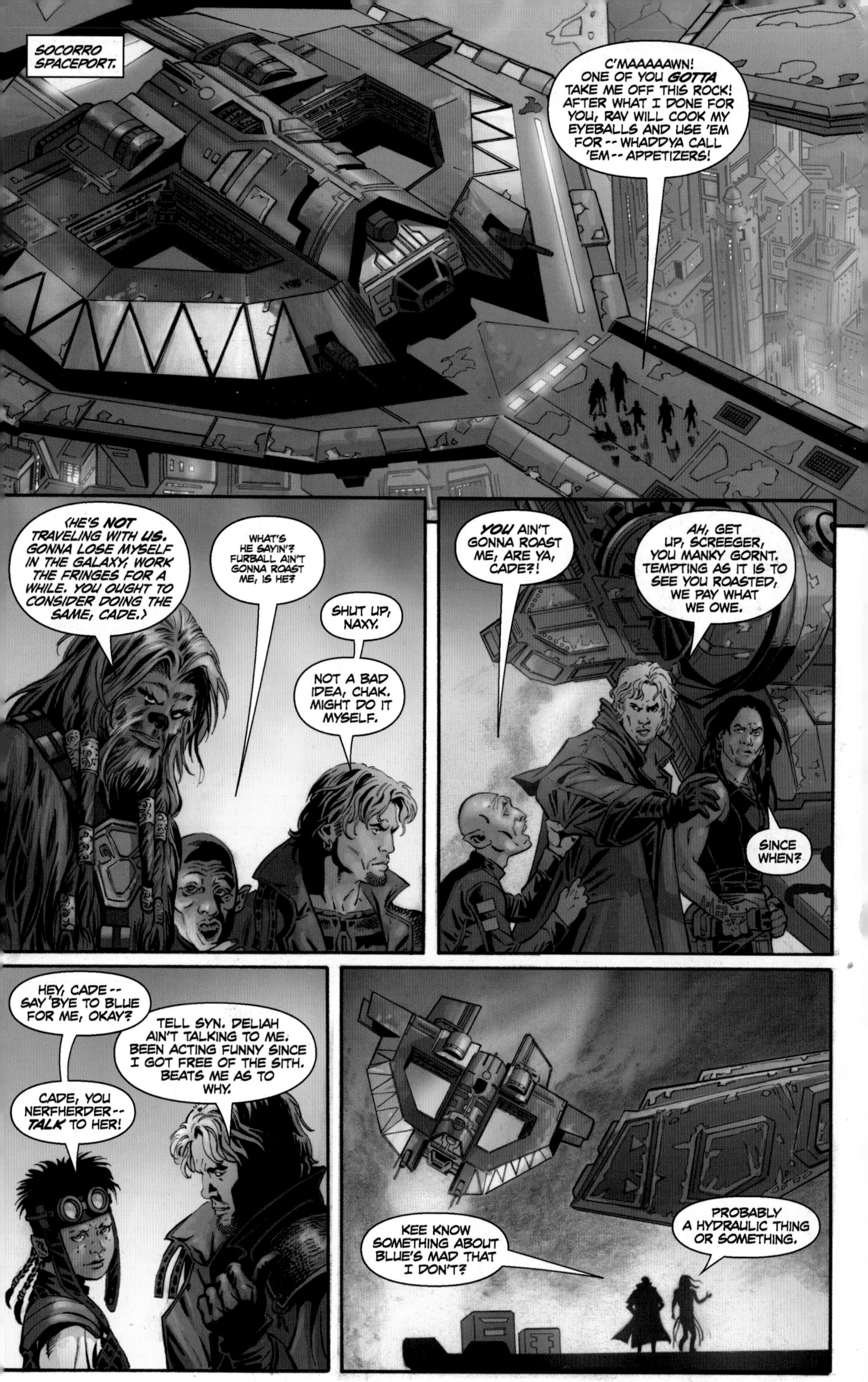
SOCORRO SPACEPORT.
C'MAAAAAWN! ONE OF YOU GOTTA TAKE ME OFF THIS ROCK! AFTER WHAT I DONE FOR YOU, RAV WILL COOK MY EYEBALLS AND USE 'EM FOR -- WHADDYA CALL 'EM -- APPETIZERS!
‹HE'S NOT TRAVELING WITH US. GONNA LOSE MYSELF IN THE GALAXY, WORK THE FRINGES FOR A WHILE. YOU OUGHT TO CONSIDER DOING THE SAME, CADE.›
WHAT'S HE SAYIN'? FURBALL AIN'T GONNA ROAST ME, IS HE?
SHUT UP, NAXY.
NOT A BAD IDEA, CHAK. MIGHT DO IT MYSELF.
YOU AIN'T GONNA ROAST ME, ARE YA, CADE?!
AH, GET UP, SCREEGER, YOU MANKY GORNT. TEMPTING AS IT IS TO SEE YOU ROASTED, WE PAY WHAT WE OWE.
SINCE WHEN?
HEY, CADE -- SAY 'BYE TO BLUE FOR ME, OKAY?
TELL SYN. DELIAH AIN'T TALKING TO ME. BEEN ACTING FUNNY SINCE I GOT FREE OF THE SITH. BEATS ME AS TO WHY.
CADE, YOU NERFHERDER -- TALK TO HER!
KEE KNOW SOMETHING ABOUT BLUE'S MAD THAT I DON'T?
PROBABLY A HYDRAULIC THING OR SOMETHING.

JARIAH, TOSS NAXY IN THE BRIG WHILE I PUNCH IN SOME COORDINATES.

WE GOT A BRIG?

THIS GET CLEANED OUT FROM OUR LAST CARGO OF ROTTING GORGS FOR THAT FANCY HUTT PARTY?

UGH... NOPE.

THEN NAXY WILL BE RIGHT AT HOME.

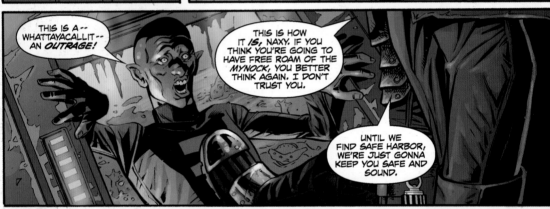

THIS IS A -- WHATTAYACALLIT -- AN *OUTRAGE!*

THIS IS HOW IT *IS*, NAXY. IF YOU THINK YOU'RE GOING TO HAVE FREE ROAM OF THE *MYNOCK*, YOU BETTER THINK AGAIN. I DON'T TRUST YOU.

UNTIL WE FIND SAFE HARBOR, WE'RE JUST GONNA KEEP YOU SAFE AND SOUND.

IT REEKS OF GORG GOO! DON'T SCUM LIKE YOU GOT ANY SENSE OF SMELL?

GET OFF IT, NAXY. YOU'VE LICKED NASTIER STUFF OFF RAV'S BOOTS!

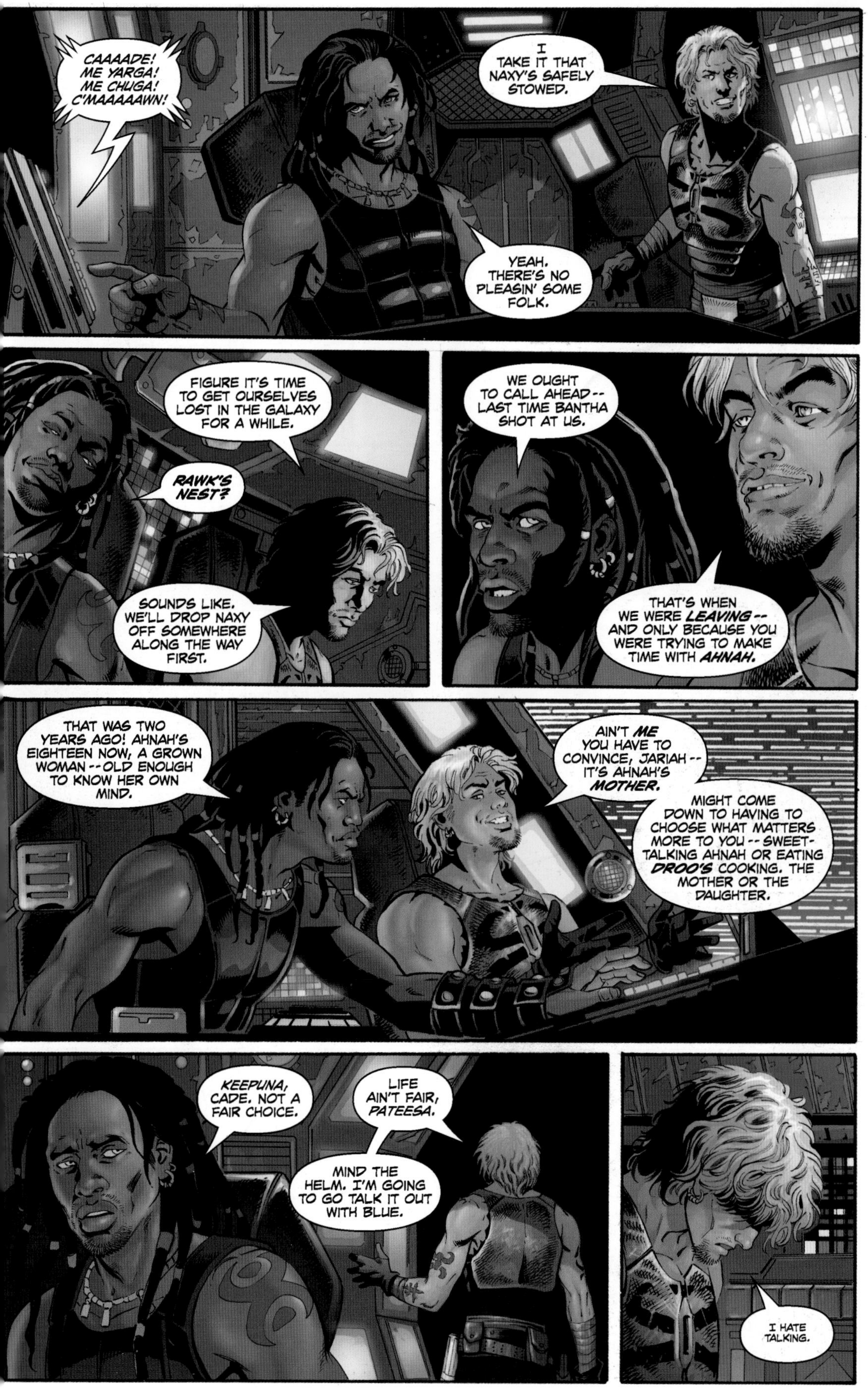
CAAAADE! ME YARGA! ME CHUGA! C'MAAAAAWN!
I TAKE IT THAT NAXY'S SAFELY STOWED.
YEAH. THERE'S NO PLEASIN' SOME FOLK.
FIGURE IT'S TIME TO GET OURSELVES LOST IN THE GALAXY FOR A WHILE.
RAWK'S NEST?
SOUNDS LIKE. WE'LL DROP NAXY OFF SOMEWHERE ALONG THE WAY FIRST.
WE OUGHT TO CALL AHEAD -- LAST TIME BANTHA SHOT AT US.
THAT'S WHEN WE WERE LEAVING -- AND ONLY BECAUSE YOU WERE TRYING TO MAKE TIME WITH AHNAH.
THAT WAS TWO YEARS AGO! AHNAH'S EIGHTEEN NOW, A GROWN WOMAN -- OLD ENOUGH TO KNOW HER OWN MIND.
AIN'T ME YOU HAVE TO CONVINCE, JARIAH -- IT'S AHNAH'S MOTHER.
MIGHT COME DOWN TO HAVING TO CHOOSE WHAT MATTERS MORE TO YOU -- SWEET-TALKING AHNAH OR EATING DROO'S COOKING. THE MOTHER OR THE DAUGHTER.
KEEPUNA, CADE. NOT A FAIR CHOICE.
LIFE AIN'T FAIR, PATEESA.
MIND THE HELM. I'M GOING TO GO TALK IT OUT WITH BLUE.
I HATE TALKING.

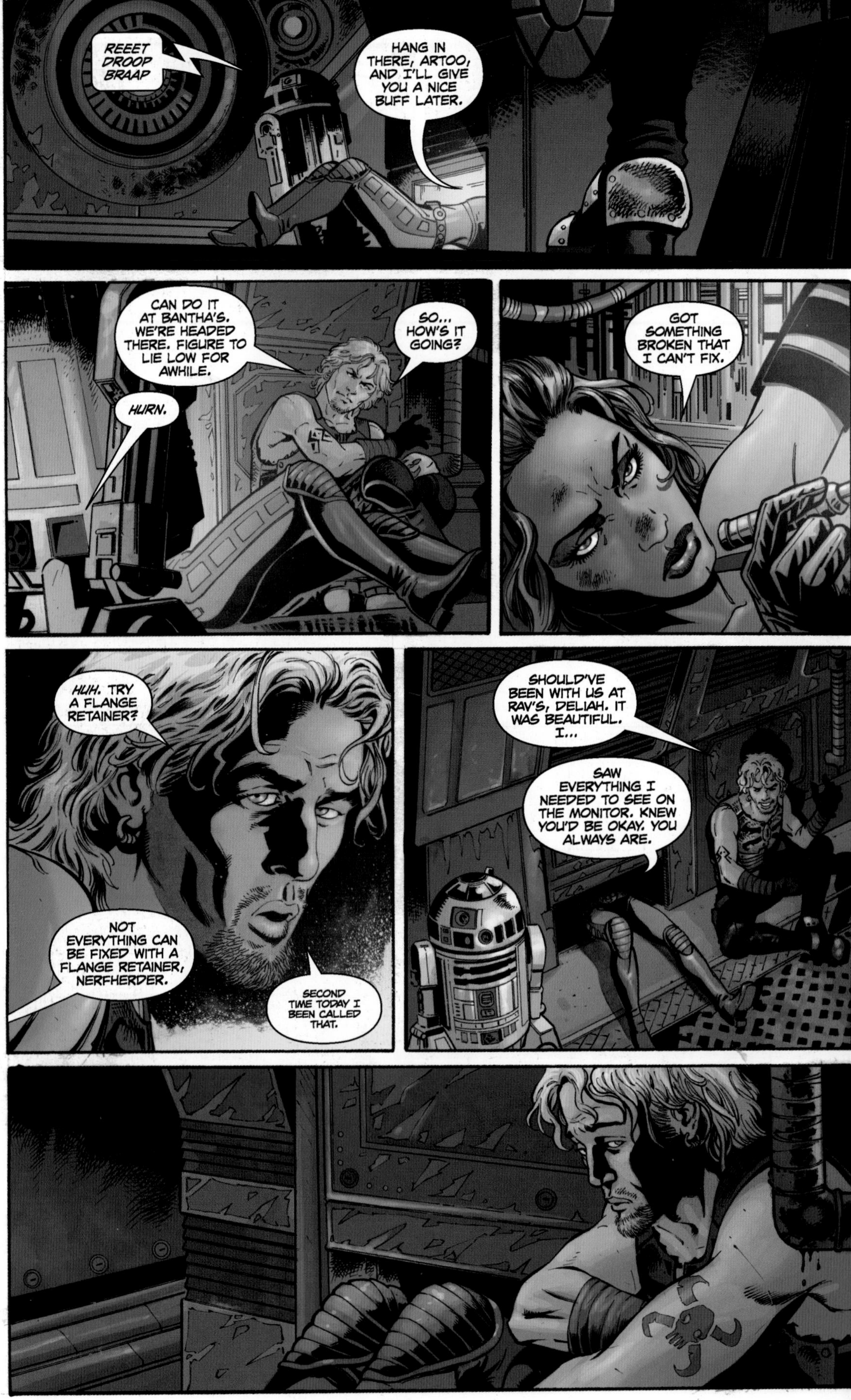
REEET DROOP BRAAP
HANG IN THERE, ARTOO, AND I'LL GIVE YOU A NICE BUFF LATER.
CAN DO IT AT BANTHA'S. WE'RE HEADED THERE. FIGURE TO LIE LOW FOR AWHILE.
HURN.
SO... HOW'S IT GOING?
GOT SOMETHING BROKEN THAT I CAN'T FIX.
HUH. TRY A FLANGE RETAINER?
NOT EVERYTHING CAN BE FIXED WITH A FLANGE RETAINER, NERFHERDER.
SECOND TIME TODAY I BEEN CALLED THAT.
SHOULD'VE BEEN WITH US AT RAV'S, DELIAH. IT WAS BEAUTIFUL. I...
SAW EVERYTHING I NEEDED TO SEE ON THE MONITOR. KNEW YOU'D BE OKAY. YOU ALWAYS ARE.

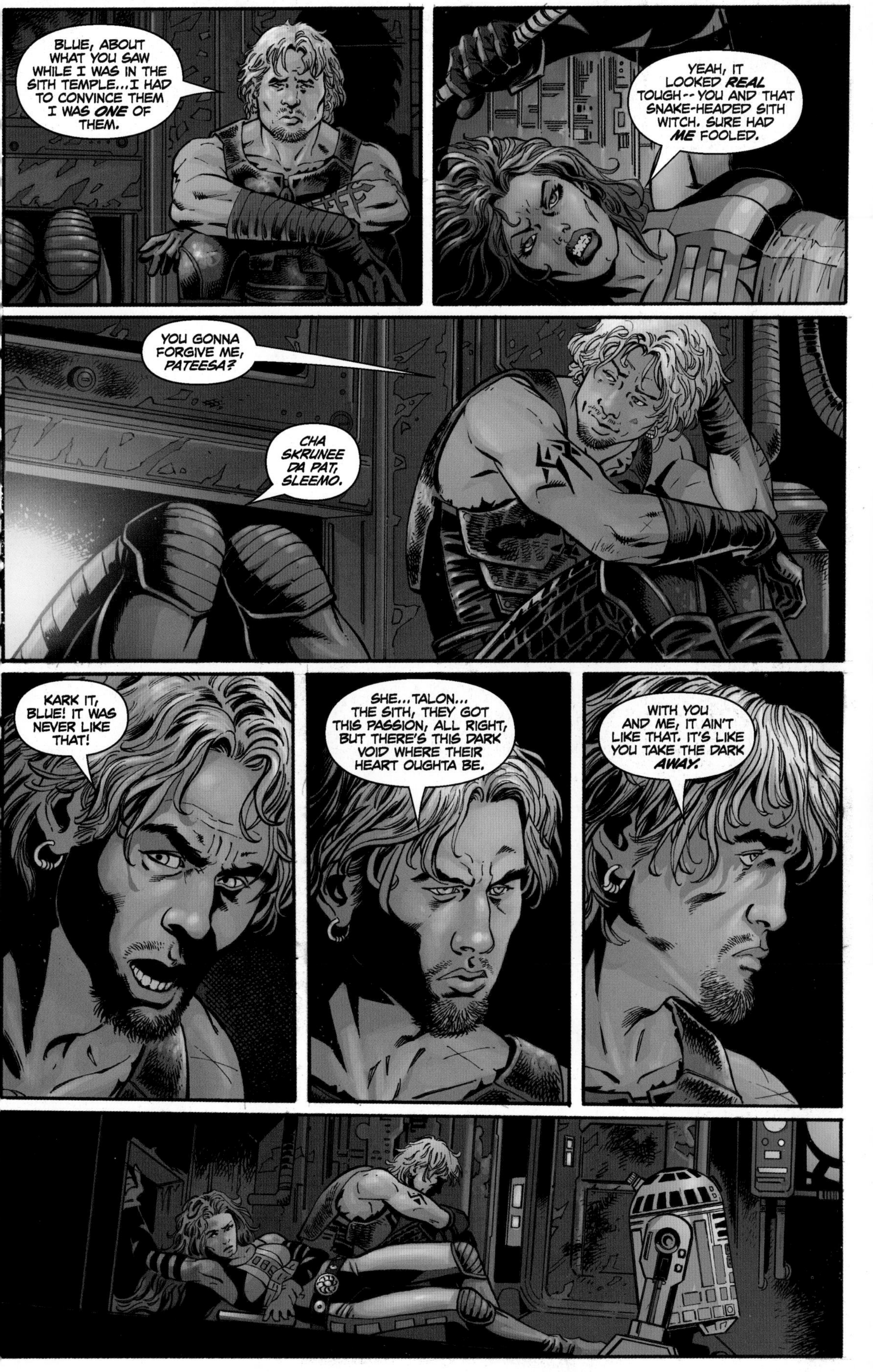
BLUE, ABOUT WHAT YOU SAW WHILE I WAS IN THE SITH TEMPLE...I HAD TO CONVINCE THEM I WAS *ONE* OF THEM.
YEAH, IT LOOKED *REAL* TOUGH--YOU AND THAT SNAKE-HEADED SITH WITCH. SURE HAD *ME* FOOLED.
YOU GONNA FORGIVE ME, *PATEESA?*
CHA SKRUNEE DA PAT, SLEEMO.
KARK IT, BLUE! IT WAS NEVER LIKE THAT!
SHE...TALON... THE SITH, THEY GOT THIS PASSION, ALL RIGHT, BUT THERE'S THIS DARK VOID WHERE THEIR HEART OUGHTA BE.
WITH YOU AND ME, IT AIN'T LIKE THAT. IT'S LIKE YOU TAKE THE DARK *AWAY.*

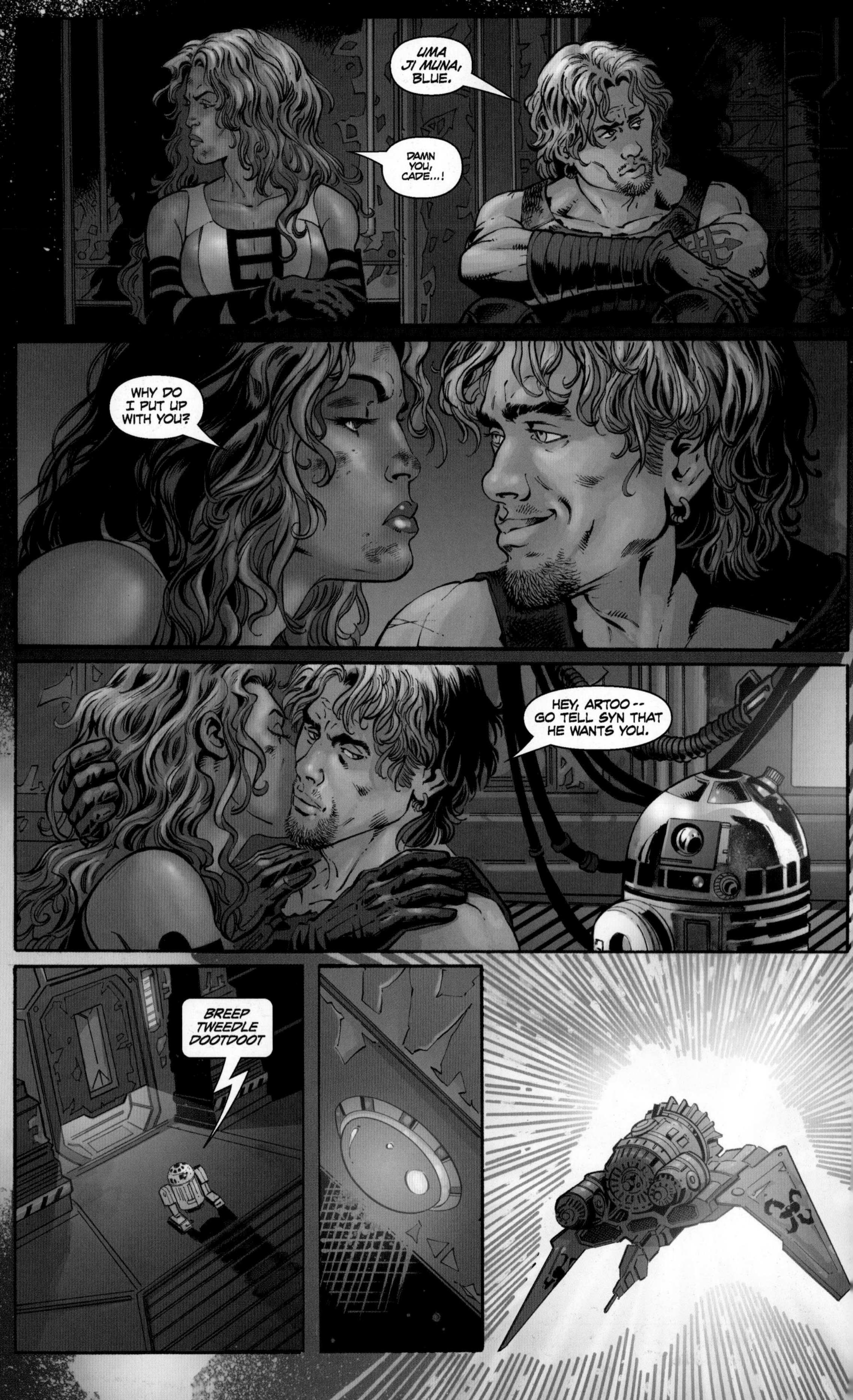
UMA JI MUNA, BLUE.
DAMN YOU, CADE...!
WHY DO I PUT UP WITH YOU?
HEY, ARTOO -- GO TELL SYN THAT HE WANTS YOU.
BREEP TWEEDLE DOOTDOOT

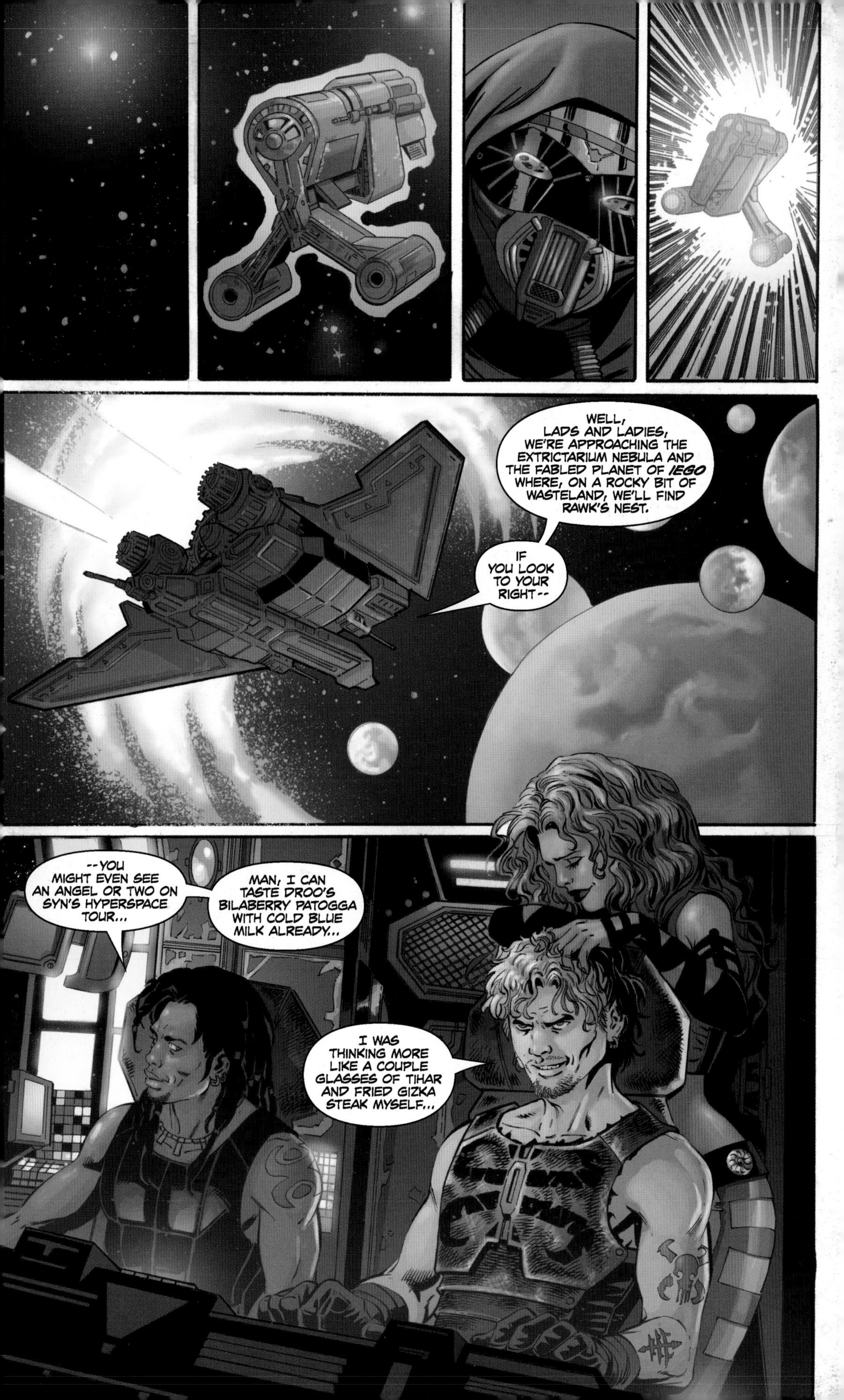
WELL, LADS AND LADIES, WE'RE APPROACHING THE EXTRICTARIUM NEBULA AND THE FABLED PLANET OF IEGO WHERE, ON A ROCKY BIT OF WASTELAND, WE'LL FIND RAWK'S NEST.
IF YOU LOOK TO YOUR RIGHT--
--YOU MIGHT EVEN SEE AN ANGEL OR TWO ON SYN'S HYPERSPACE TOUR...
MAN, I CAN TASTE DROO'S BILABERRY PATOGGA WITH COLD BLUE MILK ALREADY...
I WAS THINKING MORE LIKE A COUPLE GLASSES OF TIHAR AND FRIED GIZKA STEAK MYSELF...

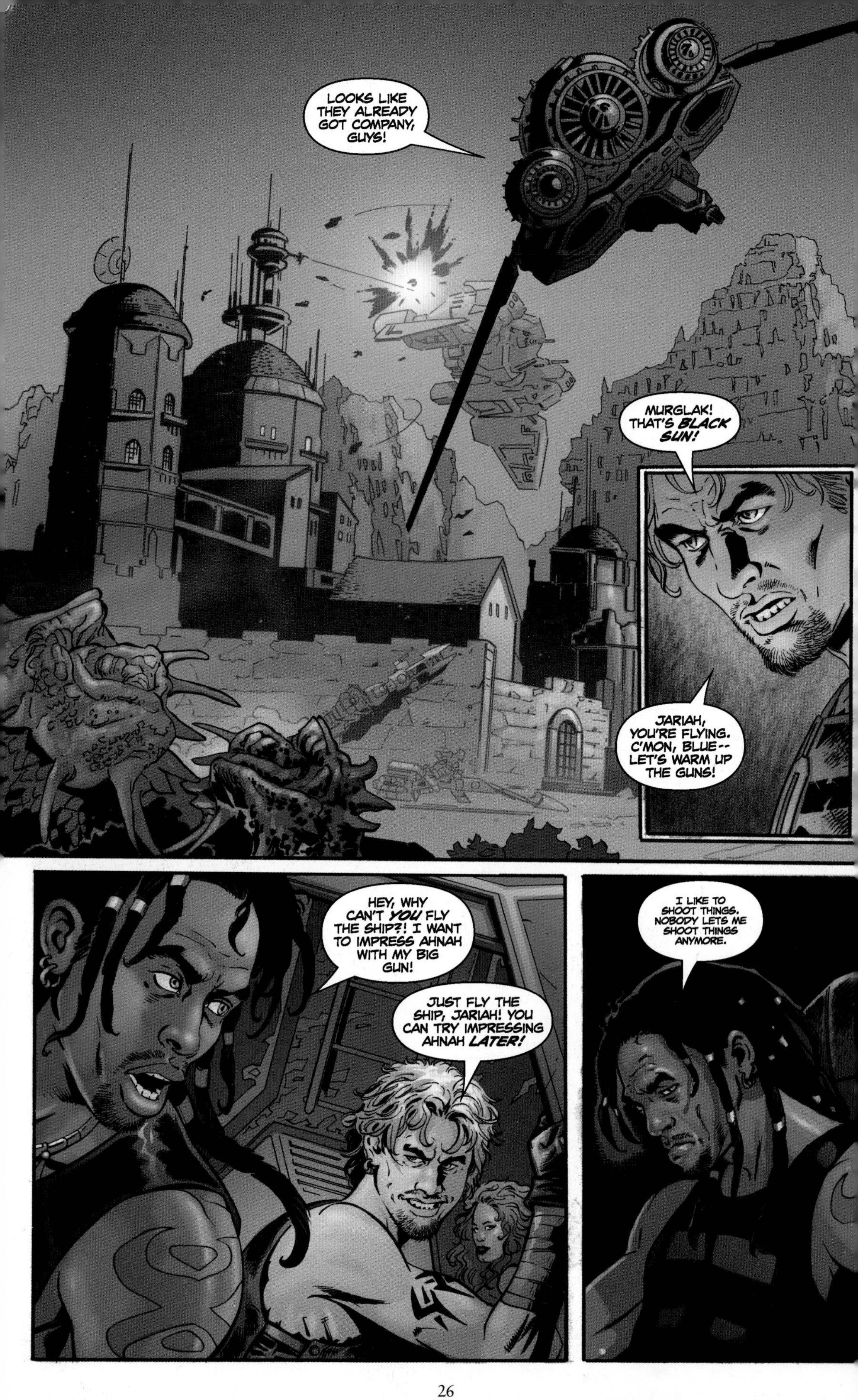
LOOKS LIKE THEY ALREADY GOT COMPANY, GUYS!
MURGLAK! THAT'S *BLACK SUN!*
JARIAH, YOU'RE FLYING. C'MON, BLUE-- LET'S WARM UP THE GUNS!
HEY, WHY CAN'T *YOU* FLY THE SHIP?! I WANT TO IMPRESS AHNAH WITH MY BIG GUN!
JUST FLY THE SHIP, JARIAH! YOU CAN TRY IMPRESSING AHNAH *LATER!*
I LIKE TO SHOOT THINGS. NOBODY LETS ME SHOOT THINGS ANYMORE.

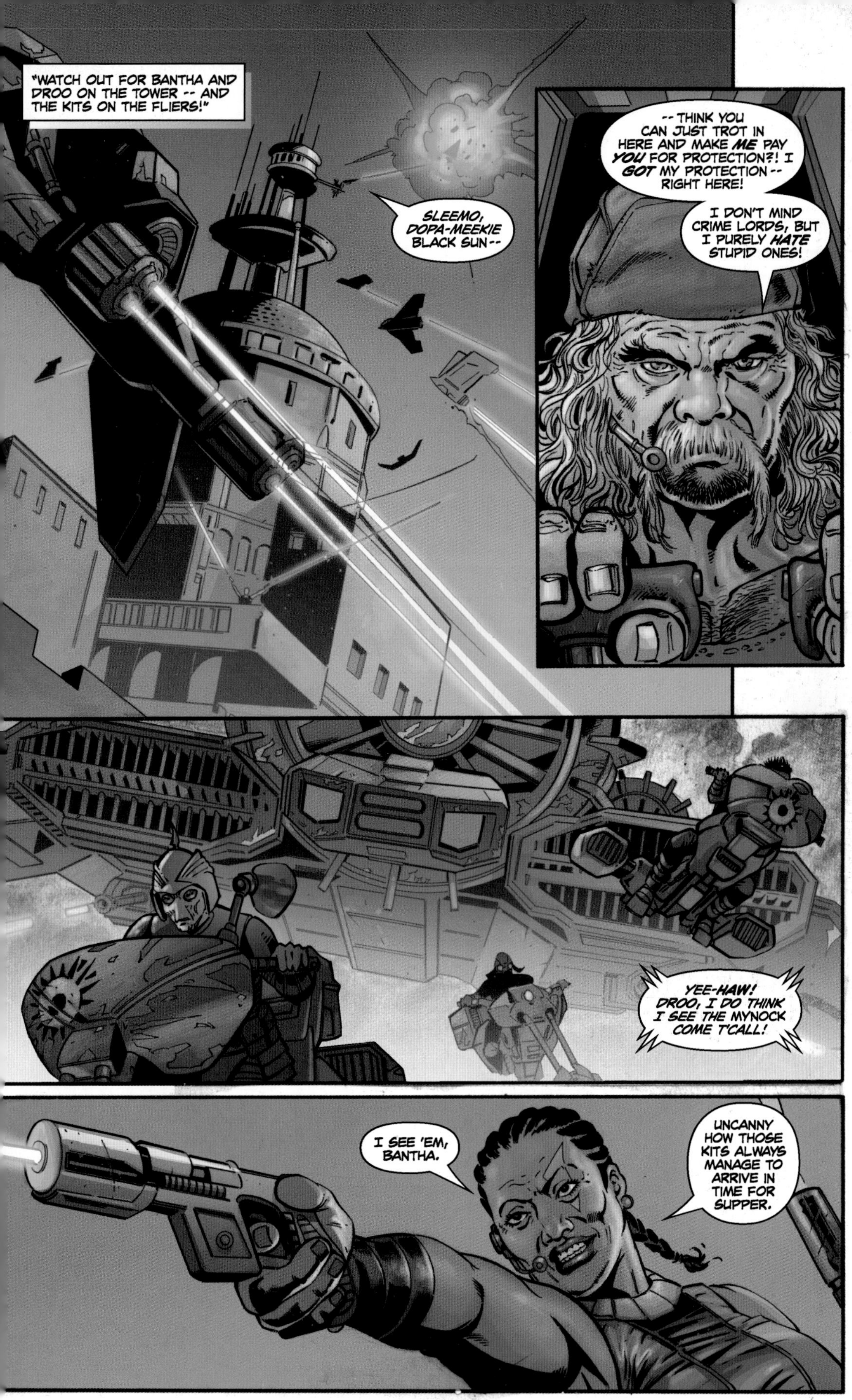
"WATCH OUT FOR BANTHA AND DROO ON THE TOWER -- AND THE KITS ON THE FLIERS!"
SLEEMO, DOPA-MEEKIE BLACK SUN--
--THINK YOU CAN JUST TROT IN HERE AND MAKE ME PAY YOU FOR PROTECTION?! I GOT MY PROTECTION -- RIGHT HERE!
I DON'T MIND CRIME LORDS, BUT I PURELY HATE STUPID ONES!
YEE-HAW! DROO, I DO THINK I SEE THE MYNOCK COME T'CALL!
I SEE 'EM, BANTHA.
UNCANNY HOW THOSE KITS ALWAYS MANAGE TO ARRIVE IN TIME FOR SUPPER.

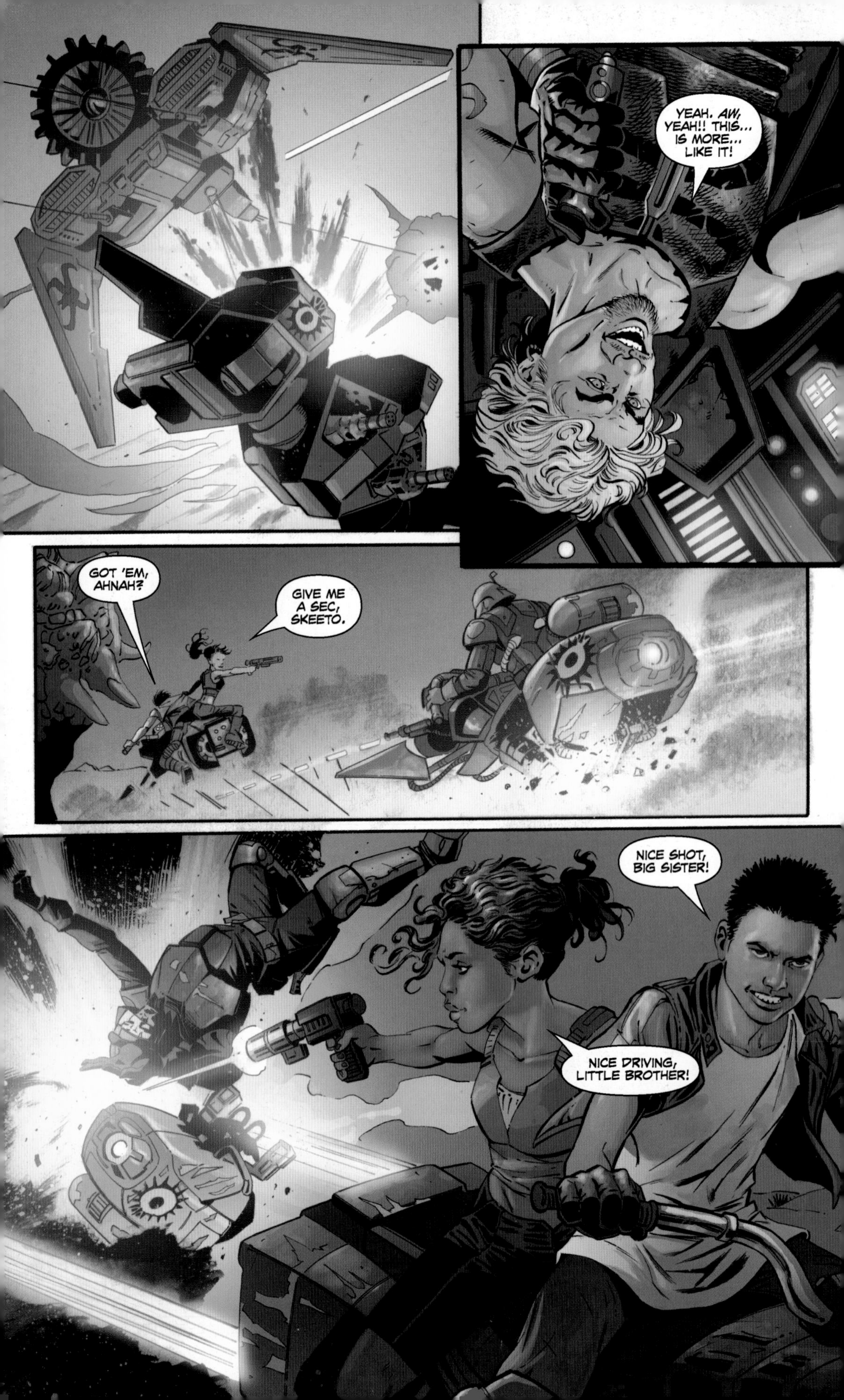
YEAH. AW, YEAH!! THIS... IS MORE... LIKE IT!
GOT 'EM, AHNAH?
GIVE ME A SEC, SKEETO.
NICE SHOT, BIG SISTER!
NICE DRIVING, LITTLE BROTHER!

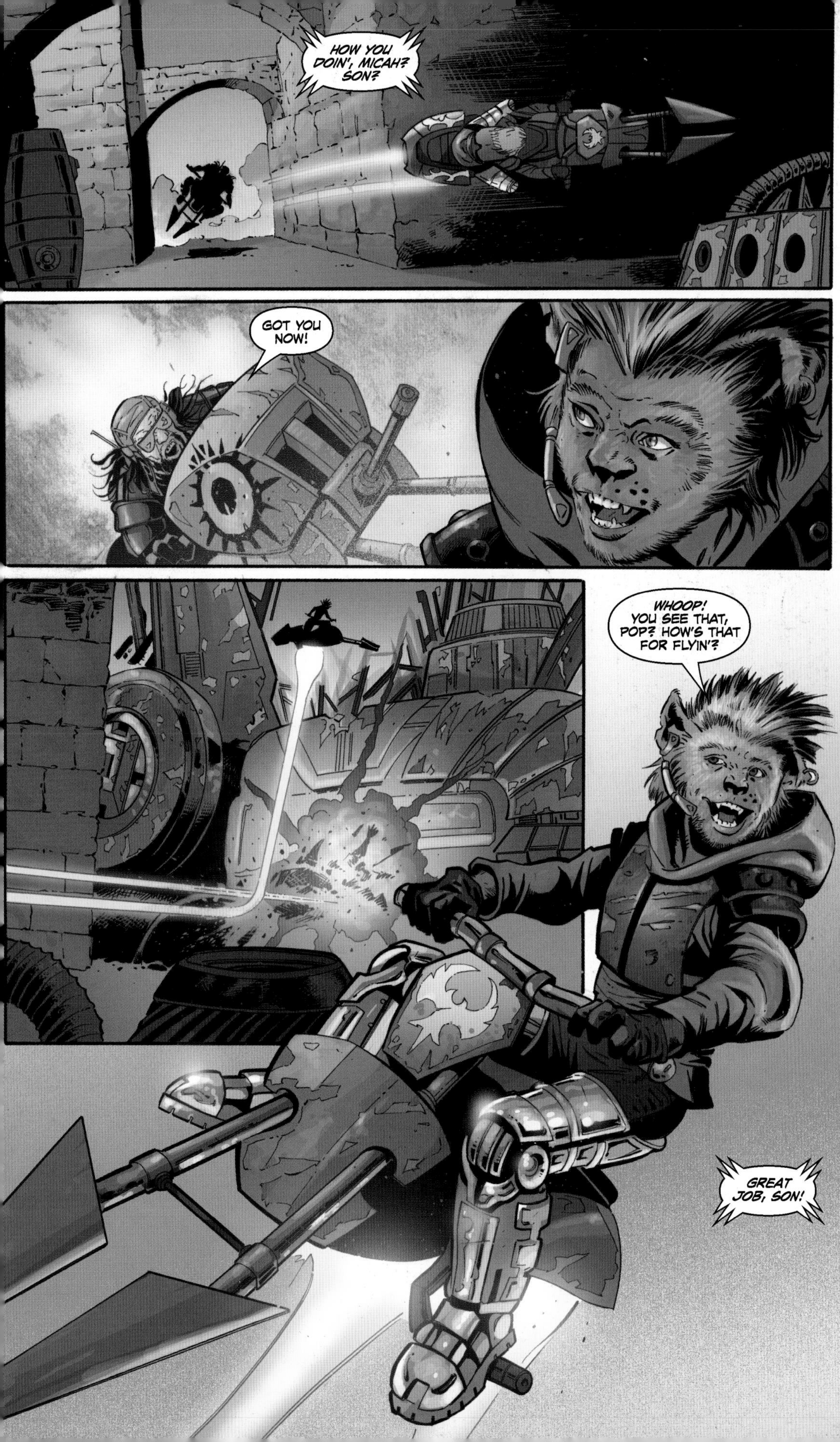
HOW YOU DOIN', MICAH? SON?
GOT YOU NOW!
WHOOP! YOU SEE THAT, POP? HOW'S THAT FOR FLYIN'?
GREAT JOB, SON!

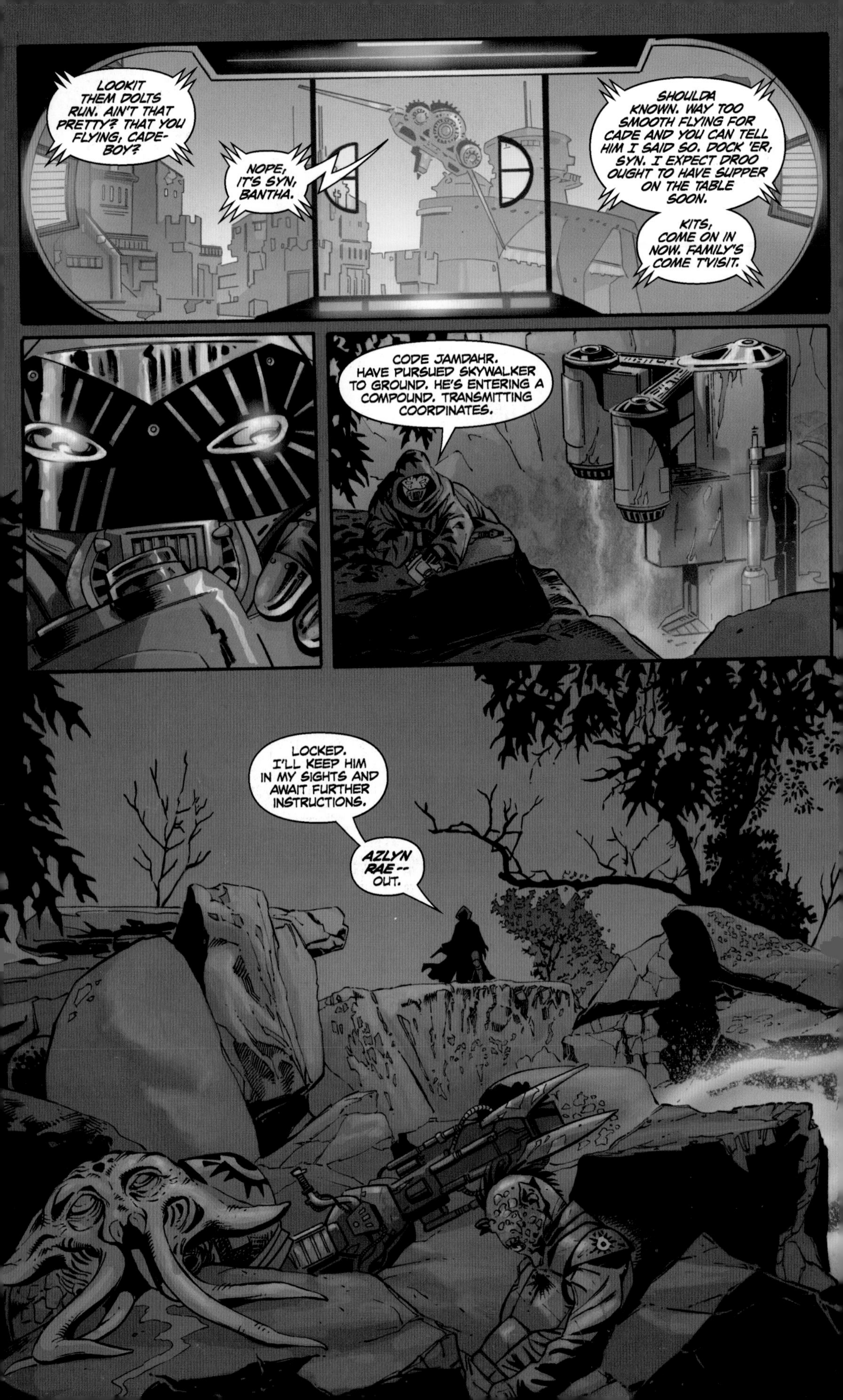
LOOKIT THEM DOLTS RUN. AIN'T THAT PRETTY? THAT YOU FLYING, CADE-BOY?
NOPE, IT'S SYN, BANTHA.
SHOULDA KNOWN. WAY TOO SMOOTH FLYING FOR CADE AND YOU CAN TELL HIM I SAID SO. DOCK 'ER, SYN. I EXPECT DROO OUGHT TO HAVE SUPPER ON THE TABLE SOON.
KITS, COME ON IN NOW. FAMILY'S COME T'VISIT.
CODE JAMDAHR. HAVE PURSUED SKYWALKER TO GROUND. HE'S ENTERING A COMPOUND. TRANSMITTING COORDINATES.
LOCKED. I'LL KEEP HIM IN MY SIGHTS AND AWAIT FURTHER INSTRUCTIONS.
AZLYN RAE-- OUT.

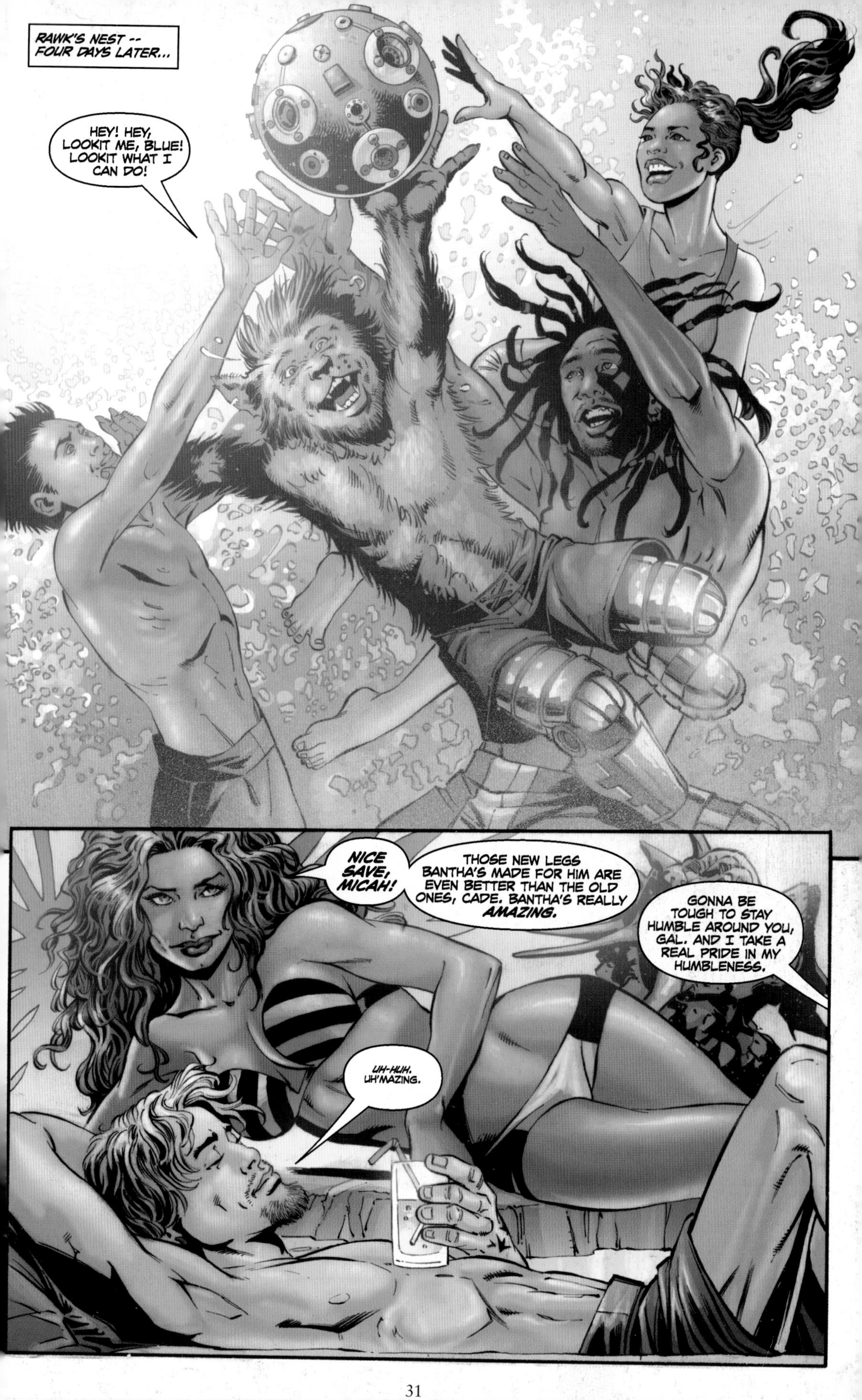
RAWK'S NEST -- FOUR DAYS LATER...
HEY! HEY, LOOKIT ME, BLUE! LOOKIT WHAT I CAN DO!
NICE SAVE, MICAH!
THOSE NEW LEGS BANTHA'S MADE FOR HIM ARE EVEN BETTER THAN THE OLD ONES, CADE. BANTHA'S REALLY AMAZING.
UH-HUH. UH'MAZING.
GONNA BE TOUGH TO STAY HUMBLE AROUND YOU, GAL. AND I TAKE A REAL PRIDE IN MY HUMBLENESS.

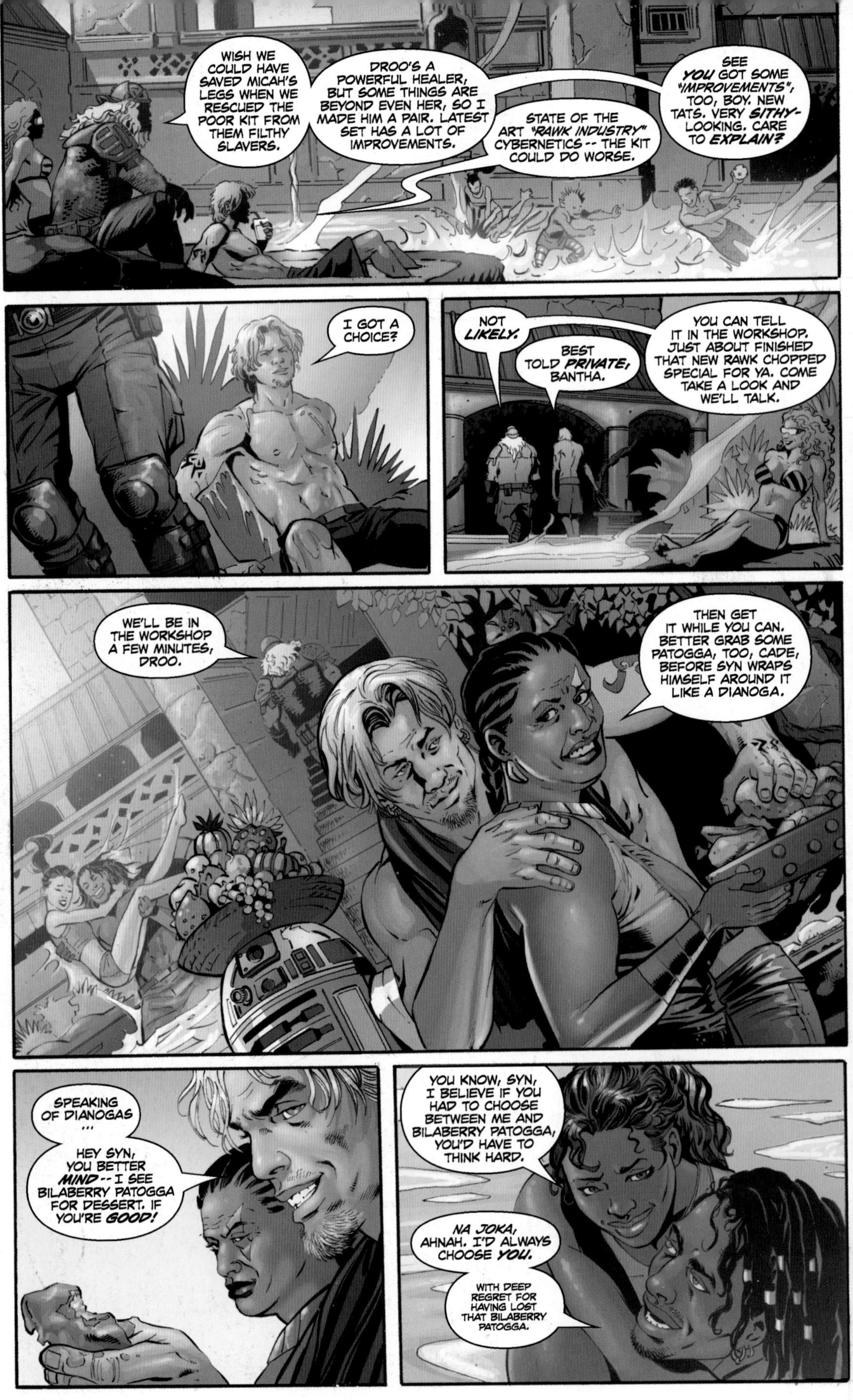
WISH WE COULD HAVE SAVED MICAH'S LEGS WHEN WE RESCUED THE POOR KIT FROM THEM FILTHY SLAVERS.
DROO'S A POWERFUL HEALER, BUT SOME THINGS ARE BEYOND EVEN HER, SO I MADE HIM A PAIR. LATEST SET HAS A LOT OF IMPROVEMENTS.
STATE OF THE ART "RAWK INDUSTRY" CYBERNETICS -- THE KIT COULD DO WORSE.
SEE YOU GOT SOME "IMPROVEMENTS", TOO, BOY. NEW TATS. VERY SITHY-LOOKING. CARE TO EXPLAIN?
I GOT A CHOICE?
NOT LIKELY.
YOU CAN TELL IT IN THE WORKSHOP. JUST ABOUT FINISHED THAT NEW RAWK CHOPPED SPECIAL FOR YA. COME TAKE A LOOK AND WE'LL TALK.
BEST TOLD PRIVATE, BANTHA.
WE'LL BE IN THE WORKSHOP A FEW MINUTES, DROO.
THEN GET IT WHILE YOU CAN. BETTER GRAB SOME PATOGGA, TOO, CADE, BEFORE SYN WRAPS HIMSELF AROUND IT LIKE A DIANOGA.
SPEAKING OF DIANOGAS ...
HEY SYN, YOU BETTER MIND -- I SEE BILABERRY PATOGGA FOR DESSERT. IF YOU'RE GOOD!
YOU KNOW, SYN, I BELIEVE IF YOU HAD TO CHOOSE BETWEEN ME AND BILABERRY PATOGGA, YOU'D HAVE TO THINK HARD.
NA JOKA, AHNAH. I'D ALWAYS CHOOSE YOU.
WITH DEEP REGRET FOR HAVING LOST THAT BILABERRY PATOGGA.

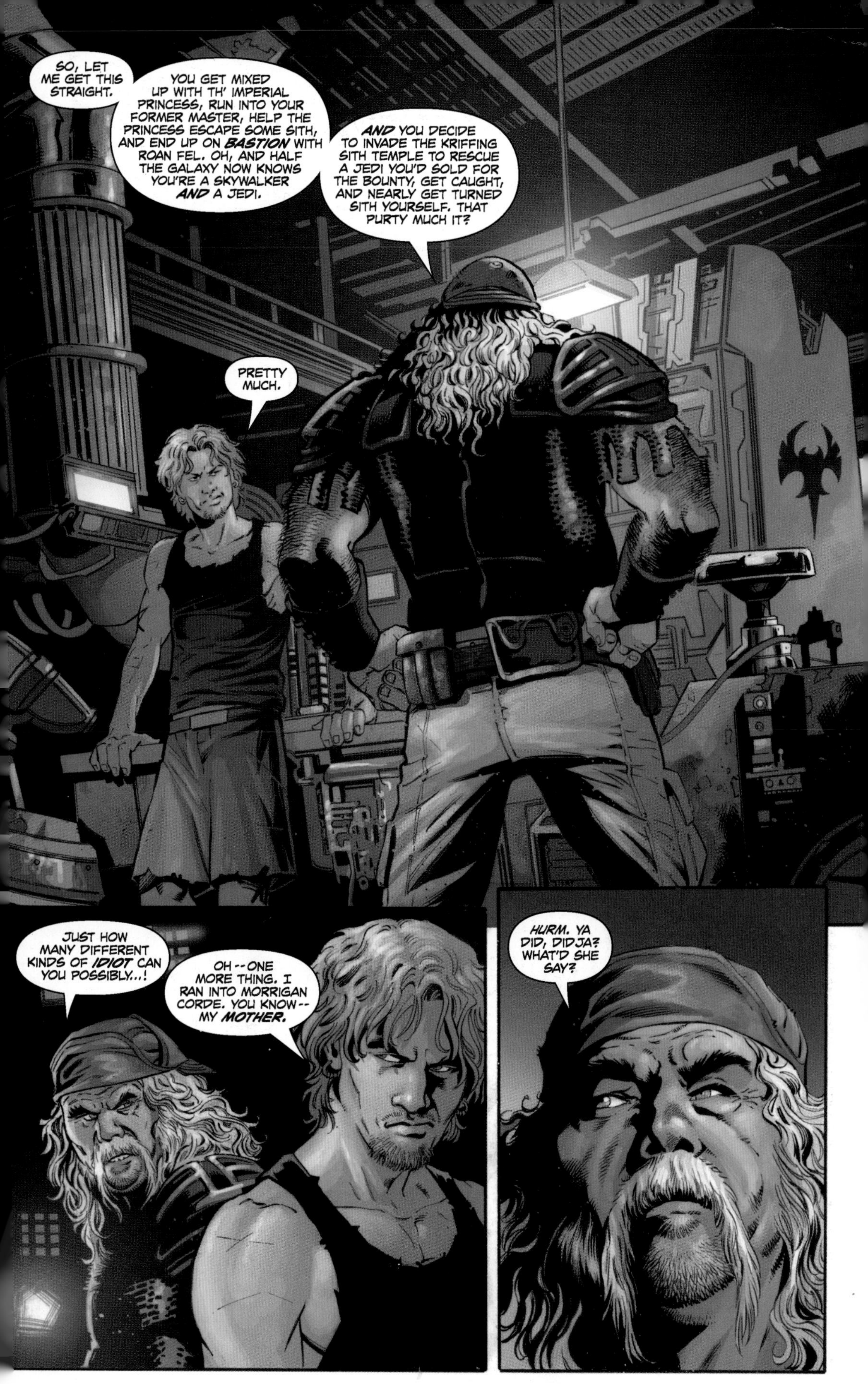

SO, LET ME GET THIS STRAIGHT.
YOU GET MIXED UP WITH TH' IMPERIAL PRINCESS, RUN INTO YOUR FORMER MASTER, HELP THE PRINCESS ESCAPE SOME SITH, AND END UP ON *BASTION* WITH ROAN FEL. OH, AND HALF THE GALAXY NOW KNOWS YOU'RE A SKYWALKER *AND* A JEDI.
AND YOU DECIDE TO INVADE THE KRIFFING SITH TEMPLE TO RESCUE A JEDI YOU'D SOLD FOR THE BOUNTY, GET CAUGHT, AND NEARLY GET TURNED SITH YOURSELF. THAT PURTY MUCH IT?
PRETTY MUCH.
JUST HOW MANY DIFFERENT KINDS OF *IDIOT* CAN YOU POSSIBLY...!
OH--ONE MORE THING. I RAN INTO MORRIGAN CORDE. YOU KNOW-- MY *MOTHER.*
HURM. YA DID, DIDJA? WHAT'D SHE SAY?

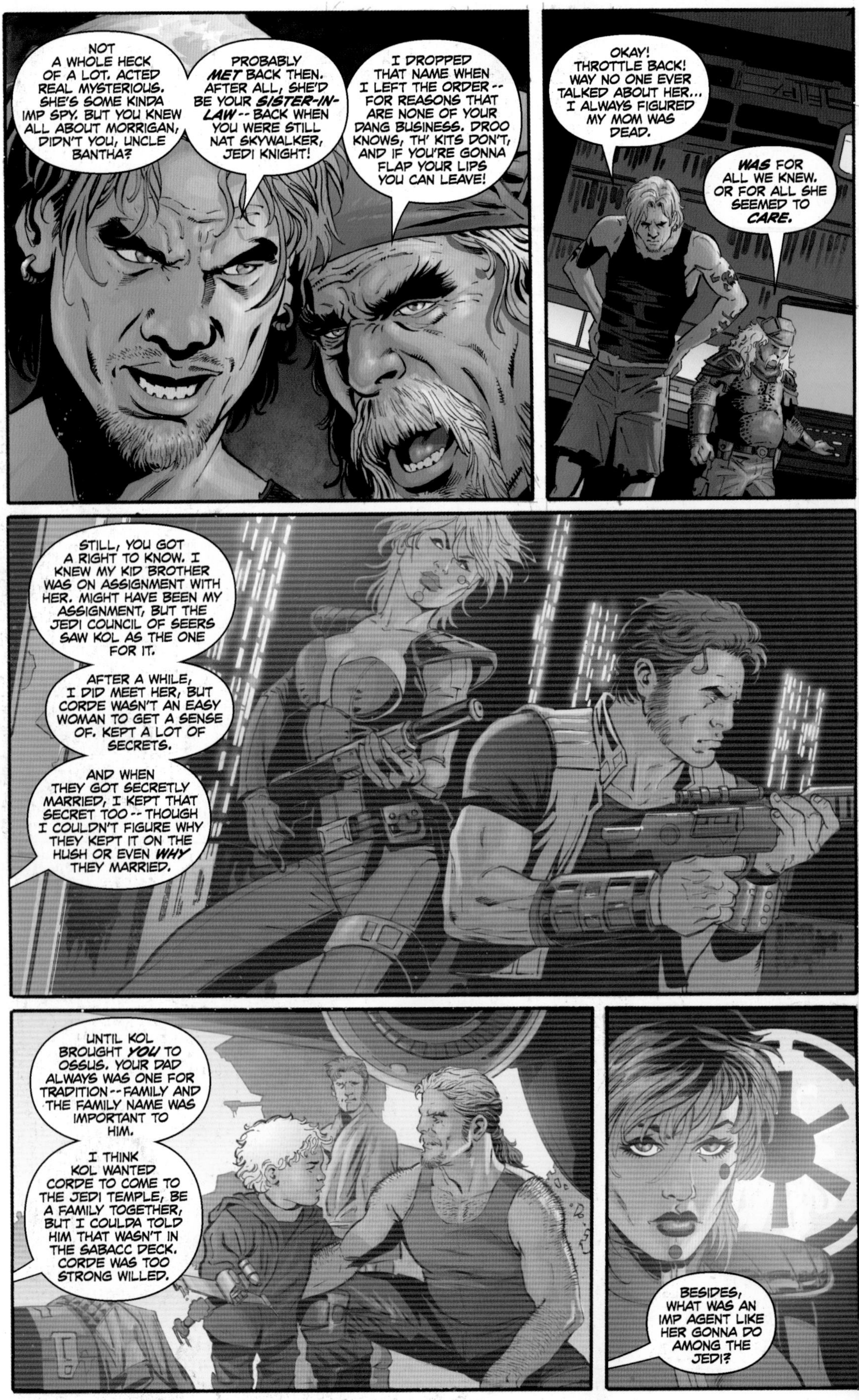
NOT A WHOLE HECK OF A LOT. ACTED REAL MYSTERIOUS. SHE'S SOME KINDA IMP SPY. BUT YOU KNEW ALL ABOUT MORRIGAN, DIDN'T YOU, UNCLE BANTHA?
PROBABLY MET BACK THEN. AFTER ALL, SHE'D BE YOUR SISTER-IN-LAW -- BACK WHEN YOU WERE STILL NAT SKYWALKER, JEDI KNIGHT!
I DROPPED THAT NAME WHEN I LEFT THE ORDER -- FOR REASONS THAT ARE NONE OF YOUR DANG BUSINESS. DROO KNOWS, TH' KITS DON'T, AND IF YOU'RE GONNA FLAP YOUR LIPS YOU CAN LEAVE!
OKAY! THROTTLE BACK! WAY NO ONE EVER TALKED ABOUT HER... I ALWAYS FIGURED MY MOM WAS DEAD.
WAS FOR ALL WE KNEW. OR FOR ALL SHE SEEMED TO CARE.
STILL, YOU GOT A RIGHT TO KNOW. I KNEW MY KID BROTHER WAS ON ASSIGNMENT WITH HER. MIGHT HAVE BEEN MY ASSIGNMENT, BUT THE JEDI COUNCIL OF SEERS SAW KOL AS THE ONE FOR IT.
AFTER A WHILE, I DID MEET HER, BUT CORDE WASN'T AN EASY WOMAN TO GET A SENSE OF. KEPT A LOT OF SECRETS.
AND WHEN THEY GOT SECRETLY MARRIED, I KEPT THAT SECRET TOO -- THOUGH I COULDN'T FIGURE WHY THEY KEPT IT ON THE HUSH OR EVEN WHY THEY MARRIED.
UNTIL KOL BROUGHT YOU TO OSSUS. YOUR DAD ALWAYS WAS ONE FOR TRADITION -- FAMILY AND THE FAMILY NAME WAS IMPORTANT TO HIM.
I THINK KOL WANTED CORDE TO COME TO THE JEDI TEMPLE, BE A FAMILY TOGETHER, BUT I COULDA TOLD HIM THAT WASN'T IN THE SABACC DECK. CORDE WAS TOO STRONG WILLED.
BESIDES, WHAT WAS AN IMP AGENT LIKE HER GONNA DO AMONG THE JEDI?

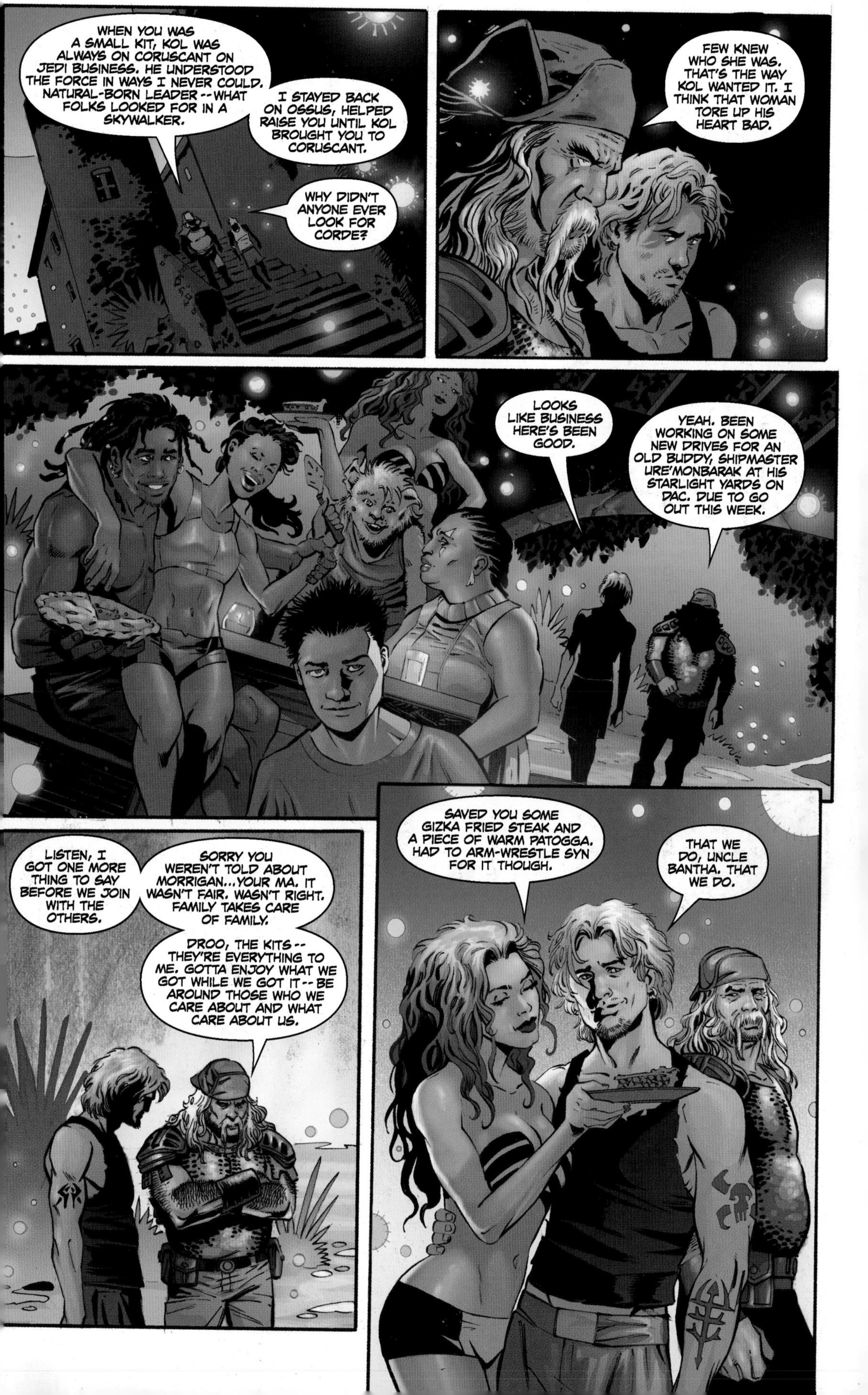
WHEN YOU WAS A SMALL KIT, KOL WAS ALWAYS ON CORUSCANT ON JEDI BUSINESS. HE UNDERSTOOD THE FORCE IN WAYS I NEVER COULD. NATURAL-BORN LEADER -- WHAT FOLKS LOOKED FOR IN A SKYWALKER.
I STAYED BACK ON OSSUS, HELPED RAISE YOU UNTIL KOL BROUGHT YOU TO CORUSCANT.
WHY DIDN'T ANYONE EVER LOOK FOR CORDE?
FEW KNEW WHO SHE WAS. THAT'S THE WAY KOL WANTED IT. I THINK THAT WOMAN TORE UP HIS HEART BAD.
LOOKS LIKE BUSINESS HERE'S BEEN GOOD.
YEAH. BEEN WORKING ON SOME NEW DRIVES FOR AN OLD BUDDY, SHIPMASTER URE'MONBARAK AT HIS STARLIGHT YARDS ON DAC. DUE TO GO OUT THIS WEEK.
LISTEN, I GOT ONE MORE THING TO SAY BEFORE WE JOIN WITH THE OTHERS.
SORRY YOU WEREN'T TOLD ABOUT MORRIGAN...YOUR MA. IT WASN'T FAIR. WASN'T RIGHT. FAMILY TAKES CARE OF FAMILY.
DROO, THE KITS -- THEY'RE EVERYTHING TO ME. GOTTA ENJOY WHAT WE GOT WHILE WE GOT IT -- BE AROUND THOSE WHO WE CARE ABOUT AND WHAT CARE ABOUT US.
SAVED YOU SOME GIZKA FRIED STEAK AND A PIECE OF WARM PATOGGA. HAD TO ARM-WRESTLE SYN FOR IT THOUGH.
THAT WE DO, UNCLE BANTHA. THAT WE DO.

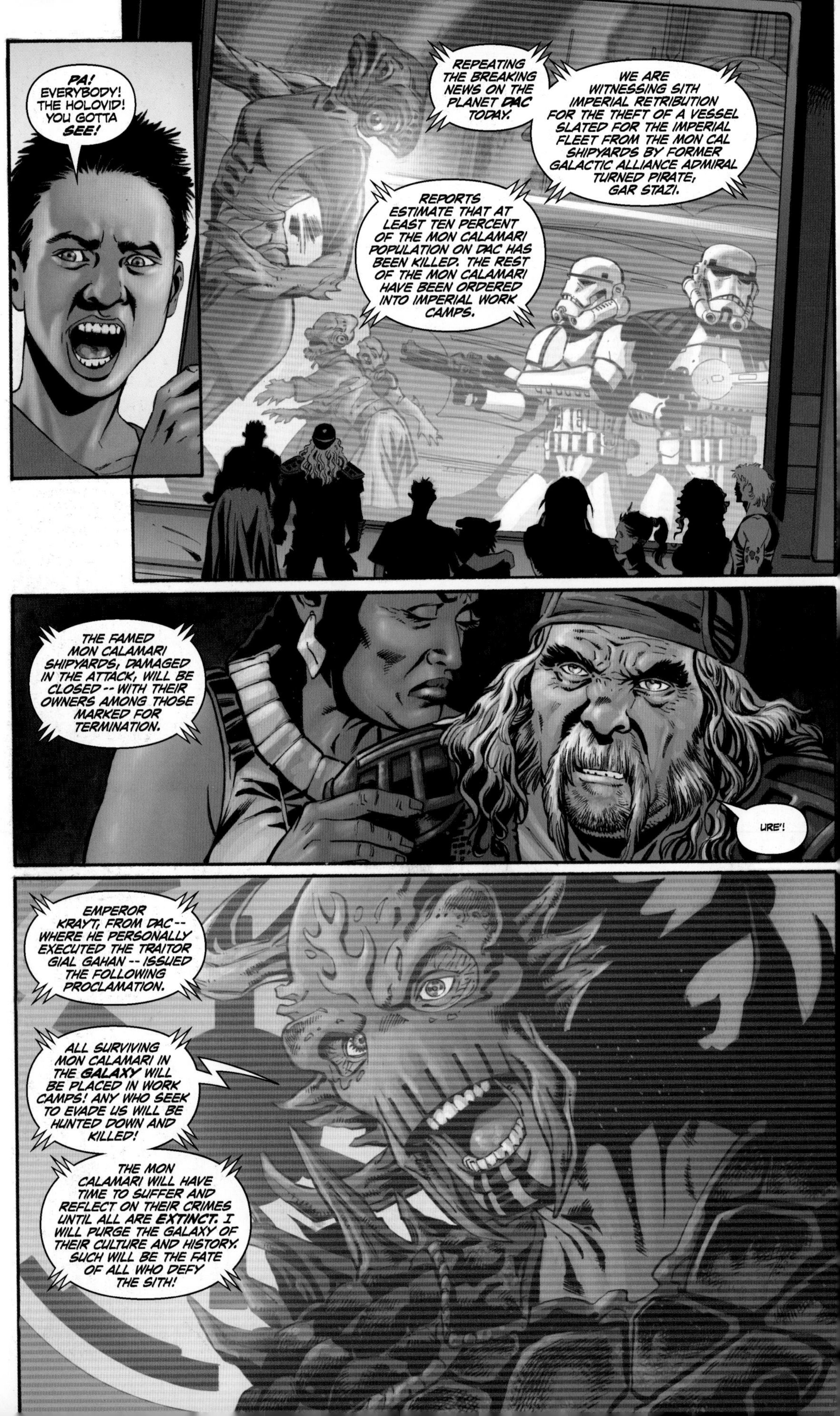
PA! EVERYBODY! THE HOLOVID! YOU GOTTA SEE!
REPEATING THE BREAKING NEWS ON THE PLANET DAC TODAY.
WE ARE WITNESSING SITH IMPERIAL RETRIBUTION FOR THE THEFT OF A VESSEL SLATED FOR THE IMPERIAL FLEET FROM THE MON CAL SHIPYARDS BY FORMER GALACTIC ALLIANCE ADMIRAL TURNED PIRATE, GAR STAZI.
REPORTS ESTIMATE THAT AT LEAST TEN PERCENT OF THE MON CALAMARI POPULATION ON DAC HAS BEEN KILLED. THE REST OF THE MON CALAMARI HAVE BEEN ORDERED INTO IMPERIAL WORK CAMPS.
THE FAMED MON CALAMARI SHIPYARDS, DAMAGED IN THE ATTACK, WILL BE CLOSED -- WITH THEIR OWNERS AMONG THOSE MARKED FOR TERMINATION.
URE'!
EMPEROR KRAYT, FROM DAC -- WHERE HE PERSONALLY EXECUTED THE TRAITOR GIAL GAHAN -- ISSUED THE FOLLOWING PROCLAMATION.
ALL SURVIVING MON CALAMARI IN THE GALAXY WILL BE PLACED IN WORK CAMPS! ANY WHO SEEK TO EVADE US WILL BE HUNTED DOWN AND KILLED!
THE MON CALAMARI WILL HAVE TIME TO SUFFER AND REFLECT ON THEIR CRIMES UNTIL ALL ARE EXTINCT. I WILL PURGE THE GALAXY OF THEIR CULTURE AND HISTORY. SUCH WILL BE THE FATE OF ALL WHO DEFY THE SITH!

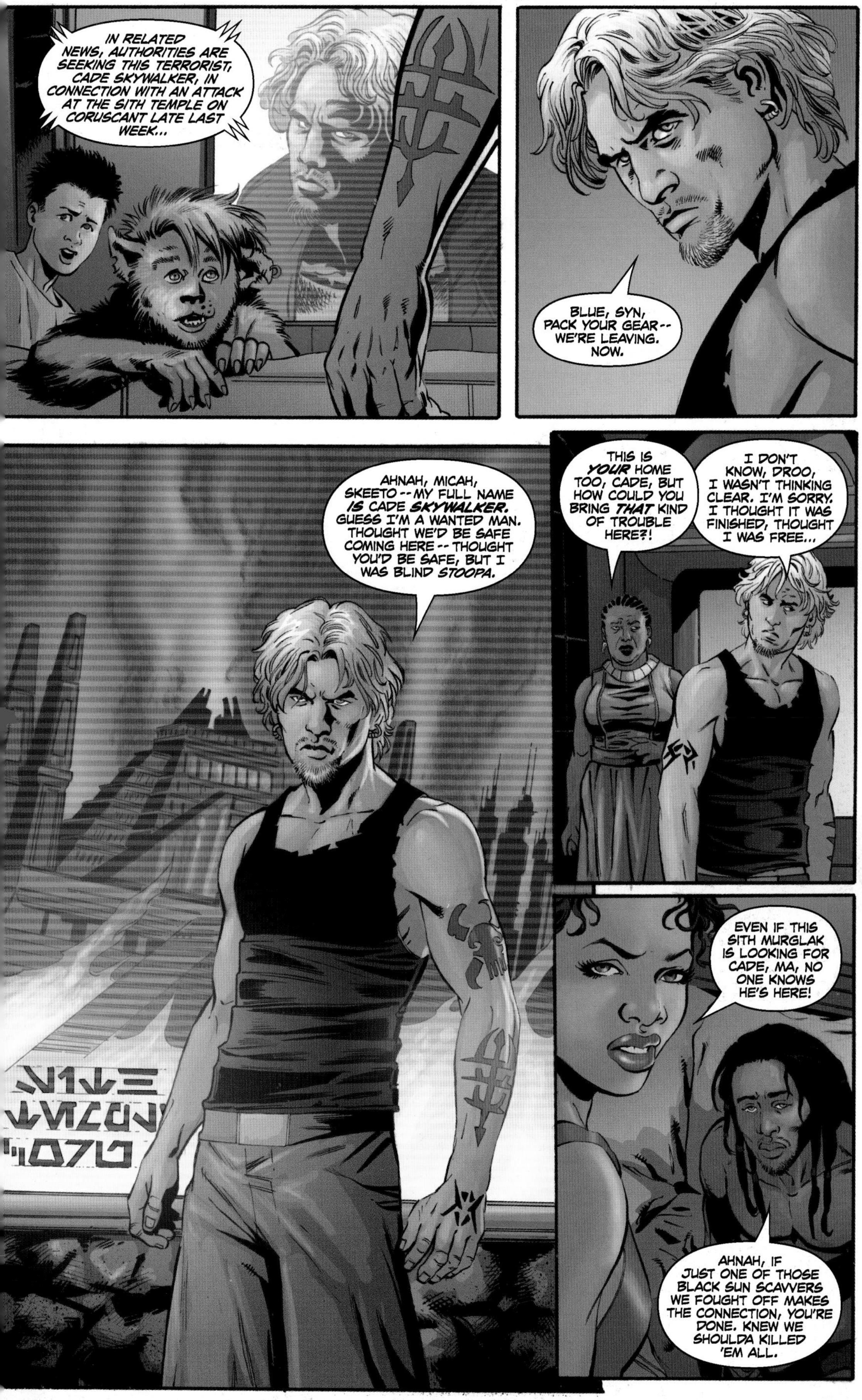
IN RELATED NEWS, AUTHORITIES ARE SEEKING THIS TERRORIST, CADE SKYWALKER, IN CONNECTION WITH AN ATTACK AT THE SITH TEMPLE ON CORUSCANT LATE LAST WEEK...
BLUE, SYN, PACK YOUR GEAR-- WE'RE LEAVING. NOW.
AHNAH, MICAH, SKEETO--MY FULL NAME *IS* CADE ***SKYWALKER.*** GUESS I'M A WANTED MAN. THOUGHT WE'D BE SAFE COMING HERE--THOUGHT YOU'D BE SAFE, BUT I WAS BLIND *STOOPA.*
THIS IS ***YOUR*** HOME TOO, CADE, BUT HOW COULD YOU BRING ***THAT*** KIND OF TROUBLE HERE?!
I DON'T KNOW, DROO, I WASN'T THINKING CLEAR. I'M SORRY. I THOUGHT IT WAS FINISHED, THOUGHT I WAS FREE...
EVEN IF THIS SITH MURGLAK IS LOOKING FOR CADE, MA, NO ONE KNOWS HE'S HERE!
AHNAH, IF JUST ONE OF THOSE BLACK SUN SCAVVERS WE FOUGHT OFF MAKES THE CONNECTION, YOU'RE DONE. KNEW WE SHOULDA KILLED 'EM ALL.

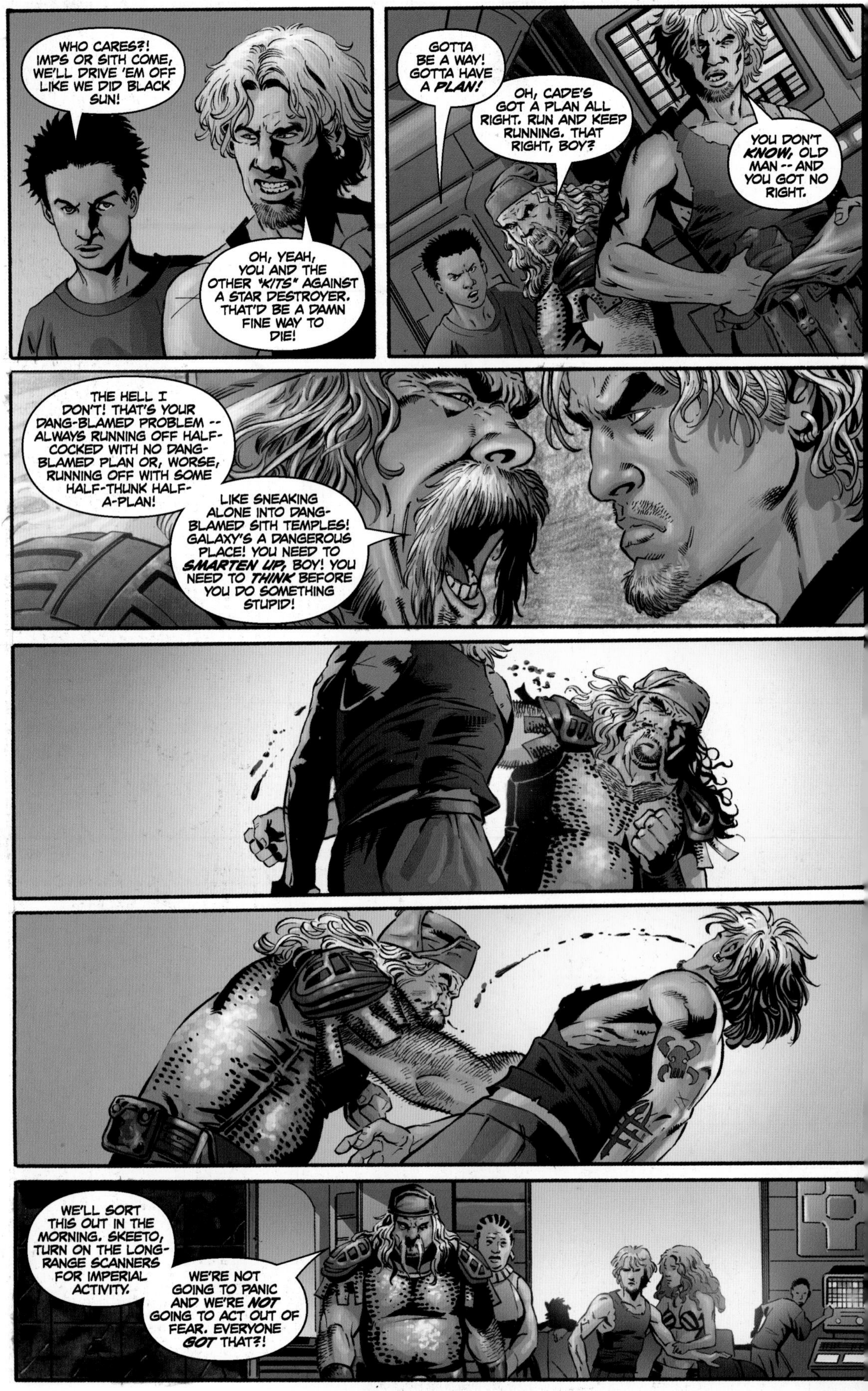
WHO CARES?! IMPS OR SITH COME, WE'LL DRIVE 'EM OFF LIKE WE DID BLACK SUN!
OH, YEAH, YOU AND THE OTHER "K'ITS" AGAINST A STAR DESTROYER. THAT'D BE A DAMN FINE WAY TO DIE!
GOTTA BE A WAY! GOTTA HAVE A PLAN!
OH, CADE'S GOT A PLAN ALL RIGHT. RUN AND KEEP RUNNING. THAT RIGHT, BOY?
YOU DON'T KNOW, OLD MAN -- AND YOU GOT NO RIGHT.
THE HELL I DON'T! THAT'S YOUR DANG-BLAMED PROBLEM -- ALWAYS RUNNING OFF HALF-COCKED WITH NO DANG-BLAMED PLAN OR, WORSE, RUNNING OFF WITH SOME HALF-THUNK HALF-A-PLAN!
LIKE SNEAKING ALONE INTO DANG-BLAMED SITH TEMPLES! GALAXY'S A DANGEROUS PLACE! YOU NEED TO SMARTEN UP, BOY! YOU NEED TO THINK BEFORE YOU DO SOMETHING STUPID!
WE'LL SORT THIS OUT IN THE MORNING. SKEETO, TURN ON THE LONG-RANGE SCANNERS FOR IMPERIAL ACTIVITY.
WE'RE NOT GOING TO PANIC AND WE'RE NOT GOING TO ACT OUT OF FEAR. EVERYONE GOT THAT?!

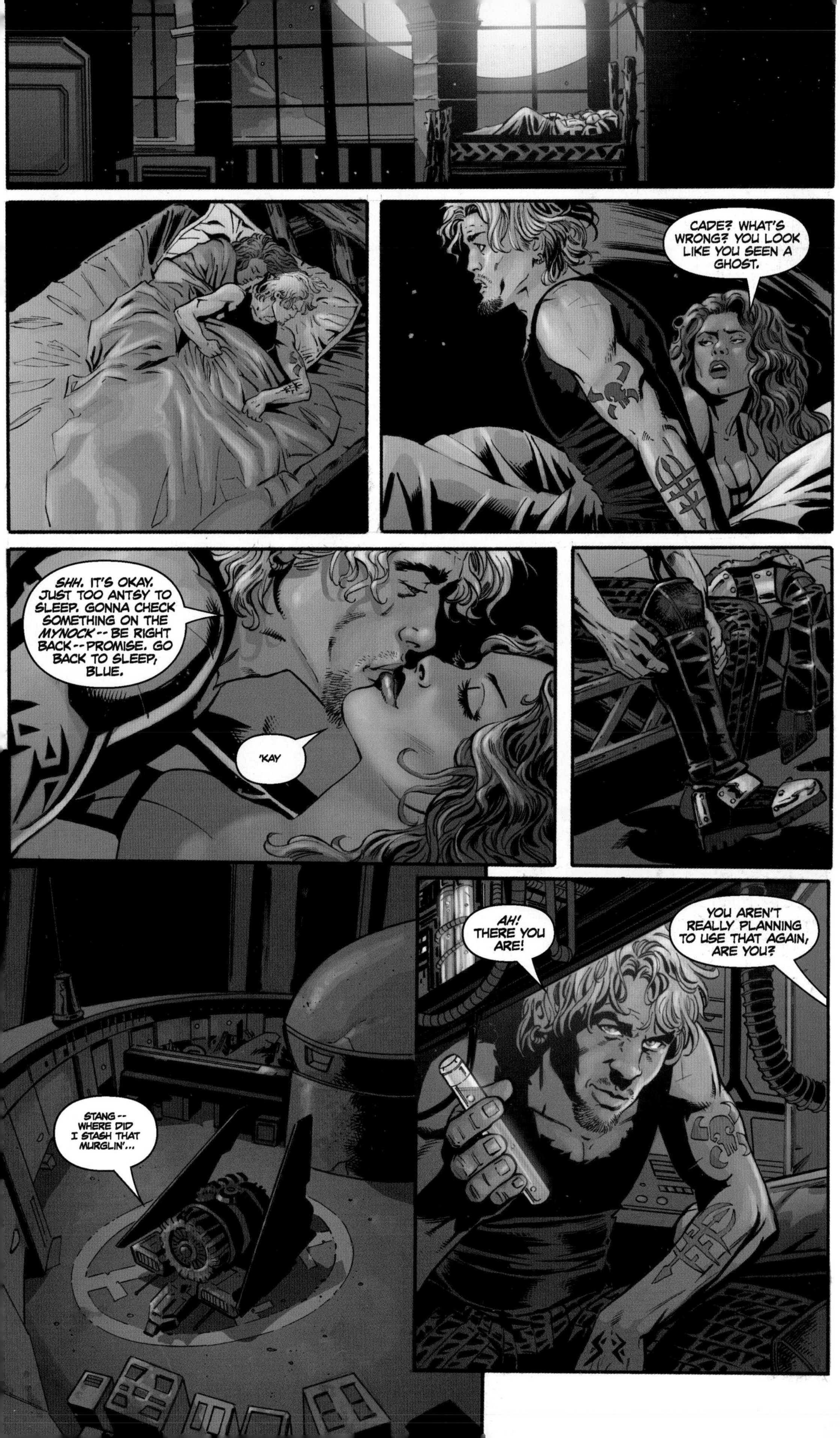
CADE? WHAT'S WRONG? YOU LOOK LIKE YOU SEEN A GHOST.
SHH. IT'S OKAY. JUST TOO ANTSY TO SLEEP. GONNA CHECK SOMETHING ON THE *MYNOCK*--BE RIGHT BACK--PROMISE. GO BACK TO SLEEP, BLUE.
'KAY
STANG--WHERE DID I STASH THAT MURGLIN'...
AH! THERE YOU ARE!
YOU AREN'T REALLY PLANNING TO USE THAT AGAIN, ARE YOU?

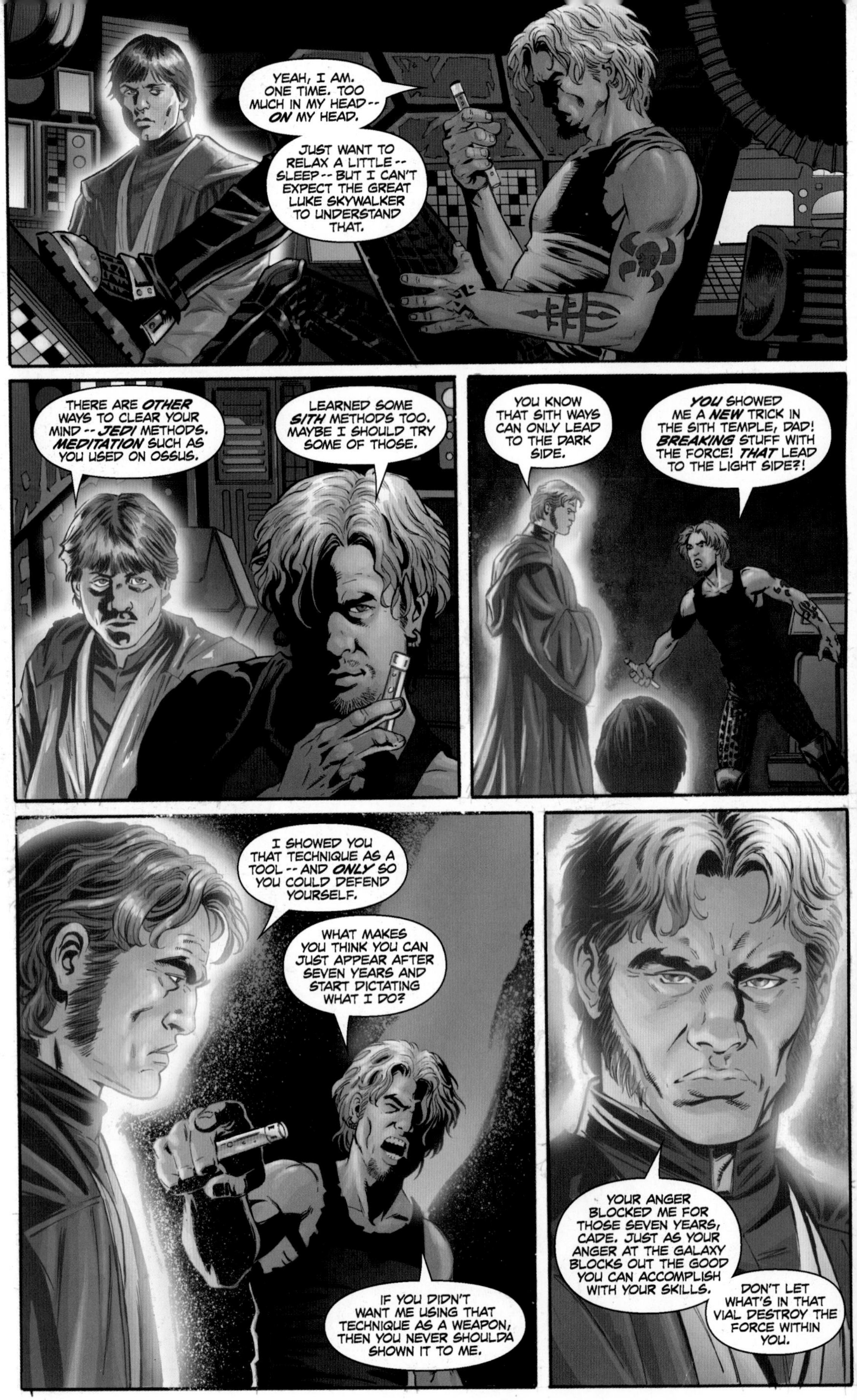
YEAH, I AM. ONE TIME. TOO MUCH IN MY HEAD-- ON MY HEAD.
JUST WANT TO RELAX A LITTLE-- SLEEP--BUT I CAN'T EXPECT THE GREAT LUKE SKYWALKER TO UNDERSTAND THAT.
THERE ARE OTHER WAYS TO CLEAR YOUR MIND--JEDI METHODS. MEDITATION SUCH AS YOU USED ON OSSUS.
LEARNED SOME SITH METHODS TOO. MAYBE I SHOULD TRY SOME OF THOSE.
YOU KNOW THAT SITH WAYS CAN ONLY LEAD TO THE DARK SIDE.
YOU SHOWED ME A NEW TRICK IN THE SITH TEMPLE, DAD! BREAKING STUFF WITH THE FORCE! THAT LEAD TO THE LIGHT SIDE?!
I SHOWED YOU THAT TECHNIQUE AS A TOOL--AND ONLY SO YOU COULD DEFEND YOURSELF.
WHAT MAKES YOU THINK YOU CAN JUST APPEAR AFTER SEVEN YEARS AND START DICTATING WHAT I DO?
IF YOU DIDN'T WANT ME USING THAT TECHNIQUE AS A WEAPON, THEN YOU NEVER SHOULDA SHOWN IT TO ME.
YOUR ANGER BLOCKED ME FOR THOSE SEVEN YEARS, CADE. JUST AS YOUR ANGER AT THE GALAXY BLOCKS OUT THE GOOD YOU CAN ACCOMPLISH WITH YOUR SKILLS.
DON'T LET WHAT'S IN THAT VIAL DESTROY THE FORCE WITHIN YOU.

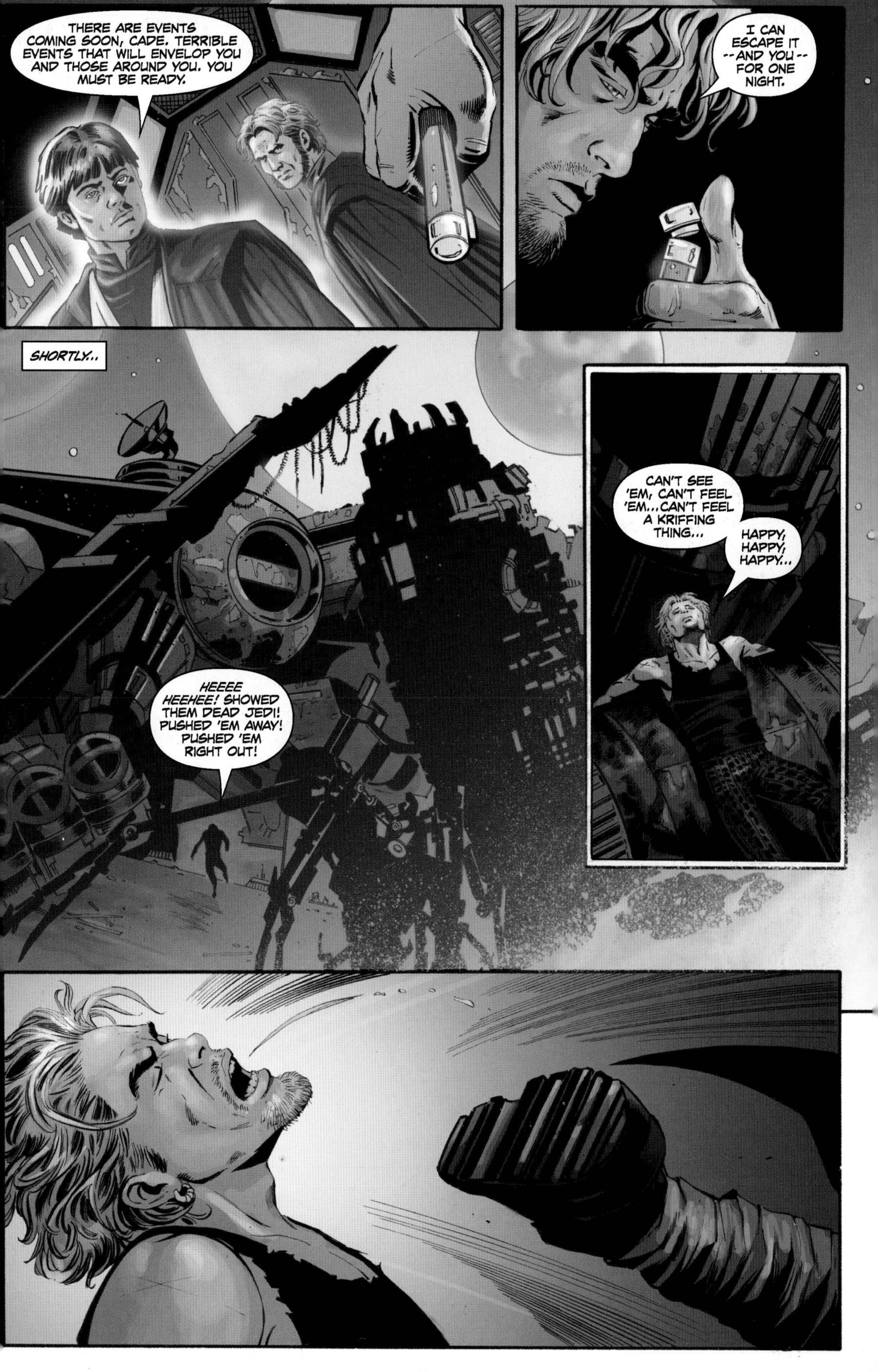
THERE ARE EVENTS COMING SOON, CADE. TERRIBLE EVENTS THAT WILL ENVELOP YOU AND THOSE AROUND YOU. YOU MUST BE READY.
I CAN ESCAPE IT --AND YOU-- FOR ONE NIGHT.
SHORTLY...
HEEEE HEEHEE! SHOWED THEM DEAD JEDI! PUSHED 'EM AWAY! PUSHED 'EM RIGHT OUT!
CAN'T SEE 'EM, CAN'T FEEL 'EM...CAN'T FEEL A KRIFFING THING...
HAPPY, HAPPY, HAPPY...

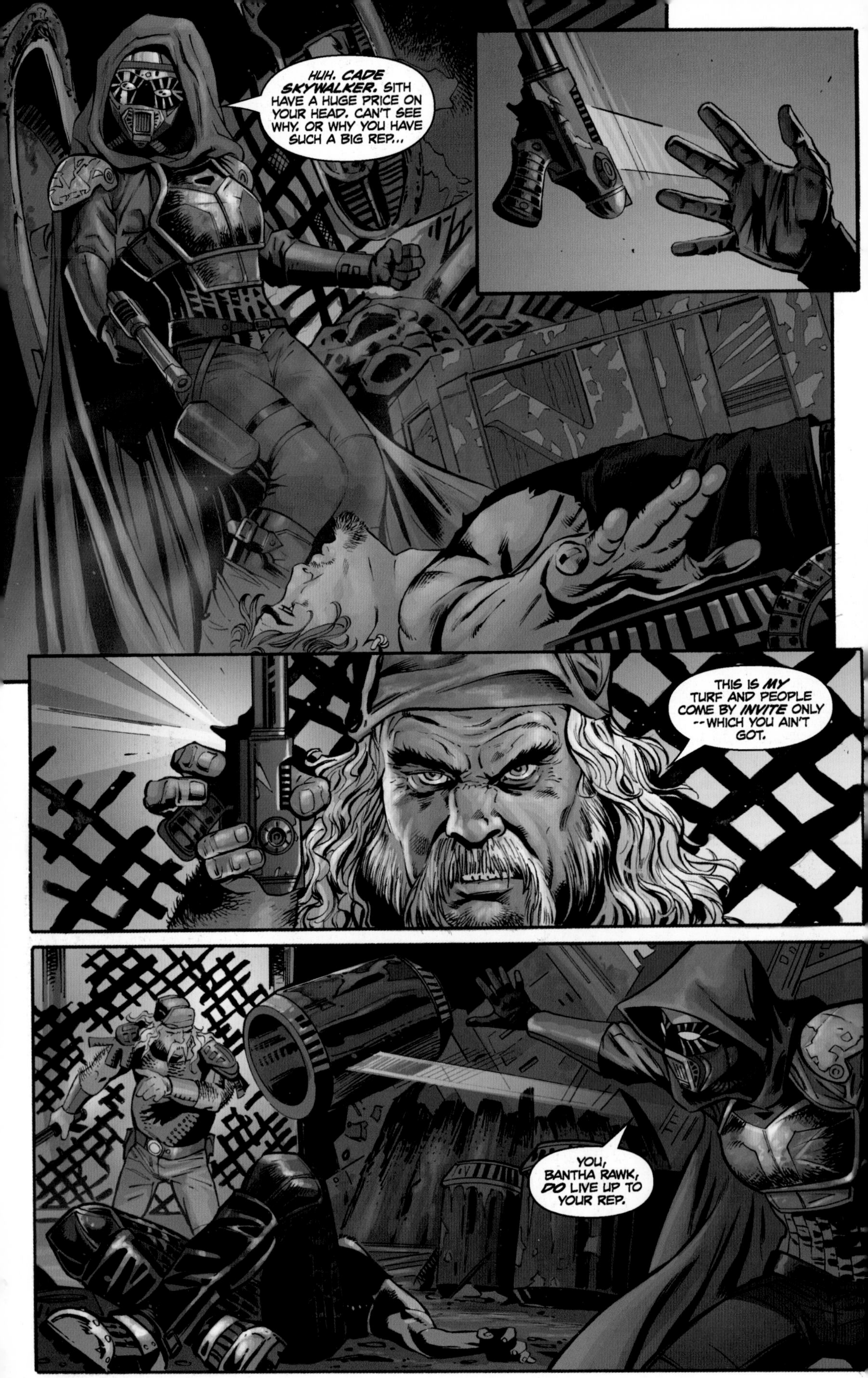
HUH. CADE SKYWALKER. SITH HAVE A HUGE PRICE ON YOUR HEAD. CAN'T SEE WHY. OR WHY YOU HAVE SUCH A BIG REP...
THIS IS MY TURF AND PEOPLE COME BY INVITE ONLY --WHICH YOU AIN'T GOT.
YOU, BANTHA RAWK, DO LIVE UP TO YOUR REP.

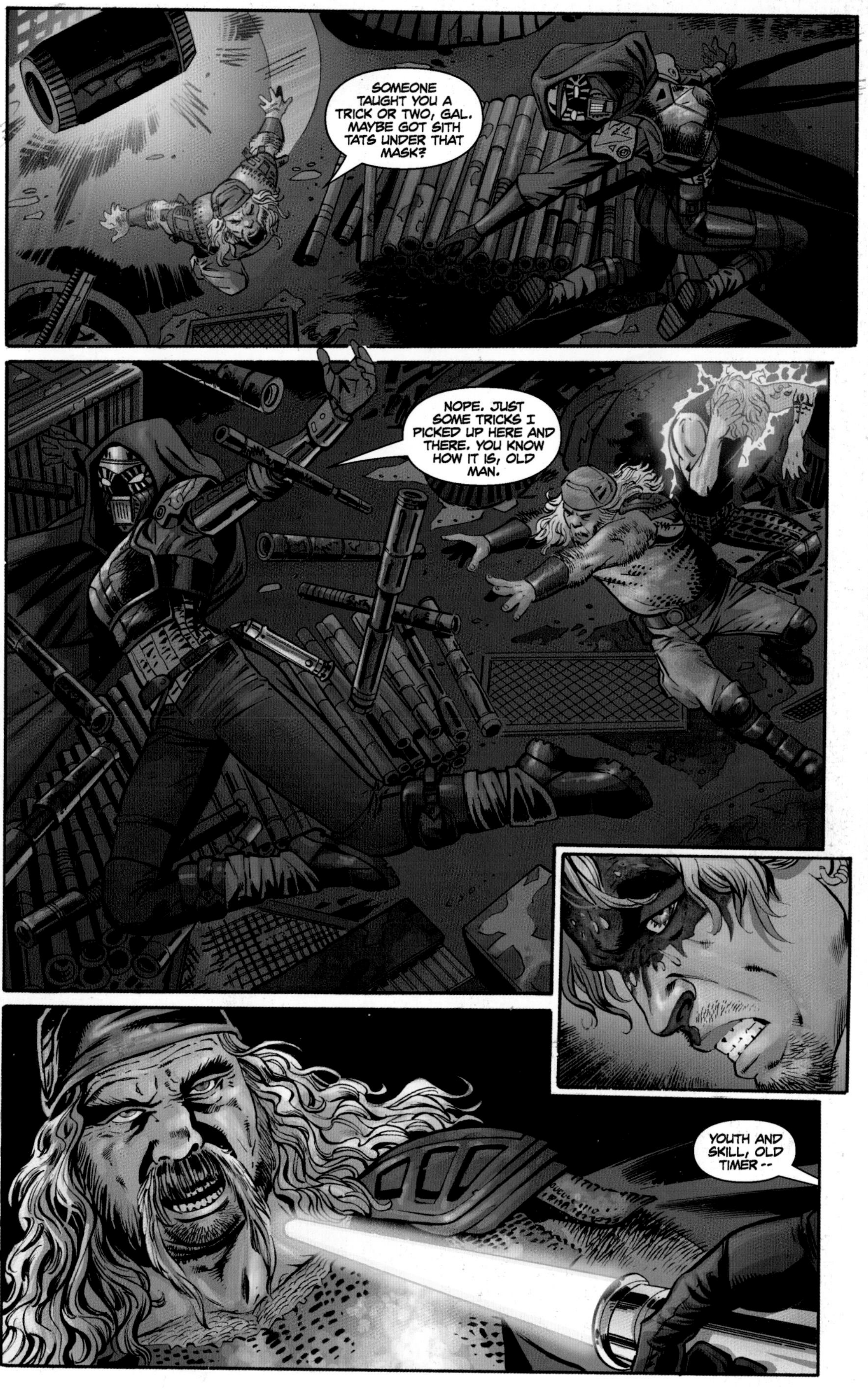
SOMEONE TAUGHT YOU A TRICK OR TWO, GAL. MAYBE GOT SITH TATS UNDER THAT MASK?
NOPE. JUST SOME TRICKS I PICKED UP HERE AND THERE. YOU KNOW HOW IT IS, OLD MAN.
YOUTH AND SKILL, OLD TIMER --

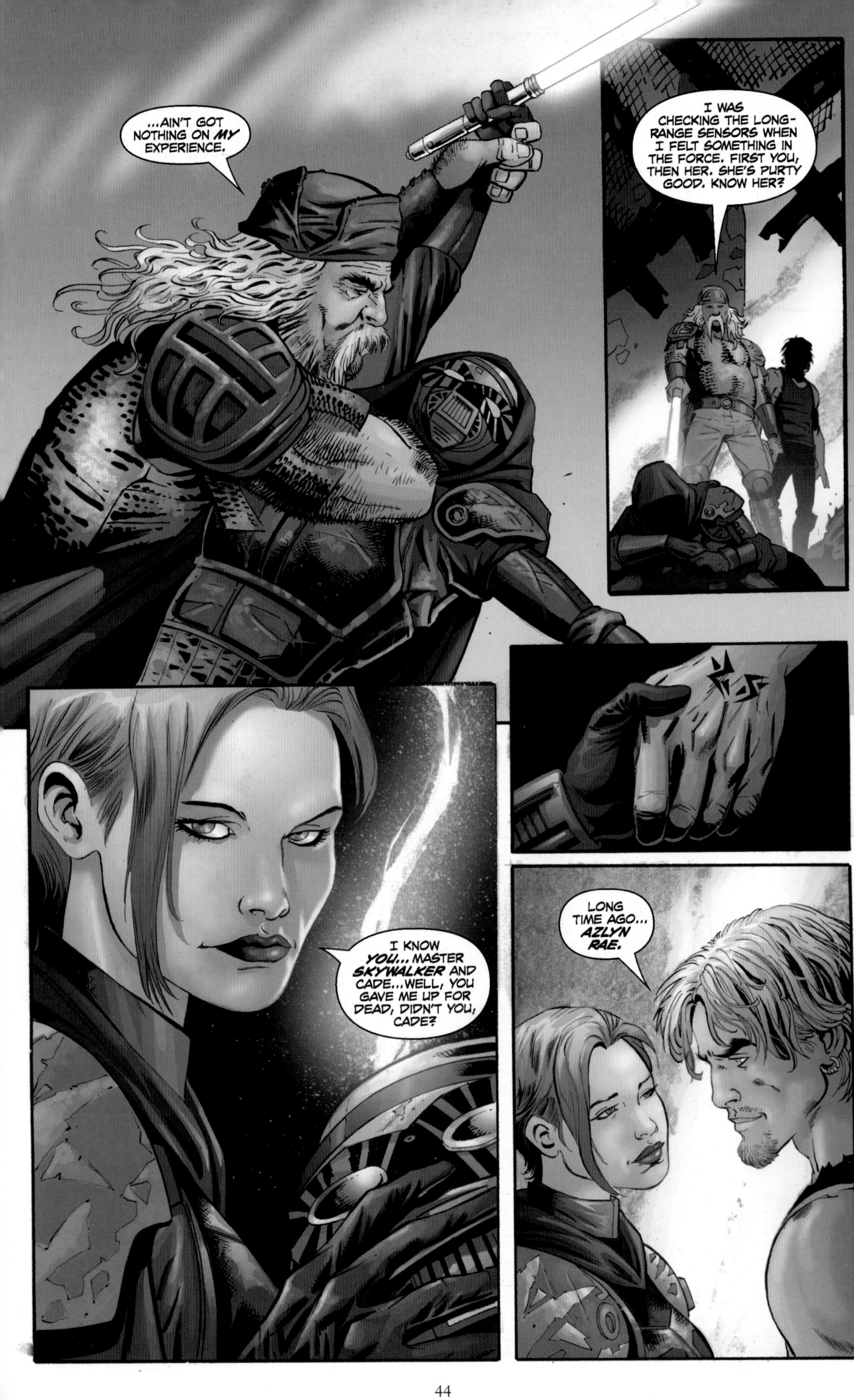
...AIN'T GOT NOTHING ON MY EXPERIENCE.
I WAS CHECKING THE LONG-RANGE SENSORS WHEN I FELT SOMETHING IN THE FORCE. FIRST YOU, THEN HER. SHE'S PURTY GOOD. KNOW HER?
I KNOW YOU... MASTER SKYWALKER AND CADE...WELL, YOU GAVE ME UP FOR DEAD, DIDN'T YOU, CADE?
LONG TIME AGO... AZLYN RAE.

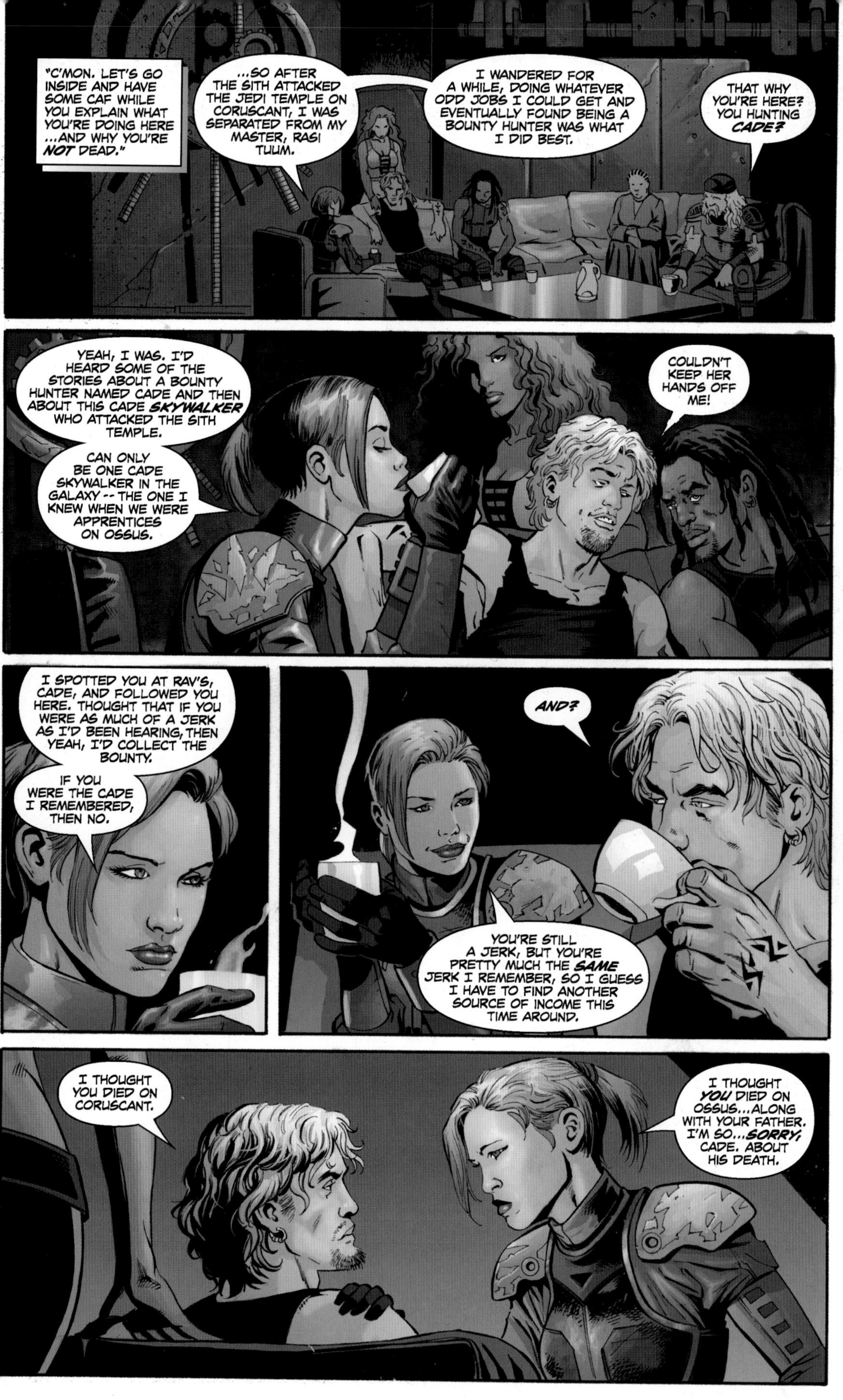
"C'MON. LET'S GO INSIDE AND HAVE SOME CAF WHILE YOU EXPLAIN WHAT YOU'RE DOING HERE ...AND WHY YOU'RE NOT DEAD."
...SO AFTER THE SITH ATTACKED THE JEDI TEMPLE ON CORUSCANT, I WAS SEPARATED FROM MY MASTER, RASI TUUM.
I WANDERED FOR A WHILE, DOING WHATEVER ODD JOBS I COULD GET AND EVENTUALLY FOUND BEING A BOUNTY HUNTER WAS WHAT I DID BEST.
THAT WHY YOU'RE HERE? YOU HUNTING CADE?
YEAH, I WAS. I'D HEARD SOME OF THE STORIES ABOUT A BOUNTY HUNTER NAMED CADE AND THEN ABOUT THIS CADE SKYWALKER WHO ATTACKED THE SITH TEMPLE.
CAN ONLY BE ONE CADE SKYWALKER IN THE GALAXY -- THE ONE I KNEW WHEN WE WERE APPRENTICES ON OSSUS.
COULDN'T KEEP HER HANDS OFF ME!
I SPOTTED YOU AT RAV'S, CADE, AND FOLLOWED YOU HERE. THOUGHT THAT IF YOU WERE AS MUCH OF A JERK AS I'D BEEN HEARING, THEN YEAH, I'D COLLECT THE BOUNTY.
IF YOU WERE THE CADE I REMEMBERED, THEN NO.
AND?
YOU'RE STILL A JERK, BUT YOU'RE PRETTY MUCH THE SAME JERK I REMEMBER, SO I GUESS I HAVE TO FIND ANOTHER SOURCE OF INCOME THIS TIME AROUND.
I THOUGHT YOU DIED ON CORUSCANT.
I THOUGHT YOU DIED ON OSSUS...ALONG WITH YOUR FATHER. I'M SO...SORRY, CADE. ABOUT HIS DEATH.

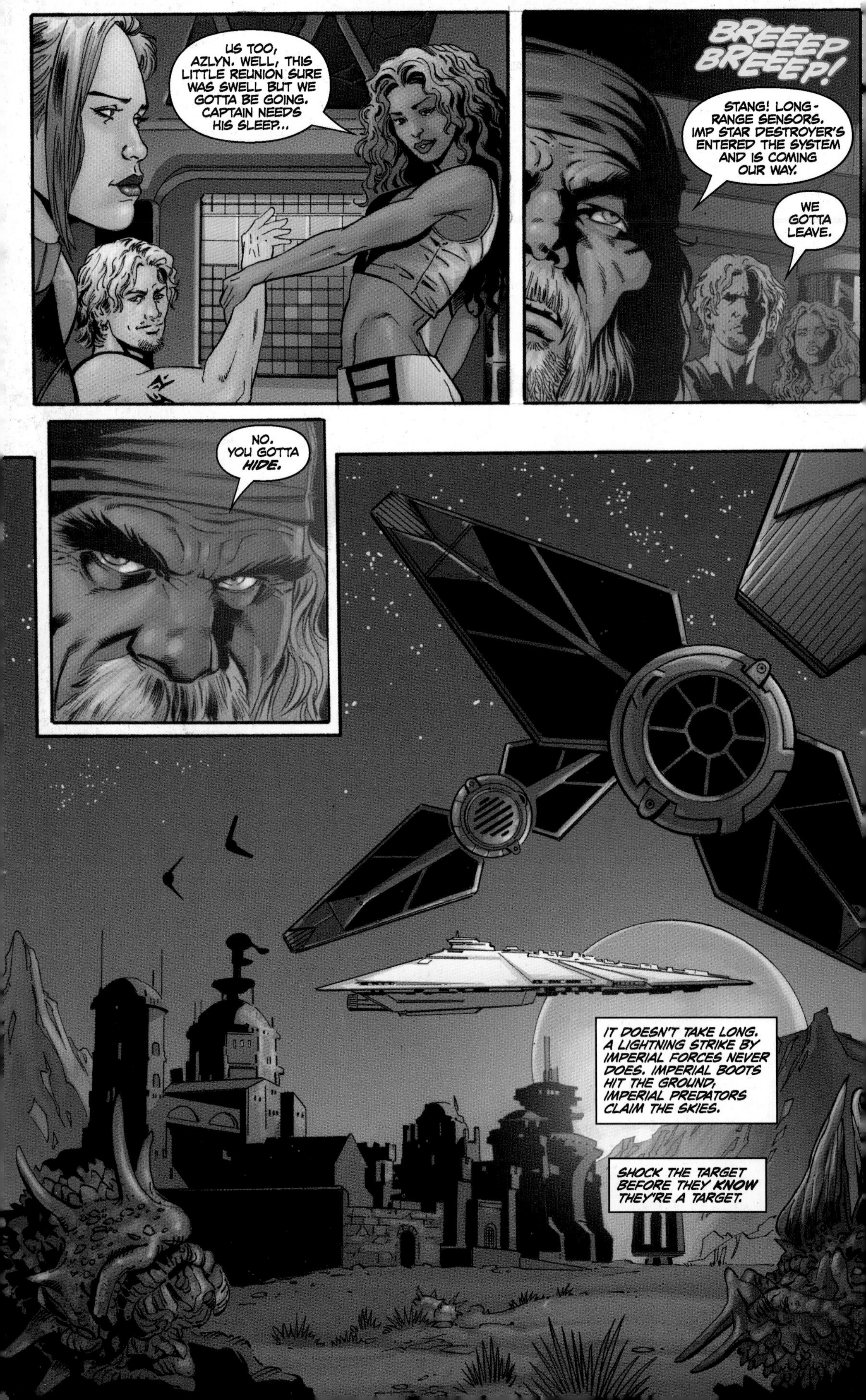
US TOO, AZLYN. WELL, THIS LITTLE REUNION SURE WAS SWELL BUT WE GOTTA BE GOING. CAPTAIN NEEDS HIS SLEEP...
BREEEP BREEEP!
STANG! LONG-RANGE SENSORS. IMP STAR DESTROYER'S ENTERED THE SYSTEM AND IS COMING OUR WAY.
WE GOTTA LEAVE.
NO. YOU GOTTA *HIDE.*
IT DOESN'T TAKE LONG. A LIGHTNING STRIKE BY IMPERIAL FORCES NEVER DOES. IMPERIAL BOOTS HIT THE GROUND, IMPERIAL PREDATORS CLAIM THE SKIES.
SHOCK THE TARGET BEFORE THEY *KNOW* THEY'RE A TARGET.

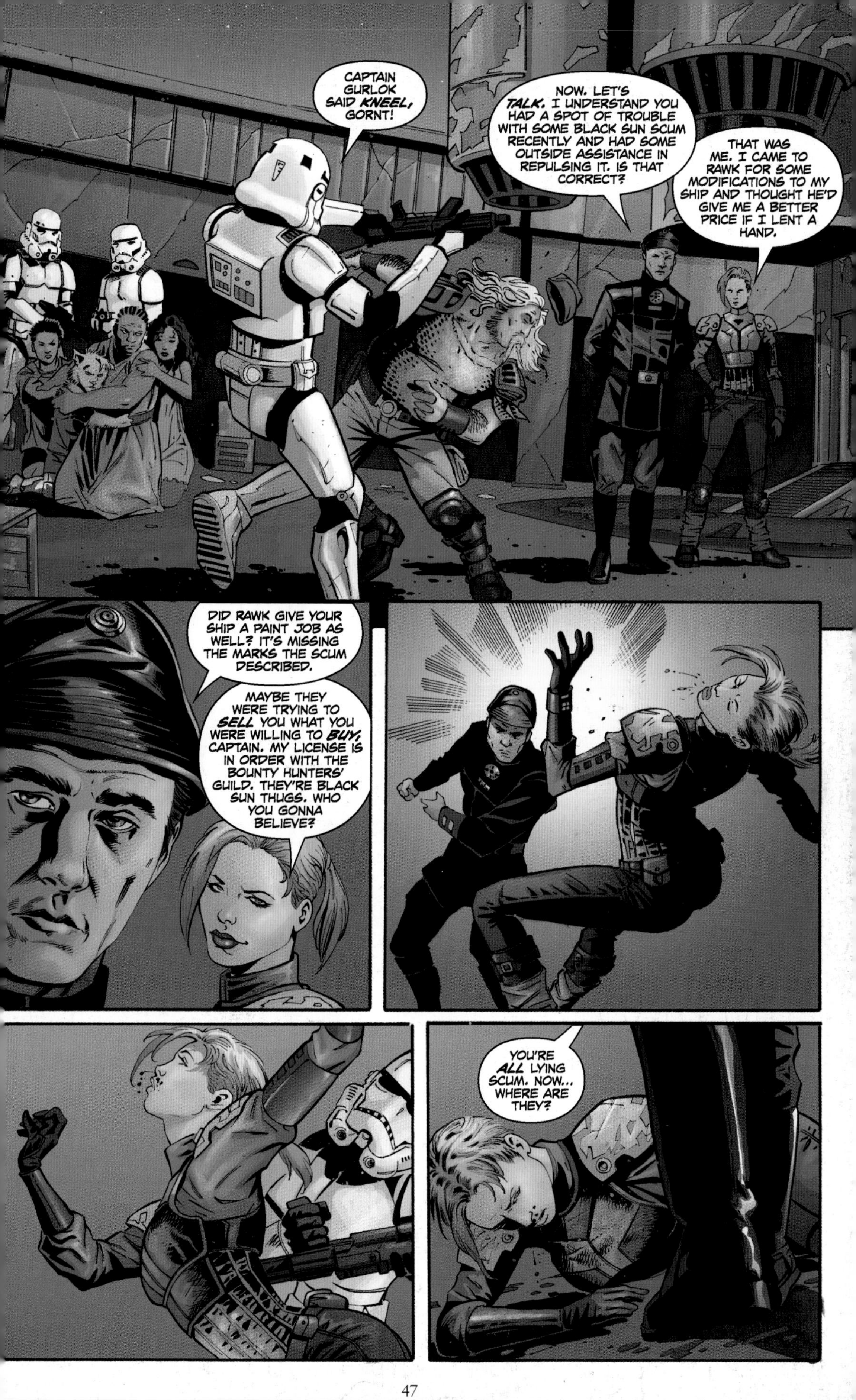
CAPTAIN GURLOK SAID KNEEL, GORNT!
NOW. LET'S TALK. I UNDERSTAND YOU HAD A SPOT OF TROUBLE WITH SOME BLACK SUN SCUM RECENTLY AND HAD SOME OUTSIDE ASSISTANCE IN REPULSING IT. IS THAT CORRECT?
THAT WAS ME. I CAME TO RAWK FOR SOME MODIFICATIONS TO MY SHIP AND THOUGHT HE'D GIVE ME A BETTER PRICE IF I LENT A HAND.
DID RAWK GIVE YOUR SHIP A PAINT JOB AS WELL? IT'S MISSING THE MARKS THE SCUM DESCRIBED.
MAYBE THEY WERE TRYING TO SELL YOU WHAT YOU WERE WILLING TO BUY, CAPTAIN. MY LICENSE IS IN ORDER WITH THE BOUNTY HUNTERS' GUILD. THEY'RE BLACK SUN THUGS. WHO YOU GONNA BELIEVE?
YOU'RE ALL LYING SCUM. NOW... WHERE ARE THEY?

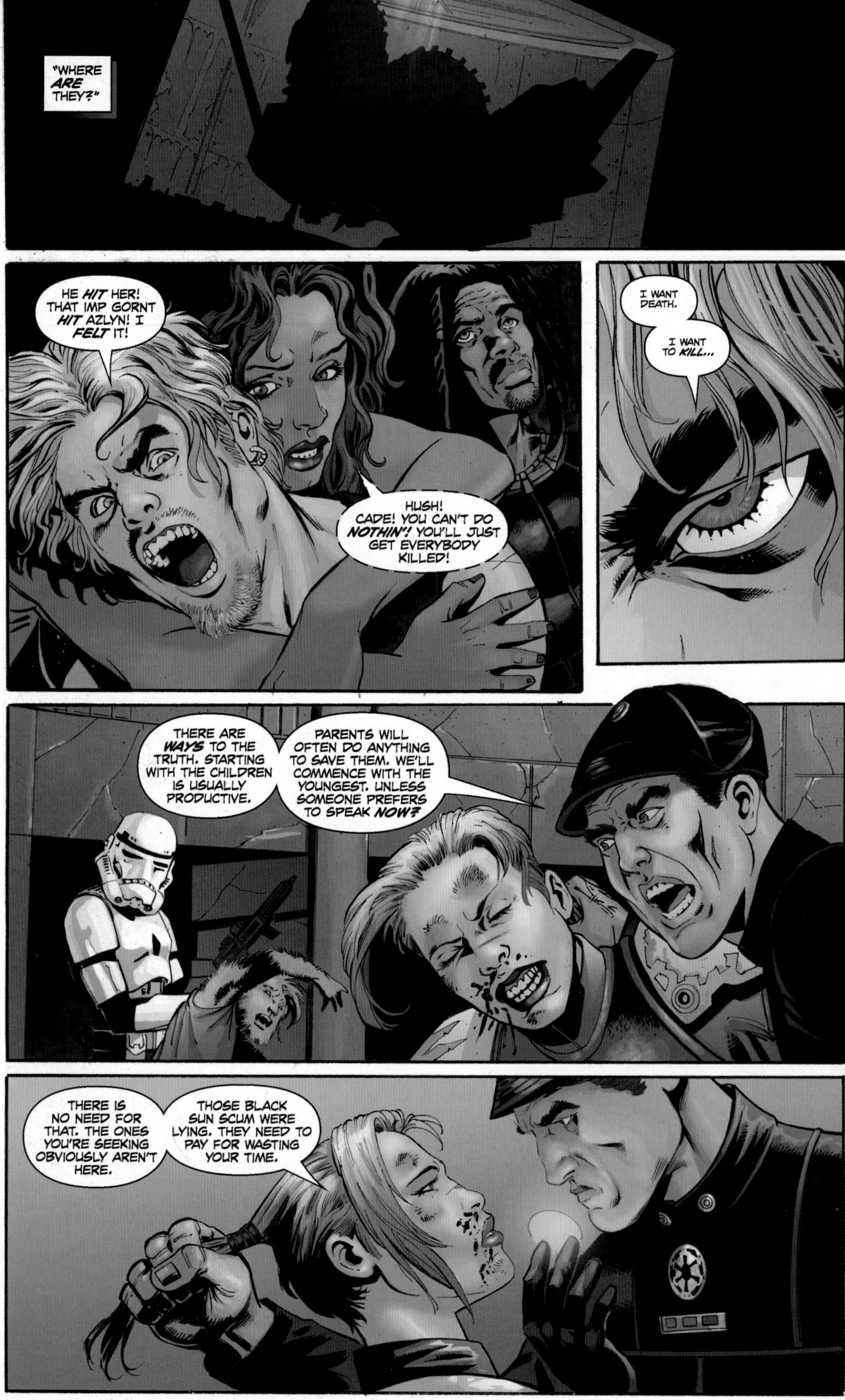
"WHERE ARE THEY?"
HE HIT HER! THAT IMP GORNT HIT AZLYN! I FELT IT!
HUSH! CADE! YOU CAN'T DO NOTHIN'! YOU'LL JUST GET EVERYBODY KILLED!
I WANT DEATH.
I WANT TO KILL...
THERE ARE WAYS TO THE TRUTH. STARTING WITH THE CHILDREN IS USUALLY PRODUCTIVE.
PARENTS WILL OFTEN DO ANYTHING TO SAVE THEM. WE'LL COMMENCE WITH THE YOUNGEST. UNLESS SOMEONE PREFERS TO SPEAK NOW?
THERE IS NO NEED FOR THAT. THE ONES YOU'RE SEEKING OBVIOUSLY AREN'T HERE.
THOSE BLACK SUN SCUM WERE LYING. THEY NEED TO PAY FOR WASTING YOUR TIME.

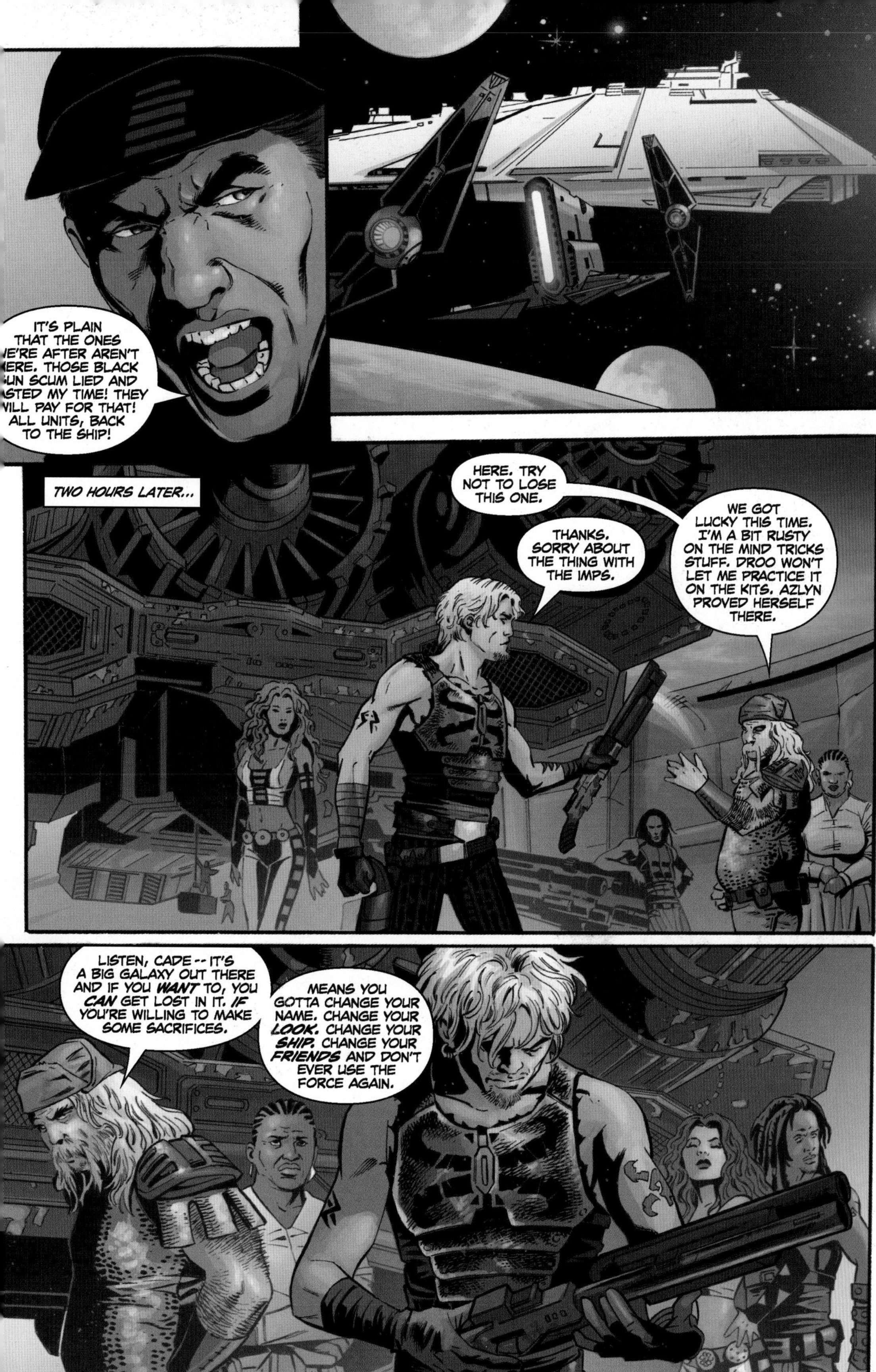

IT'S PLAIN THAT THE ONES
E'RE AFTER AREN'T
ERE. THOSE BLACK
UN SCUM LIED AND
STED MY TIME! THEY
ILL PAY FOR THAT!
ALL UNITS, BACK TO THE SHIP!
TWO HOURS LATER...
HERE. TRY NOT TO LOSE THIS ONE.
THANKS. SORRY ABOUT THE THING WITH THE IMPS.
WE GOT LUCKY THIS TIME. I'M A BIT RUSTY ON THE MIND TRICKS STUFF. DROO WON'T LET ME PRACTICE IT ON THE KITS. AZLYN PROVED HERSELF THERE.
LISTEN, CADE -- IT'S A BIG GALAXY OUT THERE AND IF YOU WANT TO, YOU CAN GET LOST IN IT. IF YOU'RE WILLING TO MAKE SOME SACRIFICES.
MEANS YOU GOTTA CHANGE YOUR NAME. CHANGE YOUR LOOK. CHANGE YOUR SHIP. CHANGE YOUR FRIENDS AND DON'T EVER USE THE FORCE AGAIN.

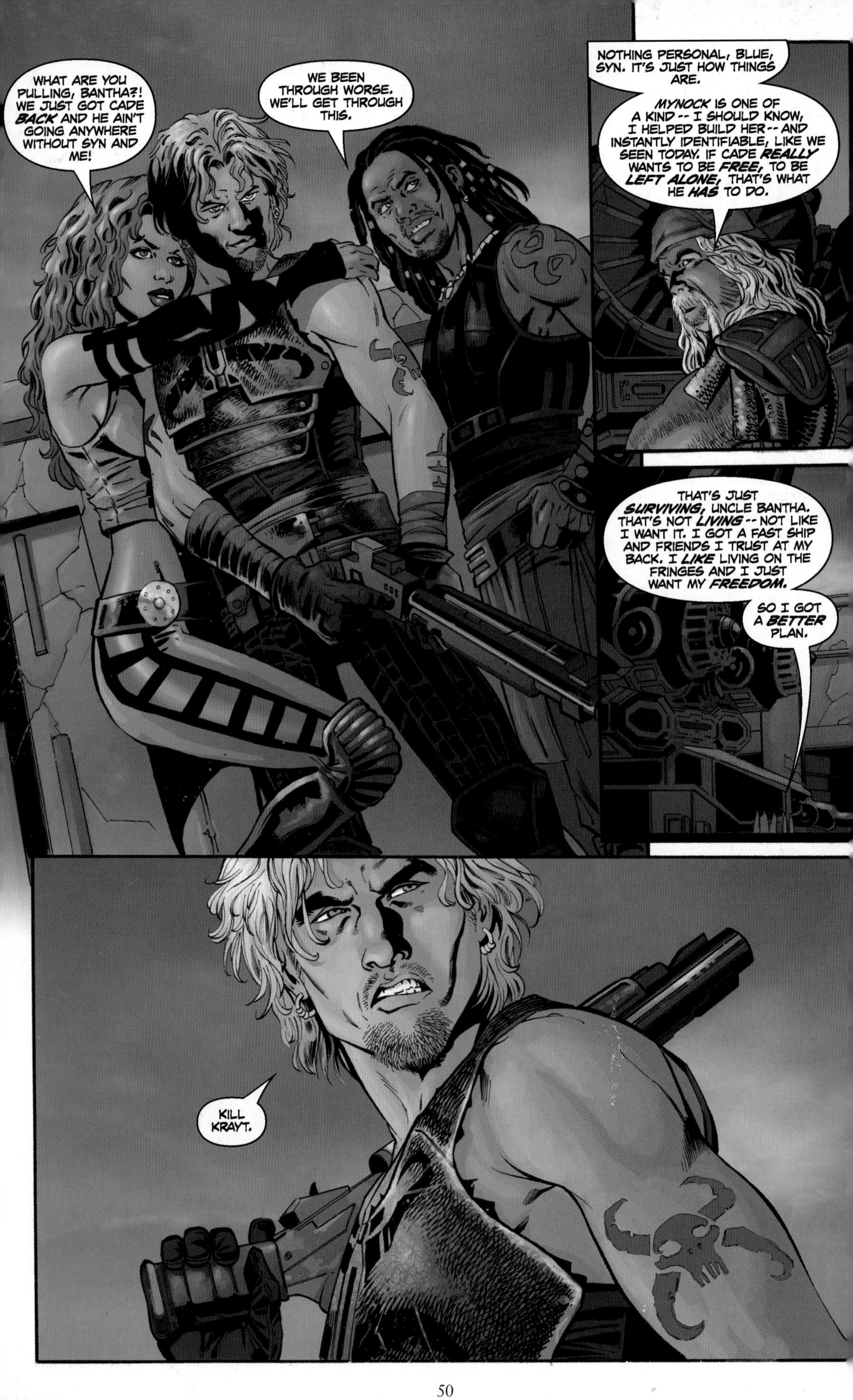
WHAT ARE YOU PULLING, BANTHA?! WE JUST GOT CADE BACK AND HE AIN'T GOING ANYWHERE WITHOUT SYN AND ME!
WE BEEN THROUGH WORSE. WE'LL GET THROUGH THIS.
NOTHING PERSONAL, BLUE, SYN. IT'S JUST HOW THINGS ARE.
MYNOCK IS ONE OF A KIND -- I SHOULD KNOW, I HELPED BUILD HER -- AND INSTANTLY IDENTIFIABLE, LIKE WE SEEN TODAY. IF CADE REALLY WANTS TO BE FREE, TO BE LEFT ALONE, THAT'S WHAT HE HAS TO DO.
THAT'S JUST SURVIVING, UNCLE BANTHA. THAT'S NOT LIVING -- NOT LIKE I WANT IT. I GOT A FAST SHIP AND FRIENDS I TRUST AT MY BACK. I LIKE LIVING ON THE FRINGES AND I JUST WANT MY FREEDOM.
SO I GOT A BETTER PLAN.
KILL KRAYT.

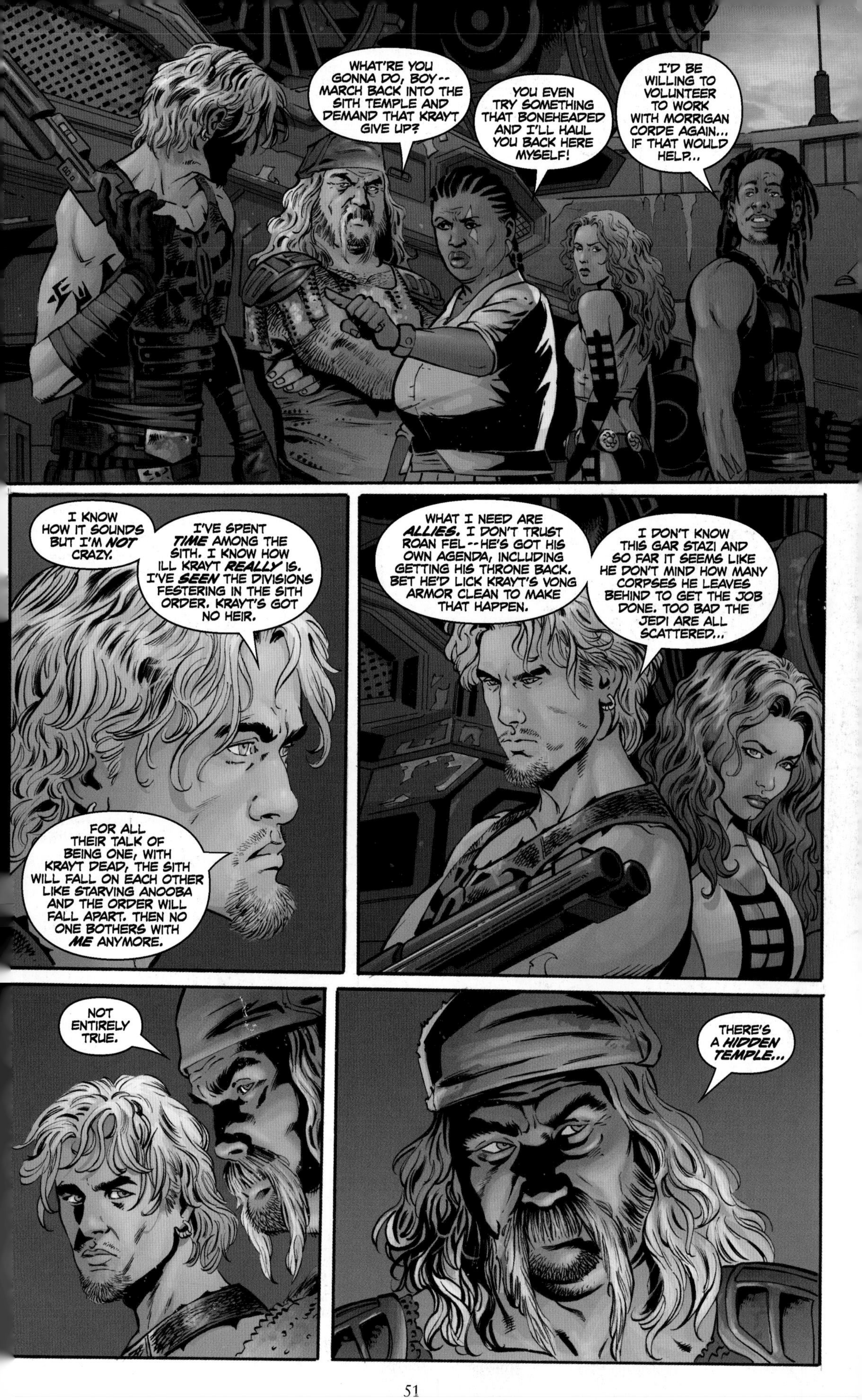
WHAT'RE YOU GONNA DO, BOY--MARCH BACK INTO THE SITH TEMPLE AND DEMAND THAT KRAYT GIVE UP?
YOU EVEN TRY SOMETHING THAT BONEHEADED AND I'LL HAUL YOU BACK HERE MYSELF!
I'D BE WILLING TO VOLUNTEER TO WORK WITH MORRIGAN CORDE AGAIN... IF THAT WOULD HELP...
I KNOW HOW IT SOUNDS BUT I'M NOT CRAZY.
I'VE SPENT TIME AMONG THE SITH. I KNOW HOW ILL KRAYT REALLY IS. I'VE SEEN THE DIVISIONS FESTERING IN THE SITH ORDER. KRAYT'S GOT NO HEIR.
FOR ALL THEIR TALK OF BEING ONE, WITH KRAYT DEAD, THE SITH WILL FALL ON EACH OTHER LIKE STARVING ANOOBA AND THE ORDER WILL FALL APART. THEN NO ONE BOTHERS WITH ME ANYMORE.
WHAT I NEED ARE ALLIES. I DON'T TRUST ROAN FEL--HE'S GOT HIS OWN AGENDA, INCLUDING GETTING HIS THRONE BACK. BET HE'D LICK KRAYT'S VONG ARMOR CLEAN TO MAKE THAT HAPPEN.
I DON'T KNOW THIS GAR STAZI AND SO FAR IT SEEMS LIKE HE DON'T MIND HOW MANY CORPSES HE LEAVES BEHIND TO GET THE JOB DONE. TOO BAD THE JEDI ARE ALL SCATTERED...
NOT ENTIRELY TRUE.
THERE'S A HIDDEN TEMPLE...

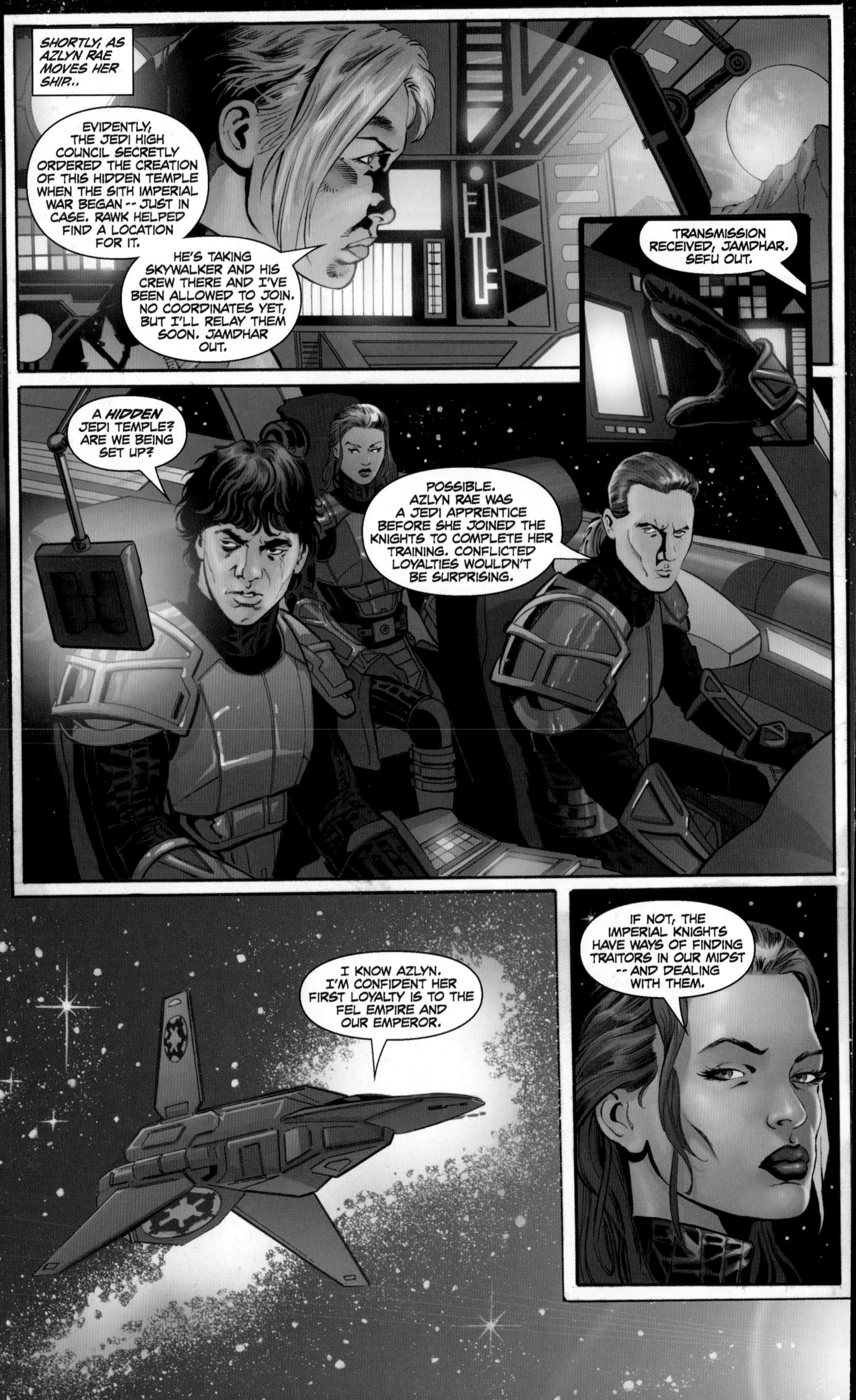
SHORTLY, AS AZLYN RAE MOVES HER SHIP...
EVIDENTLY, THE JEDI HIGH COUNCIL SECRETLY ORDERED THE CREATION OF THIS HIDDEN TEMPLE WHEN THE SITH IMPERIAL WAR BEGAN -- JUST IN CASE. RAWK HELPED FIND A LOCATION FOR IT.
HE'S TAKING SKYWALKER AND HIS CREW THERE AND I'VE BEEN ALLOWED TO JOIN. NO COORDINATES YET, BUT I'LL RELAY THEM SOON. JAMDHAR OUT.
TRANSMISSION RECEIVED, JAMDHAR. SEFU OUT.
A HIDDEN JEDI TEMPLE? ARE WE BEING SET UP?
POSSIBLE. AZLYN RAE WAS A JEDI APPRENTICE BEFORE SHE JOINED THE KNIGHTS TO COMPLETE HER TRAINING. CONFLICTED LOYALTIES WOULDN'T BE SURPRISING.
I KNOW AZLYN. I'M CONFIDENT HER FIRST LOYALTY IS TO THE FEL EMPIRE AND OUR EMPEROR.
IF NOT, THE IMPERIAL KNIGHTS HAVE WAYS OF FINDING TRAITORS IN OUR MIDST -- AND DEALING WITH THEM.

STAR WARS

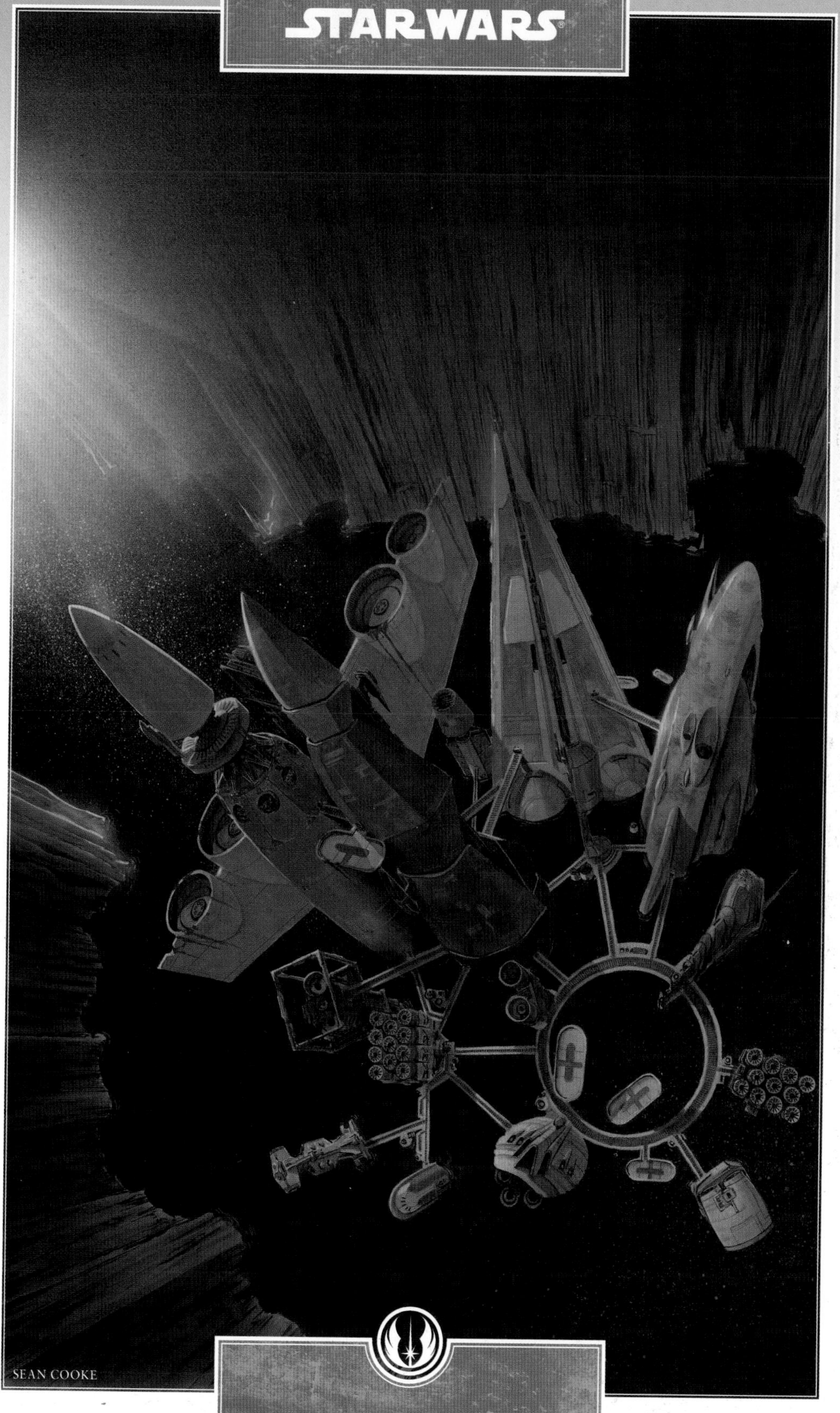
SEAN COOKE

THE HIDDEN TEMPLE

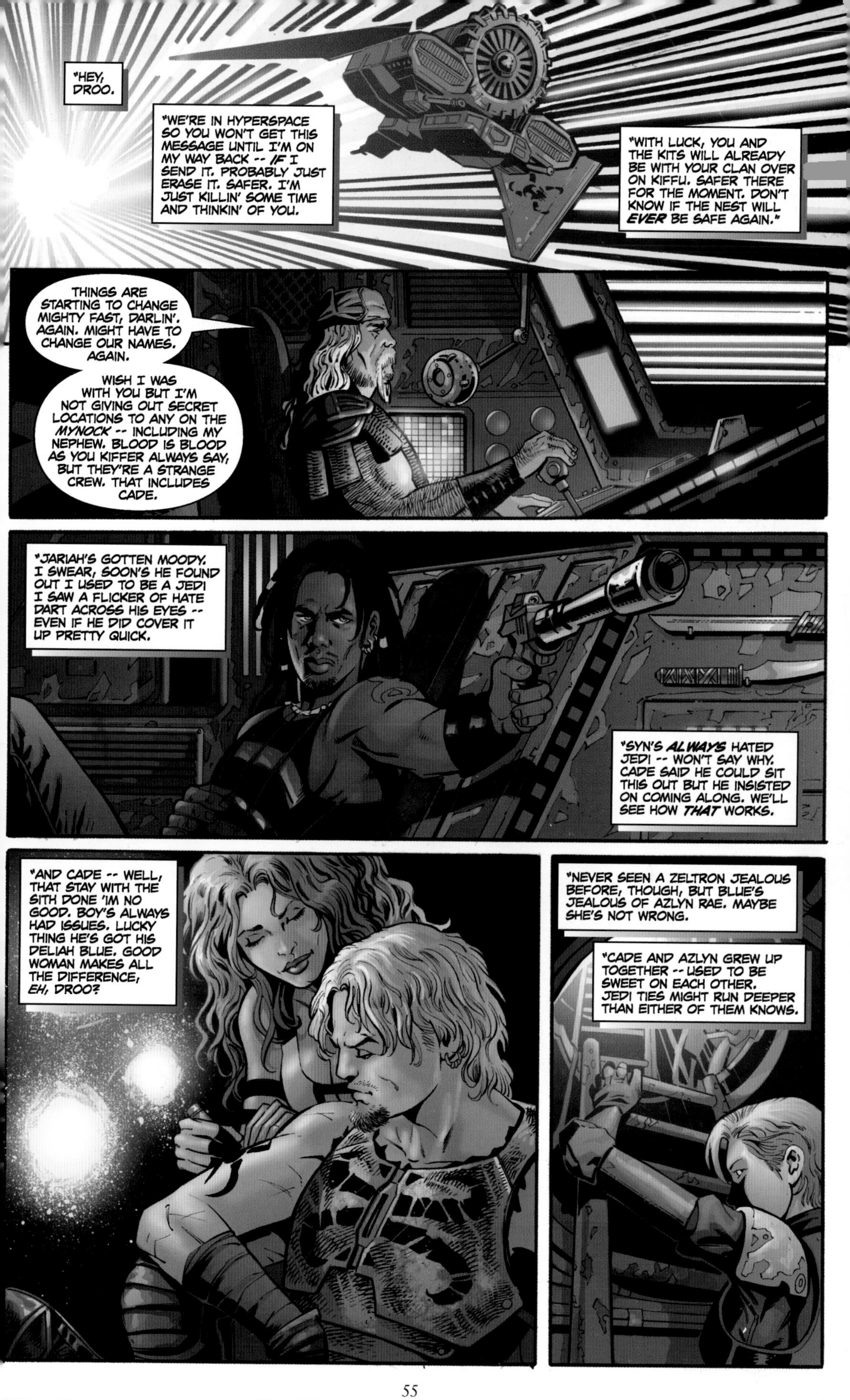
"HEY, DROO.
"WE'RE IN HYPERSPACE SO YOU WON'T GET THIS MESSAGE UNTIL I'M ON MY WAY BACK -- IF I SEND IT. PROBABLY JUST ERASE IT. SAFER. I'M JUST KILLIN' SOME TIME AND THINKIN' OF YOU.
"WITH LUCK, YOU AND THE KITS WILL ALREADY BE WITH YOUR CLAN OVER ON KIFFU. SAFER THERE FOR THE MOMENT. DON'T KNOW IF THE NEST WILL EVER BE SAFE AGAIN."
THINGS ARE STARTING TO CHANGE MIGHTY FAST, DARLIN'. AGAIN. MIGHT HAVE TO CHANGE OUR NAMES. AGAIN.
WISH I WAS WITH YOU BUT I'M NOT GIVING OUT SECRET LOCATIONS TO ANY ON THE MYNOCK -- INCLUDING MY NEPHEW. BLOOD IS BLOOD AS YOU KIFFER ALWAYS SAY, BUT THEY'RE A STRANGE CREW. THAT INCLUDES CADE.
"JARIAH'S GOTTEN MOODY. I SWEAR, SOON'S HE FOUND OUT I USED TO BE A JEDI I SAW A FLICKER OF HATE DART ACROSS HIS EYES -- EVEN IF HE DID COVER IT UP PRETTY QUICK.
"SYN'S ALWAYS HATED JEDI -- WON'T SAY WHY. CADE SAID HE COULD SIT THIS OUT BUT HE INSISTED ON COMING ALONG. WE'LL SEE HOW THAT WORKS.
"AND CADE -- WELL, THAT STAY WITH THE SITH DONE 'IM NO GOOD. BOY'S ALWAYS HAD ISSUES. LUCKY THING HE'S GOT HIS DELIAH BLUE. GOOD WOMAN MAKES ALL THE DIFFERENCE, EH, DROO?
"NEVER SEEN A ZELTRON JEALOUS BEFORE, THOUGH, BUT BLUE'S JEALOUS OF AZLYN RAE. MAYBE SHE'S NOT WRONG.
"CADE AND AZLYN GREW UP TOGETHER -- USED TO BE SWEET ON EACH OTHER. JEDI TIES MIGHT RUN DEEPER THAN EITHER OF THEM KNOWS.

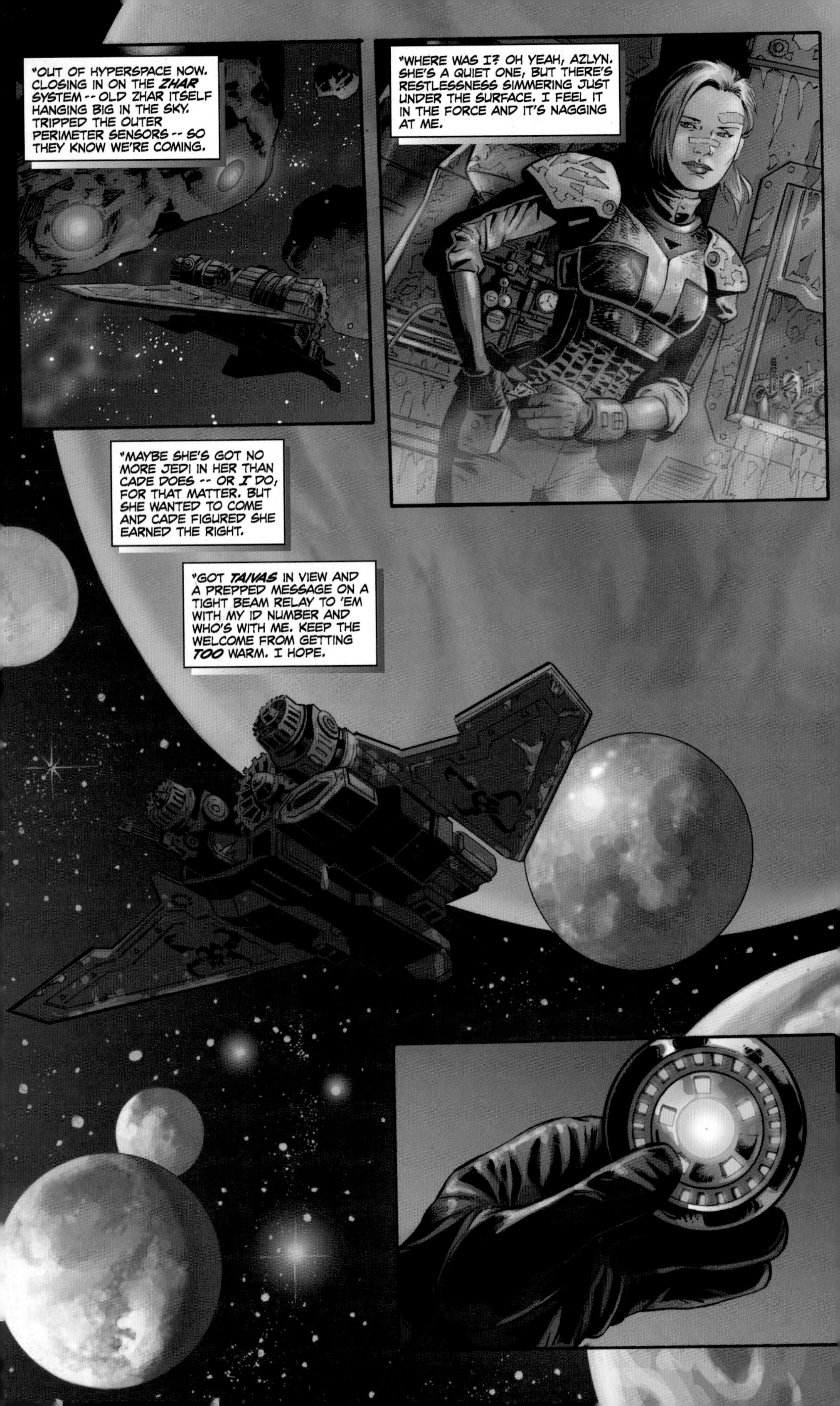
"OUT OF HYPERSPACE NOW. CLOSING IN ON THE ZHAR SYSTEM -- OLD ZHAR ITSELF HANGING BIG IN THE SKY. TRIPPED THE OUTER PERIMETER SENSORS -- SO THEY KNOW WE'RE COMING.
"WHERE WAS I? OH YEAH, AZLYN. SHE'S A QUIET ONE, BUT THERE'S RESTLESSNESS SIMMERING JUST UNDER THE SURFACE. I FEEL IT IN THE FORCE AND IT'S NAGGING AT ME.
"MAYBE SHE'S GOT NO MORE JEDI IN HER THAN CADE DOES -- OR I DO, FOR THAT MATTER. BUT SHE WANTED TO COME AND CADE FIGURED SHE EARNED THE RIGHT.
"GOT TAIVAS IN VIEW AND A PREPPED MESSAGE ON A TIGHT BEAM RELAY TO 'EM WITH MY ID NUMBER AND WHO'S WITH ME. KEEP THE WELCOME FROM GETTING TOO WARM. I HOPE.

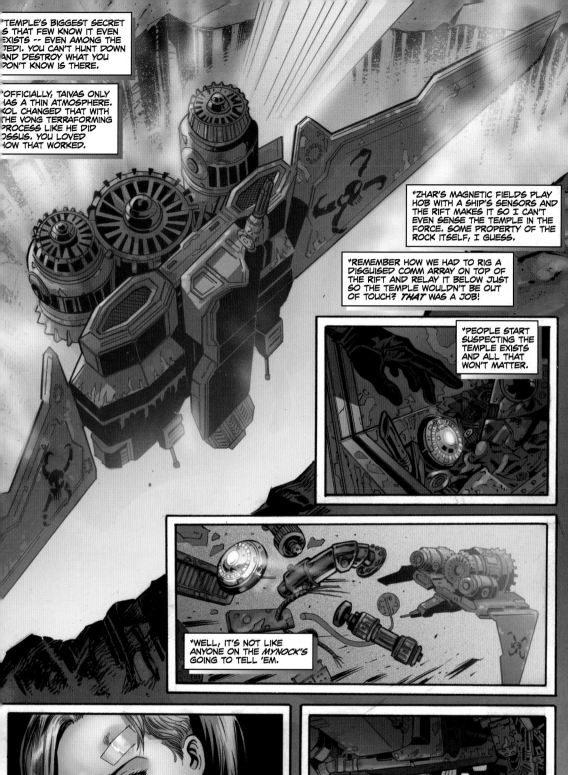

"TEMPLE'S BIGGEST SECRET IS THAT FEW KNOW IT EVEN EXISTS -- EVEN AMONG THE JEDI. YOU CAN'T HUNT DOWN AND DESTROY WHAT YOU DON'T KNOW IS THERE.

"OFFICIALLY, TAIVAS ONLY HAS A THIN ATMOSPHERE. KOL CHANGED THAT WITH THE VONG TERRAFORMING PROCESS LIKE HE DID OSSUS. YOU LOVED HOW THAT WORKED.

"ZHAR'S MAGNETIC FIELDS PLAY HOB WITH A SHIP'S SENSORS AND THE RIFT MAKES IT SO I CAN'T EVEN SENSE THE TEMPLE IN THE FORCE. SOME PROPERTY OF THE ROCK ITSELF, I GUESS.

"REMEMBER HOW WE HAD TO RIG A DISGUISED COMM ARRAY ON TOP OF THE RIFT AND RELAY IT BELOW JUST SO THE TEMPLE WOULDN'T BE OUT OF TOUCH? THAT WAS A JOB!

"PEOPLE START SUSPECTING THE TEMPLE EXISTS AND ALL THAT WON'T MATTER.

"WELL, IT'S NOT LIKE ANYONE ON THE MYNOCK'S GOING TO TELL 'EM.

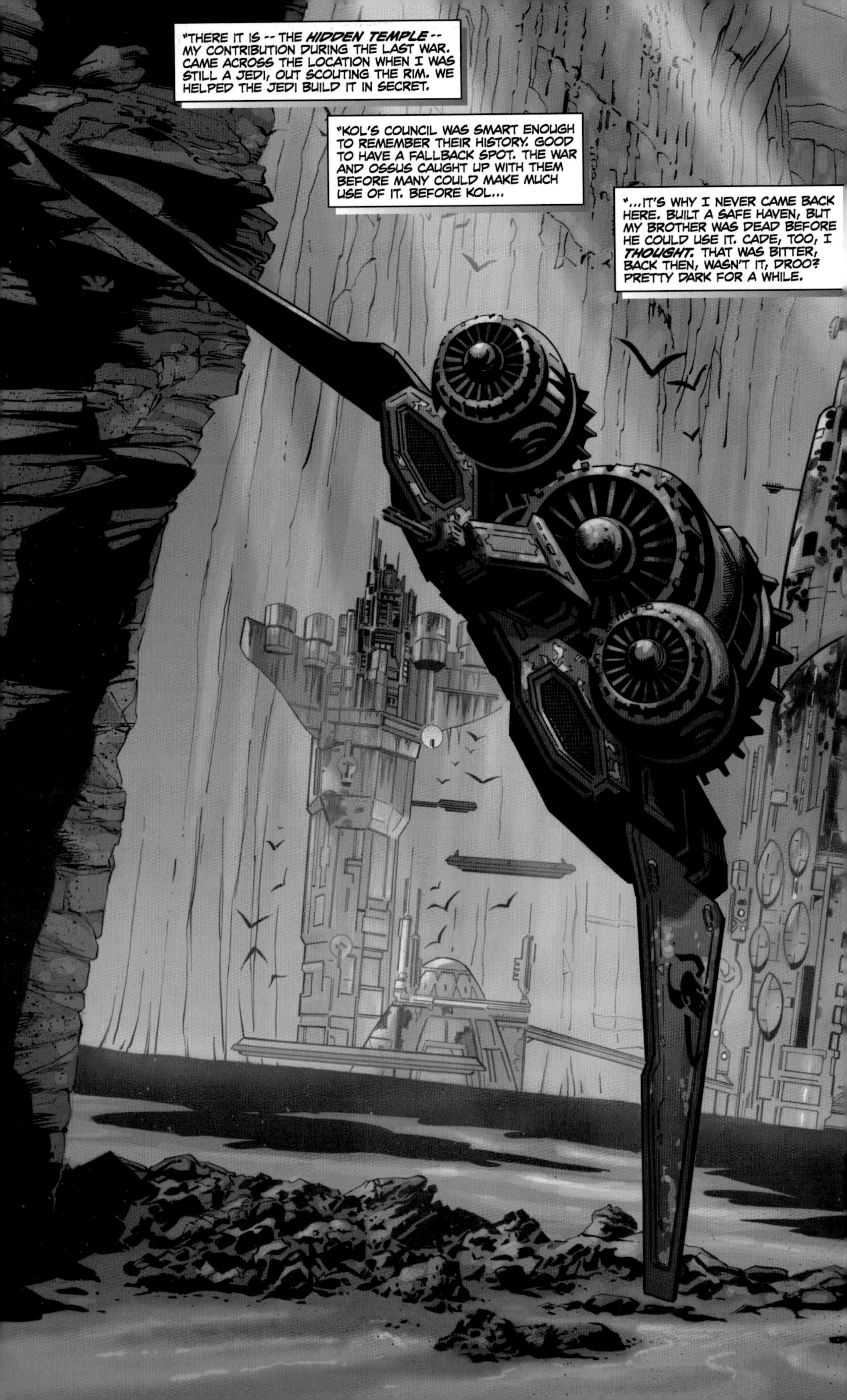
"THERE IT IS -- THE *HIDDEN TEMPLE* -- MY CONTRIBUTION DURING THE LAST WAR. CAME ACROSS THE LOCATION WHEN I WAS STILL A JEDI, OUT SCOUTING THE RIM. WE HELPED THE JEDI BUILD IT IN SECRET.
"KOL'S COUNCIL WAS SMART ENOUGH TO REMEMBER THEIR HISTORY. GOOD TO HAVE A FALLBACK SPOT. THE WAR AND OSSUS CAUGHT UP WITH THEM BEFORE MANY COULD MAKE MUCH USE OF IT. BEFORE KOL...
"...IT'S WHY I NEVER CAME BACK HERE. BUILT A SAFE HAVEN, BUT MY BROTHER WAS DEAD BEFORE HE COULD USE IT. CADE, TOO, I *THOUGHT.* THAT WAS BITTER, BACK THEN, WASN'T IT, DROO? PRETTY DARK FOR A WHILE.

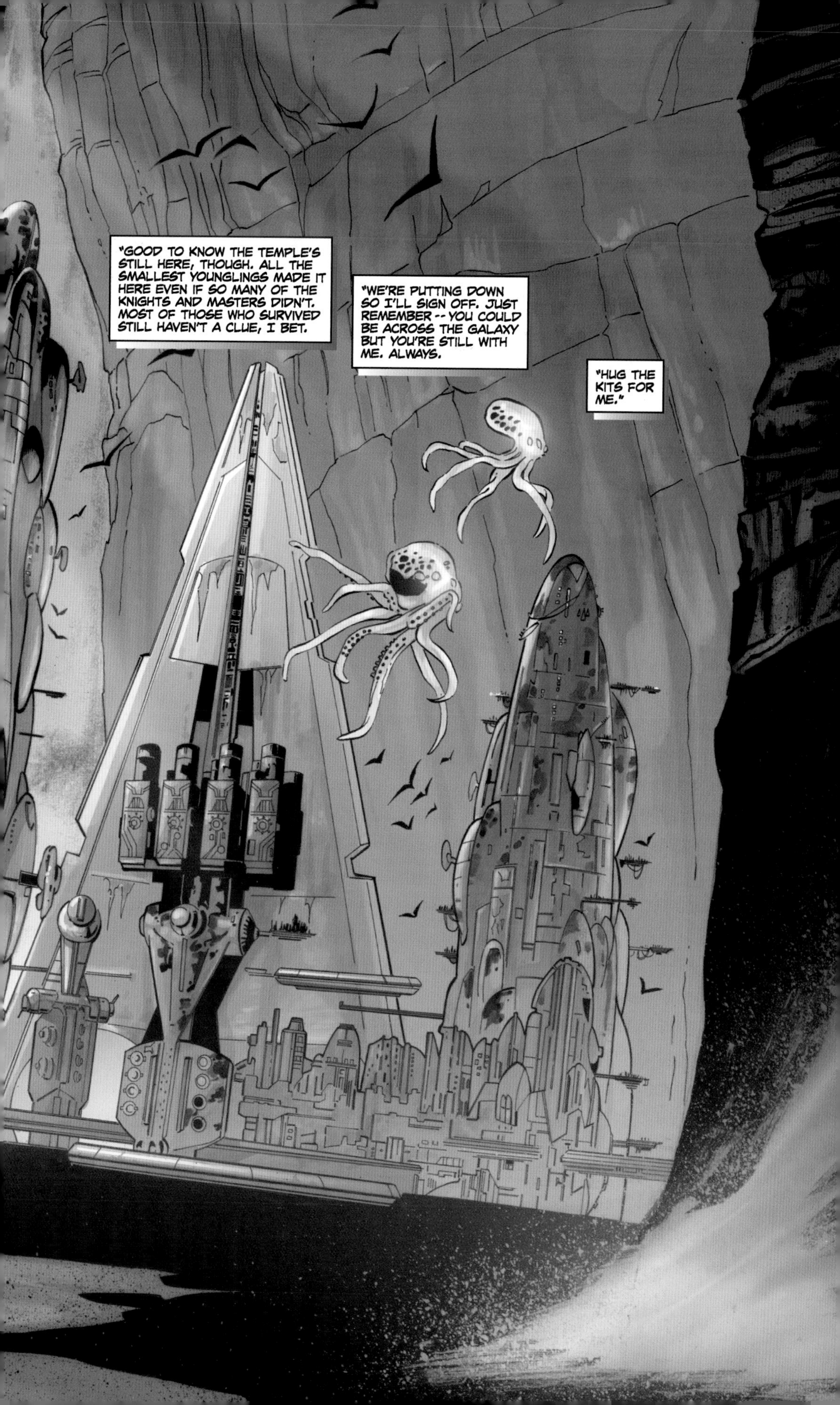
"GOOD TO KNOW THE TEMPLE'S STILL HERE, THOUGH. ALL THE SMALLEST YOUNGLINGS MADE IT HERE EVEN IF SO MANY OF THE KNIGHTS AND MASTERS DIDN'T. MOST OF THOSE WHO SURVIVED STILL HAVEN'T A CLUE, I BET.
"WE'RE PUTTING DOWN SO I'LL SIGN OFF. JUST REMEMBER -- YOU COULD BE ACROSS THE GALAXY BUT YOU'RE STILL WITH ME. ALWAYS.
"HUG THE KITS FOR ME."

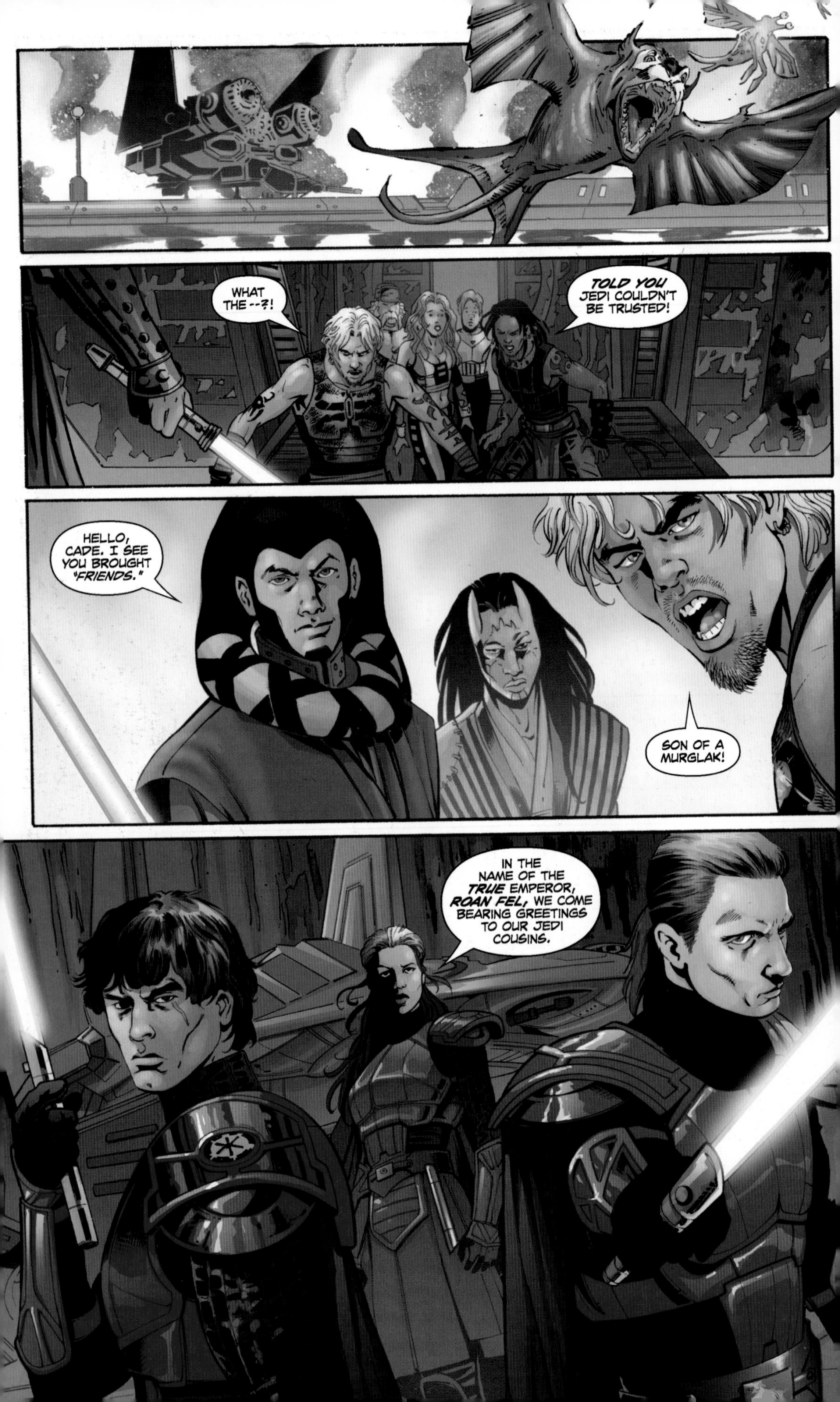
WHAT THE --?!
TOLD YOU JEDI COULDN'T BE TRUSTED!
HELLO, CADE. I SEE YOU BROUGHT "FRIENDS."
SON OF A MURGLAK!
IN THE NAME OF THE TRUE EMPEROR, ROAN FEL, WE COME BEARING GREETINGS TO OUR JEDI COUSINS.

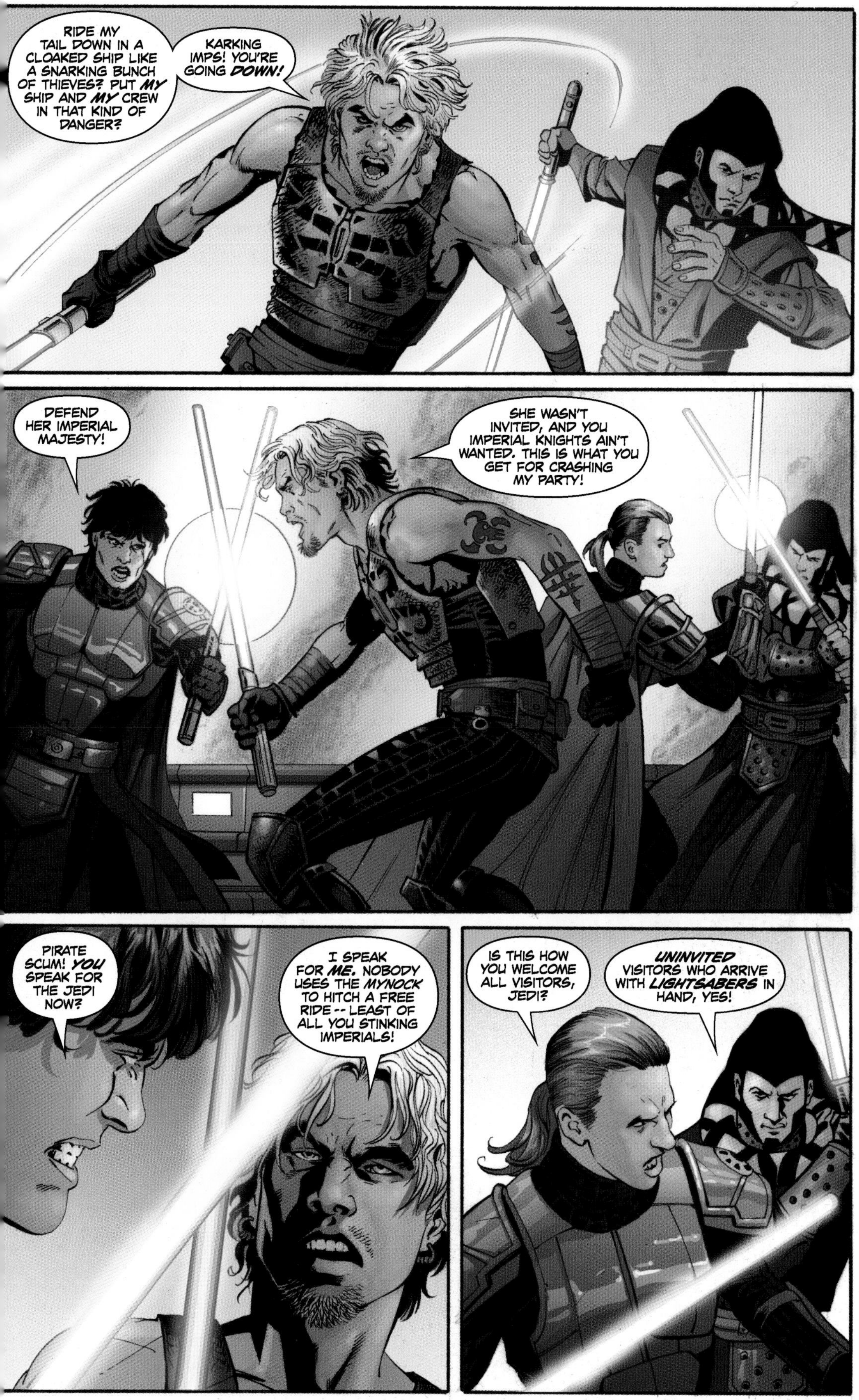
RIDE MY TAIL DOWN IN A CLOAKED SHIP LIKE A SNARKING BUNCH OF THIEVES? PUT MY SHIP AND MY CREW IN THAT KIND OF DANGER?
KARKING IMPS! YOU'RE GOING DOWN!
DEFEND HER IMPERIAL MAJESTY!
SHE WASN'T INVITED, AND YOU IMPERIAL KNIGHTS AIN'T WANTED. THIS IS WHAT YOU GET FOR CRASHING MY PARTY!
PIRATE SCUM! YOU SPEAK FOR THE JEDI NOW?
I SPEAK FOR ME. NOBODY USES THE MYNOCK TO HITCH A FREE RIDE -- LEAST OF ALL YOU STINKING IMPERIALS!
IS THIS HOW YOU WELCOME ALL VISITORS, JEDI?
UNINVITED VISITORS WHO ARRIVE WITH LIGHTSABERS IN HAND, YES!

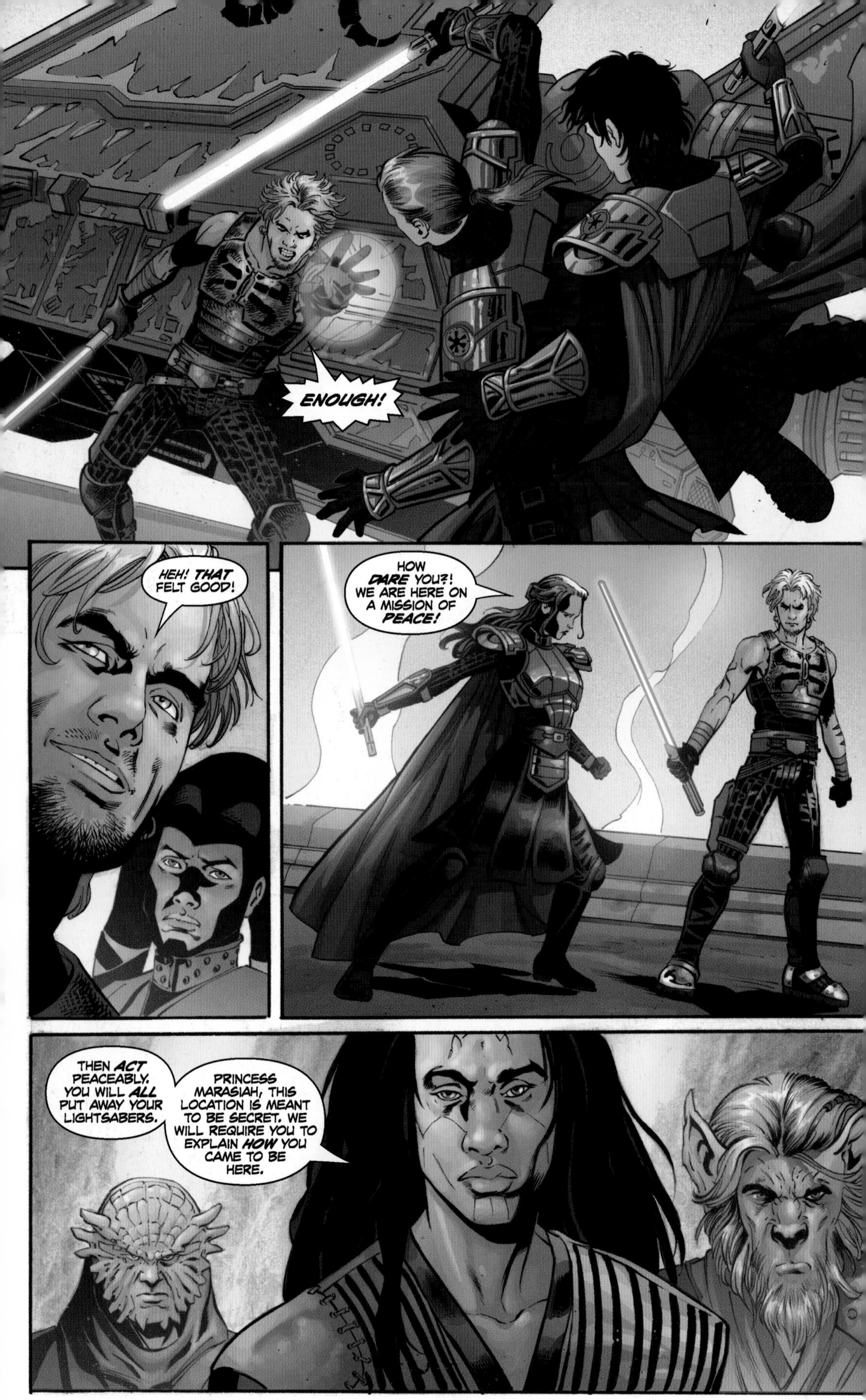
ENOUGH!
HEH! THAT FELT GOOD!
HOW DARE YOU?! WE ARE HERE ON A MISSION OF PEACE!
THEN ACT PEACEABLY. YOU WILL ALL PUT AWAY YOUR LIGHTSABERS.
PRINCESS MARASIAH, THIS LOCATION IS MEANT TO BE SECRET. WE WILL REQUIRE YOU TO EXPLAIN HOW YOU CAME TO BE HERE.

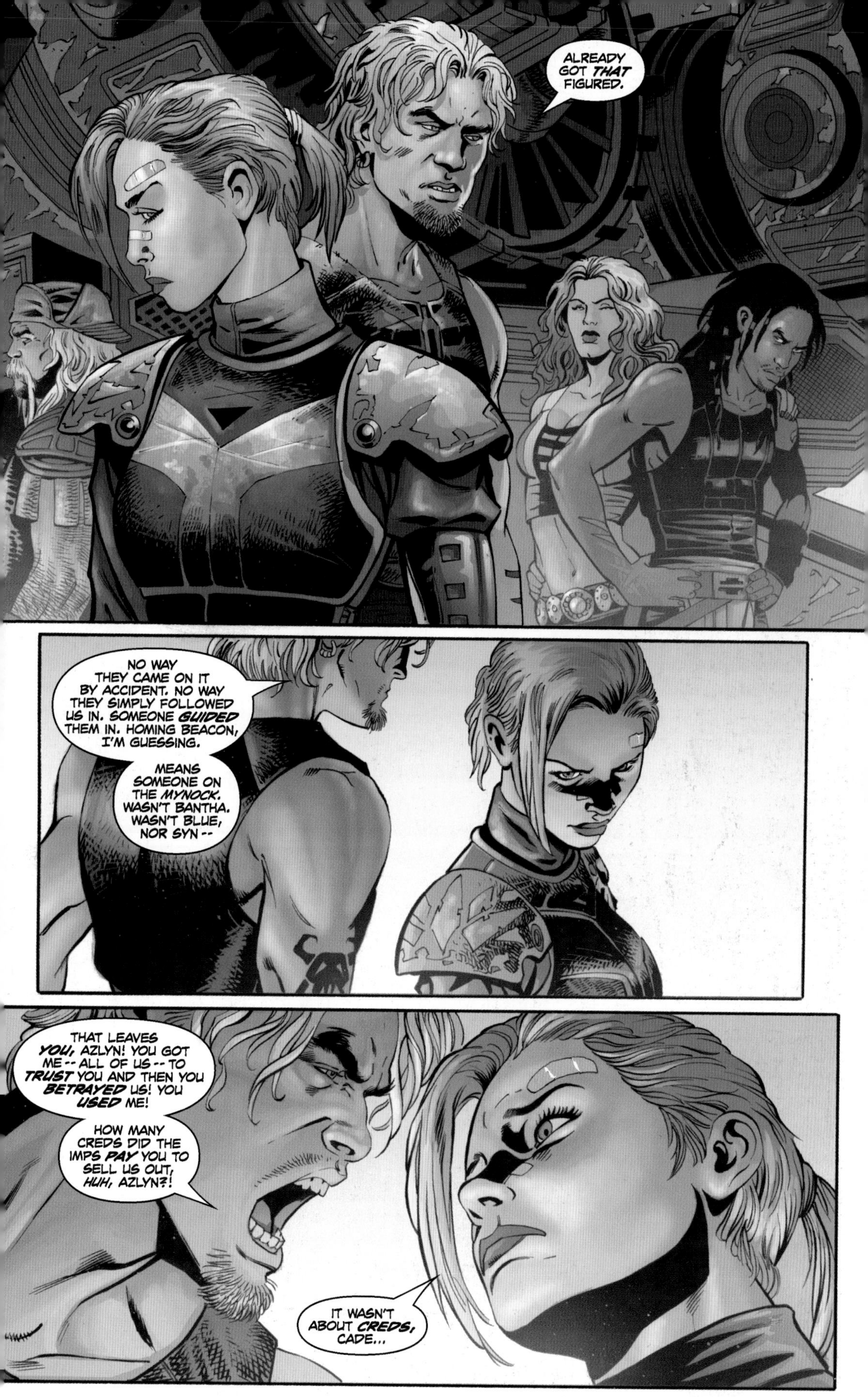
ALREADY GOT *THAT* FIGURED.
NO WAY THEY CAME ON IT BY ACCIDENT. NO WAY THEY SIMPLY FOLLOWED US IN. SOMEONE *GUIDED* THEM IN. HOMING BEACON, I'M GUESSING.
MEANS SOMEONE ON THE *MYNOCK*. WASN'T BANTHA. WASN'T BLUE, NOR SYN --
THAT LEAVES *YOU*, AZLYN! YOU GOT ME -- ALL OF US -- TO *TRUST* YOU AND THEN YOU *BETRAYED* US! YOU *USED* ME!
HOW MANY CREDS DID THE IMPS *PAY* YOU TO SELL US OUT, *HUH*, AZLYN?!
IT WASN'T ABOUT *CREDS*, CADE...

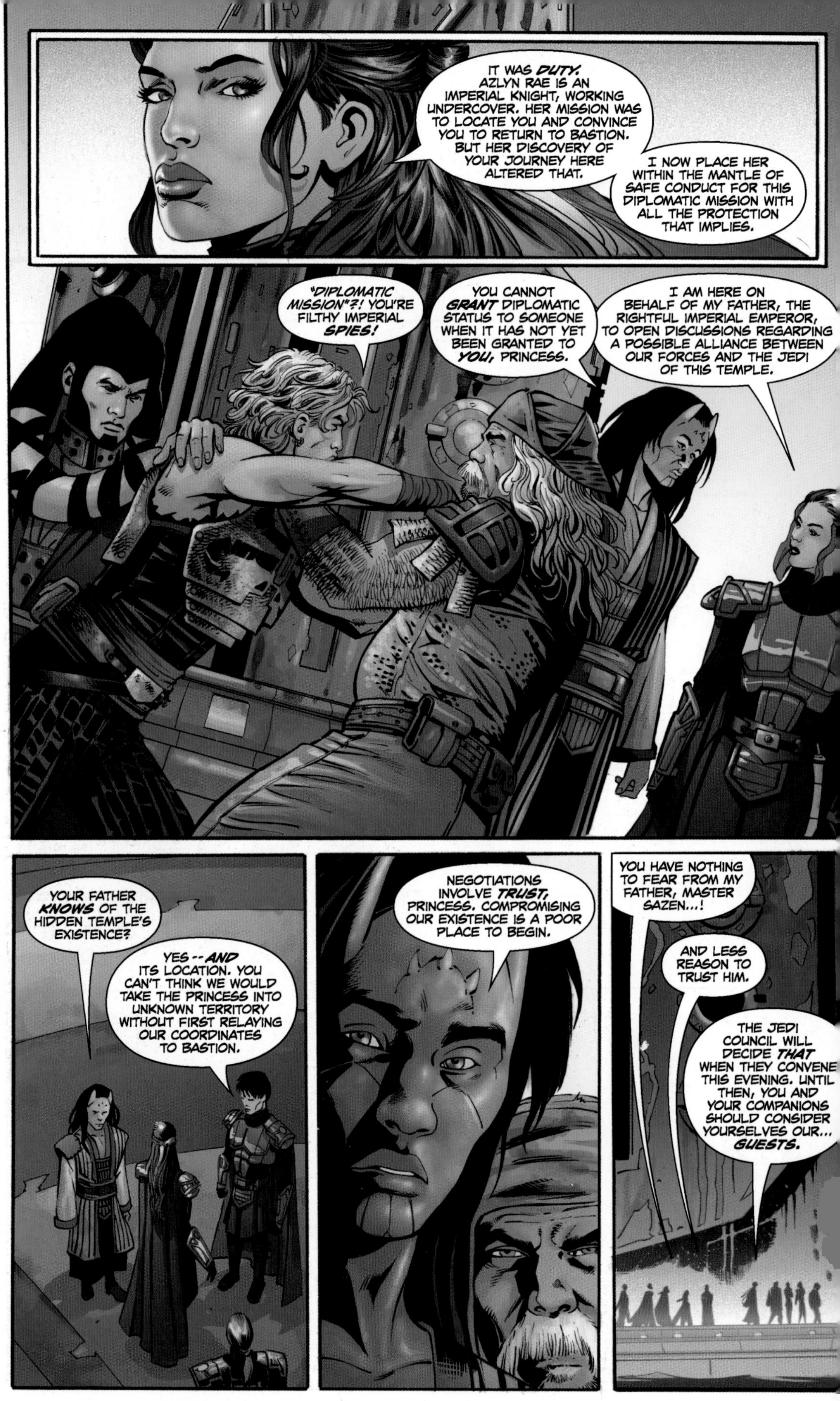
IT WAS DUTY. AZLYN RAE IS AN IMPERIAL KNIGHT, WORKING UNDERCOVER. HER MISSION WAS TO LOCATE YOU AND CONVINCE YOU TO RETURN TO BASTION. BUT HER DISCOVERY OF YOUR JOURNEY HERE ALTERED THAT.
I NOW PLACE HER WITHIN THE MANTLE OF SAFE CONDUCT FOR THIS DIPLOMATIC MISSION WITH ALL THE PROTECTION THAT IMPLIES.
"DIPLOMATIC MISSION"?! YOU'RE FILTHY IMPERIAL SPIES!
YOU CANNOT GRANT DIPLOMATIC STATUS TO SOMEONE WHEN IT HAS NOT YET BEEN GRANTED TO YOU, PRINCESS.
I AM HERE ON BEHALF OF MY FATHER, THE RIGHTFUL IMPERIAL EMPEROR, TO OPEN DISCUSSIONS REGARDING A POSSIBLE ALLIANCE BETWEEN OUR FORCES AND THE JEDI OF THIS TEMPLE.
YOUR FATHER KNOWS OF THE HIDDEN TEMPLE'S EXISTENCE?
YES -- AND ITS LOCATION. YOU CAN'T THINK WE WOULD TAKE THE PRINCESS INTO UNKNOWN TERRITORY WITHOUT FIRST RELAYING OUR COORDINATES TO BASTION.
NEGOTIATIONS INVOLVE TRUST, PRINCESS. COMPROMISING OUR EXISTENCE IS A POOR PLACE TO BEGIN.
YOU HAVE NOTHING TO FEAR FROM MY FATHER, MASTER SAZEN...!
AND LESS REASON TO TRUST HIM.
THE JEDI COUNCIL WILL DECIDE THAT WHEN THEY CONVENE THIS EVENING. UNTIL THEN, YOU AND YOUR COMPANIONS SHOULD CONSIDER YOURSELVES OUR... GUESTS.

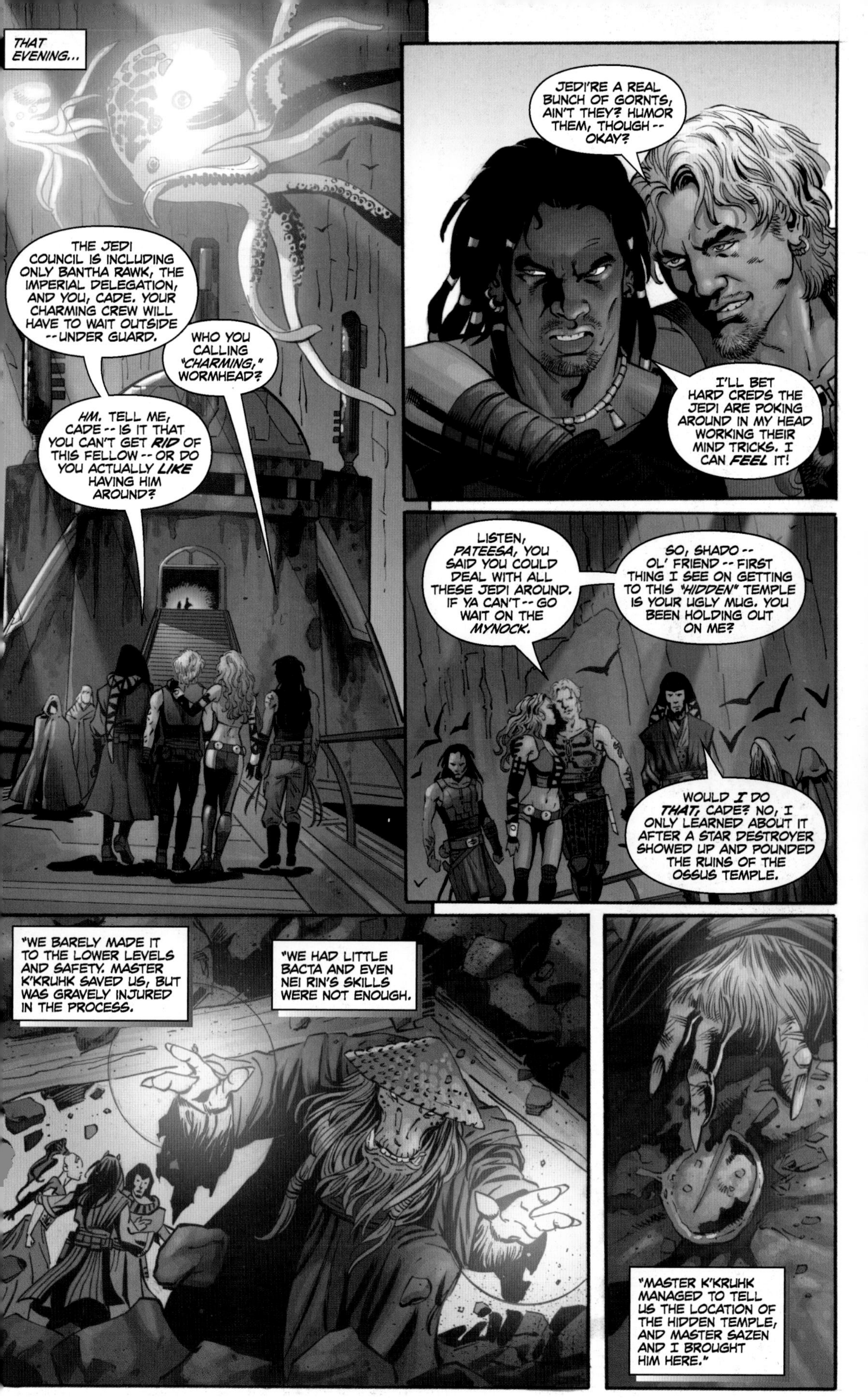
THAT EVENING...
THE JEDI COUNCIL IS INCLUDING ONLY BANTHA RAWK, THE IMPERIAL DELEGATION, AND YOU, CADE. YOUR CHARMING CREW WILL HAVE TO WAIT OUTSIDE -- UNDER GUARD.
WHO YOU CALLING "CHARMING," WORMHEAD?
HM. TELL ME, CADE -- IS IT THAT YOU CAN'T GET RID OF THIS FELLOW -- OR DO YOU ACTUALLY LIKE HAVING HIM AROUND?
JEDI'RE A REAL BUNCH OF GORNTS, AIN'T THEY? HUMOR THEM, THOUGH -- OKAY?
I'LL BET HARD CREDS THE JEDI ARE POKING AROUND IN MY HEAD WORKING THEIR MIND TRICKS. I CAN FEEL IT!
LISTEN, PATEESA, YOU SAID YOU COULD DEAL WITH ALL THESE JEDI AROUND. IF YA CAN'T -- GO WAIT ON THE MYNOCK.
SO, SHADO -- OL' FRIEND -- FIRST THING I SEE ON GETTING TO THIS "HIDDEN" TEMPLE IS YOUR UGLY MUG. YOU BEEN HOLDING OUT ON ME?
WOULD I DO THAT, CADE? NO, I ONLY LEARNED ABOUT IT AFTER A STAR DESTROYER SHOWED UP AND POUNDED THE RUINS OF THE OSSUS TEMPLE.
"WE BARELY MADE IT TO THE LOWER LEVELS AND SAFETY. MASTER K'KRUHK SAVED US, BUT WAS GRAVELY INJURED IN THE PROCESS.
"WE HAD LITTLE BACTA AND EVEN NEI RIN'S SKILLS WERE NOT ENOUGH.
"MASTER K'KRUHK MANAGED TO TELL US THE LOCATION OF THE HIDDEN TEMPLE, AND MASTER SAZEN AND I BROUGHT HIM HERE."

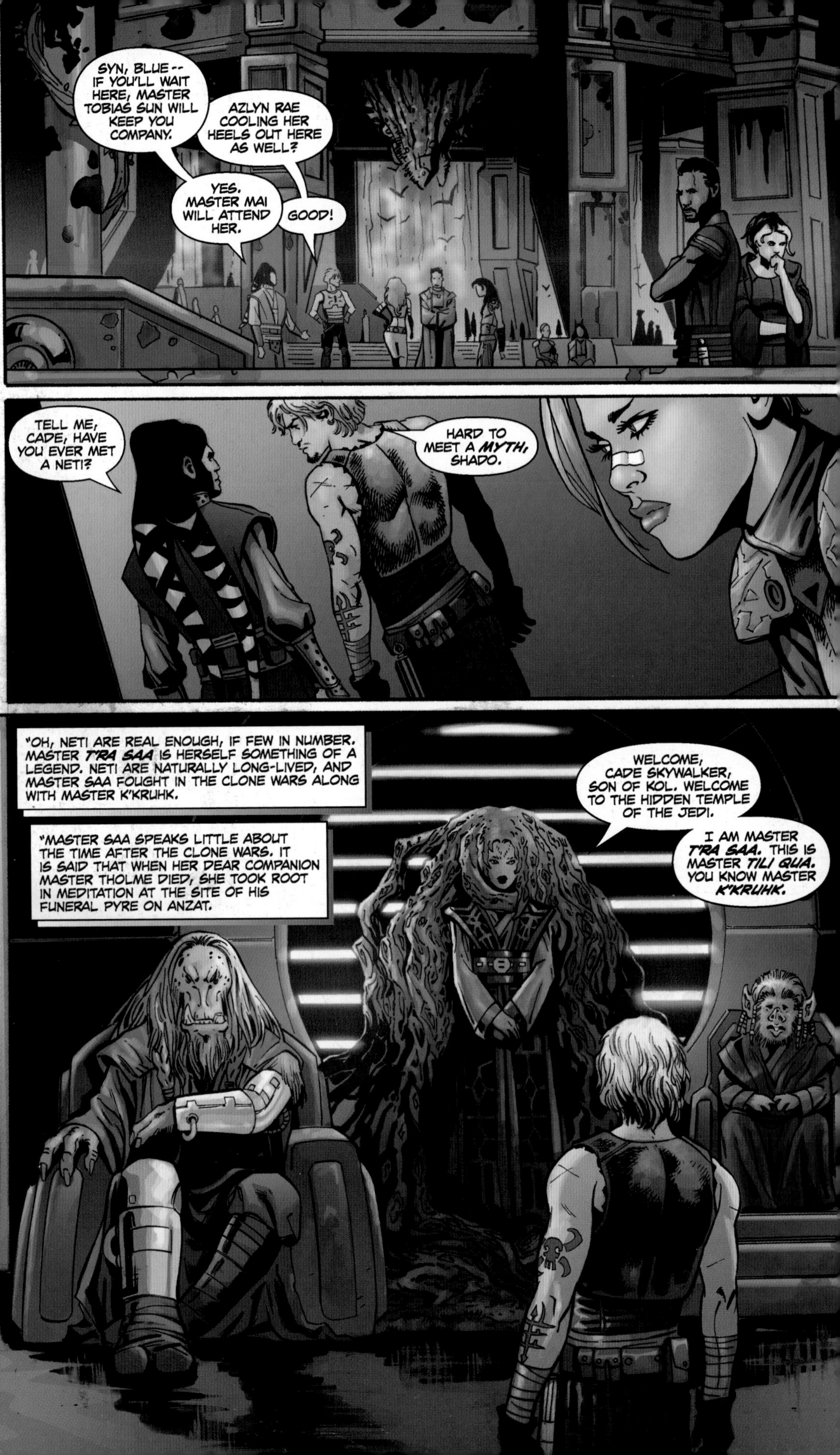
SYN, BLUE -- IF YOU'LL WAIT HERE, MASTER TOBIAS SUN WILL KEEP YOU COMPANY.
AZLYN RAE COOLING HER HEELS OUT HERE AS WELL?
YES. MASTER MAI WILL ATTEND HER.
GOOD!
TELL ME, CADE, HAVE YOU EVER MET A NETI?
HARD TO MEET A MYTH, SHADO.
"OH, NETI ARE REAL ENOUGH, IF FEW IN NUMBER. MASTER T'RA SAA IS HERSELF SOMETHING OF A LEGEND. NETI ARE NATURALLY LONG-LIVED, AND MASTER SAA FOUGHT IN THE CLONE WARS ALONG WITH MASTER K'KRUHK.
"MASTER SAA SPEAKS LITTLE ABOUT THE TIME AFTER THE CLONE WARS. IT IS SAID THAT WHEN HER DEAR COMPANION MASTER THOLME DIED, SHE TOOK ROOT IN MEDITATION AT THE SITE OF HIS FUNERAL PYRE ON ANZAT.
WELCOME, CADE SKYWALKER, SON OF KOL. WELCOME TO THE HIDDEN TEMPLE OF THE JEDI.
I AM MASTER T'RA SAA. THIS IS MASTER TILI QUA. YOU KNOW MASTER K'KRUHK.

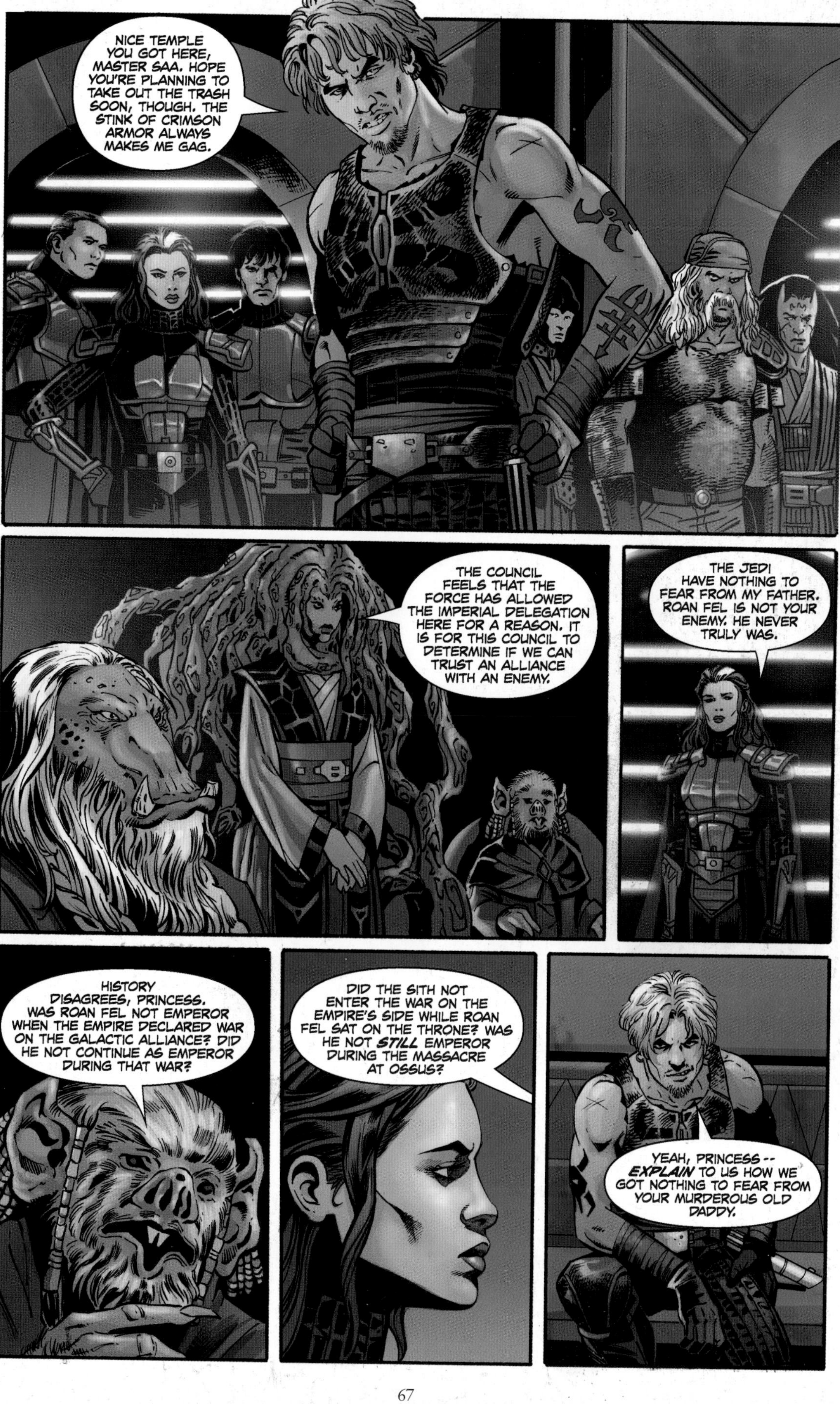
NICE TEMPLE YOU GOT HERE, MASTER SAA. HOPE YOU'RE PLANNING TO TAKE OUT THE TRASH SOON, THOUGH. THE STINK OF CRIMSON ARMOR ALWAYS MAKES ME GAG.
THE COUNCIL FEELS THAT THE FORCE HAS ALLOWED THE IMPERIAL DELEGATION HERE FOR A REASON. IT IS FOR THIS COUNCIL TO DETERMINE IF WE CAN TRUST AN ALLIANCE WITH AN ENEMY.
THE JEDI HAVE NOTHING TO FEAR FROM MY FATHER. ROAN FEL IS NOT YOUR ENEMY. HE NEVER TRULY WAS.
HISTORY DISAGREES, PRINCESS. WAS ROAN FEL NOT EMPEROR WHEN THE EMPIRE DECLARED WAR ON THE GALACTIC ALLIANCE? DID HE NOT CONTINUE AS EMPEROR DURING THAT WAR?
DID THE SITH NOT ENTER THE WAR ON THE EMPIRE'S SIDE WHILE ROAN FEL SAT ON THE THRONE? WAS HE NOT *STILL* EMPEROR DURING THE MASSACRE AT OSSUS?
YEAH, PRINCESS -- *EXPLAIN* TO US HOW WE GOT NOTHING TO FEAR FROM YOUR MURDEROUS OLD DADDY.

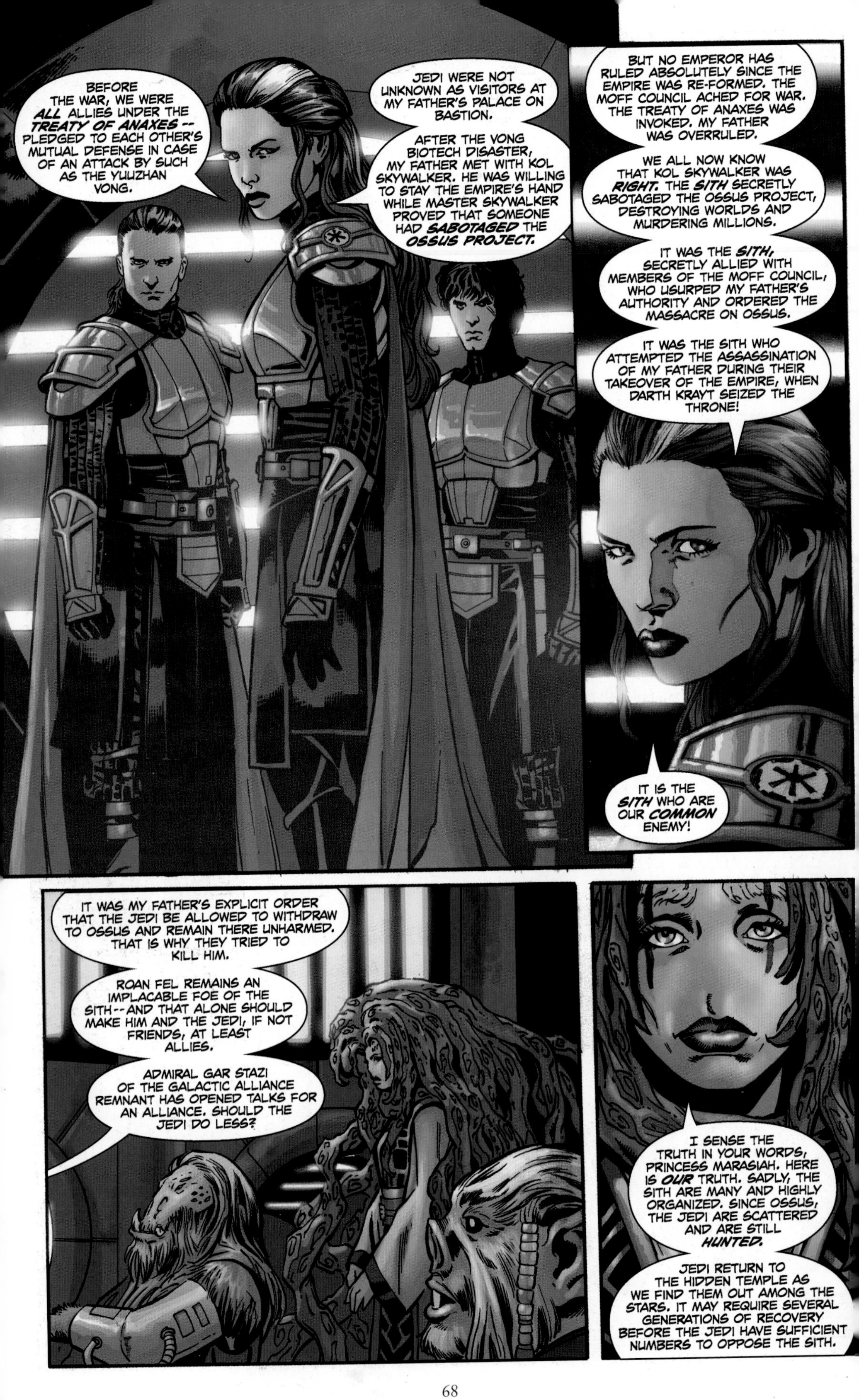
BEFORE THE WAR, WE WERE ALL ALLIES UNDER THE TREATY OF ANAXES -- PLEDGED TO EACH OTHER'S MUTUAL DEFENSE IN CASE OF AN ATTACK BY SUCH AS THE YUUZHAN VONG.
JEDI WERE NOT UNKNOWN AS VISITORS AT MY FATHER'S PALACE ON BASTION.
AFTER THE VONG BIOTECH DISASTER, MY FATHER MET WITH KOL SKYWALKER. HE WAS WILLING TO STAY THE EMPIRE'S HAND WHILE MASTER SKYWALKER PROVED THAT SOMEONE HAD SABOTAGED THE OSSUS PROJECT.
BUT NO EMPEROR HAS RULED ABSOLUTELY SINCE THE EMPIRE WAS RE-FORMED. THE MOFF COUNCIL ACHED FOR WAR. THE TREATY OF ANAXES WAS INVOKED. MY FATHER WAS OVERRULED.
WE ALL NOW KNOW THAT KOL SKYWALKER WAS RIGHT. THE SITH SECRETLY SABOTAGED THE OSSUS PROJECT, DESTROYING WORLDS AND MURDERING MILLIONS.
IT WAS THE SITH, SECRETLY ALLIED WITH MEMBERS OF THE MOFF COUNCIL, WHO USURPED MY FATHER'S AUTHORITY AND ORDERED THE MASSACRE ON OSSUS.
IT WAS THE SITH WHO ATTEMPTED THE ASSASSINATION OF MY FATHER DURING THEIR TAKEOVER OF THE EMPIRE, WHEN DARTH KRAYT SEIZED THE THRONE!
IT IS THE SITH WHO ARE OUR COMMON ENEMY!
IT WAS MY FATHER'S EXPLICIT ORDER THAT THE JEDI BE ALLOWED TO WITHDRAW TO OSSUS AND REMAIN THERE UNHARMED. THAT IS WHY THEY TRIED TO KILL HIM.
ROAN FEL REMAINS AN IMPLACABLE FOE OF THE SITH--AND THAT ALONE SHOULD MAKE HIM AND THE JEDI, IF NOT FRIENDS, AT LEAST ALLIES.
ADMIRAL GAR STAZI OF THE GALACTIC ALLIANCE REMNANT HAS OPENED TALKS FOR AN ALLIANCE. SHOULD THE JEDI DO LESS?
I SENSE THE TRUTH IN YOUR WORDS, PRINCESS MARASIAH. HERE IS OUR TRUTH. SADLY, THE SITH ARE MANY AND HIGHLY ORGANIZED. SINCE OSSUS, THE JEDI ARE SCATTERED AND ARE STILL HUNTED.
JEDI RETURN TO THE HIDDEN TEMPLE AS WE FIND THEM OUT AMONG THE STARS. IT MAY REQUIRE SEVERAL GENERATIONS OF RECOVERY BEFORE THE JEDI HAVE SUFFICIENT NUMBERS TO OPPOSE THE SITH.

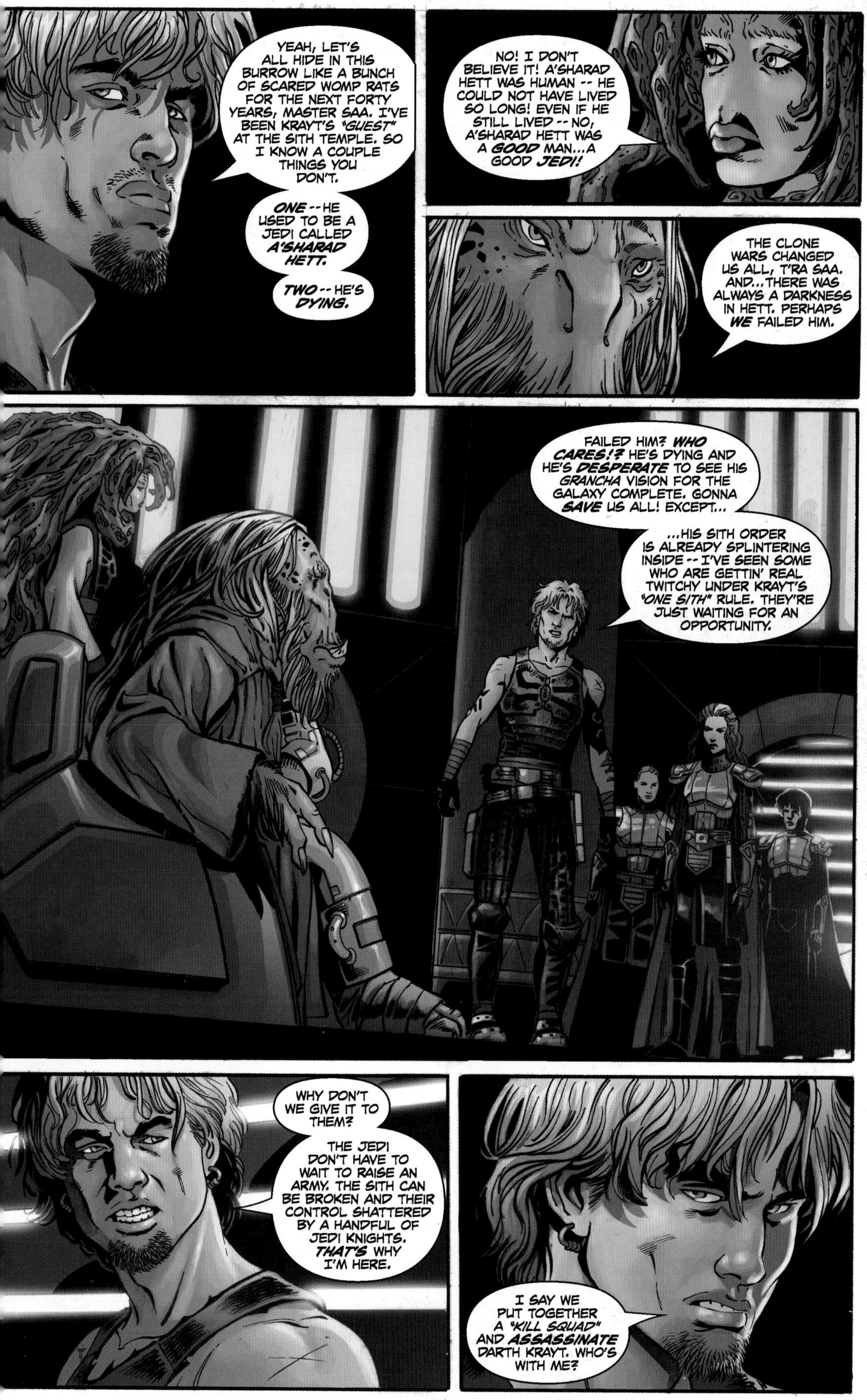
YEAH, LET'S ALL HIDE IN THIS BURROW LIKE A BUNCH OF SCARED WOMP RATS FOR THE NEXT FORTY YEARS, MASTER SAA. I'VE BEEN KRAYT'S "GUEST" AT THE SITH TEMPLE. SO I KNOW A COUPLE THINGS YOU DON'T.
ONE -- HE USED TO BE A JEDI CALLED A'SHARAD HETT.
TWO -- HE'S DYING.
NO! I DON'T BELIEVE IT! A'SHARAD HETT WAS HUMAN -- HE COULD NOT HAVE LIVED SO LONG! EVEN IF HE STILL LIVED -- NO, A'SHARAD HETT WAS A GOOD MAN... A GOOD JEDI!
THE CLONE WARS CHANGED US ALL, T'RA SAA. AND... THERE WAS ALWAYS A DARKNESS IN HETT. PERHAPS WE FAILED HIM.
FAILED HIM? WHO CARES!? HE'S DYING AND HE'S DESPERATE TO SEE HIS GRANCHA VISION FOR THE GALAXY COMPLETE. GONNA SAVE US ALL! EXCEPT...
...HIS SITH ORDER IS ALREADY SPLINTERING INSIDE -- I'VE SEEN SOME WHO ARE GETTIN' REAL TWITCHY UNDER KRAYT'S "ONE SITH" RULE. THEY'RE JUST WAITING FOR AN OPPORTUNITY.
WHY DON'T WE GIVE IT TO THEM?
THE JEDI DON'T HAVE TO WAIT TO RAISE AN ARMY. THE SITH CAN BE BROKEN AND THEIR CONTROL SHATTERED BY A HANDFUL OF JEDI KNIGHTS. THAT'S WHY I'M HERE.
I SAY WE PUT TOGETHER A "KILL SQUAD" AND ASSASSINATE DARTH KRAYT. WHO'S WITH ME?

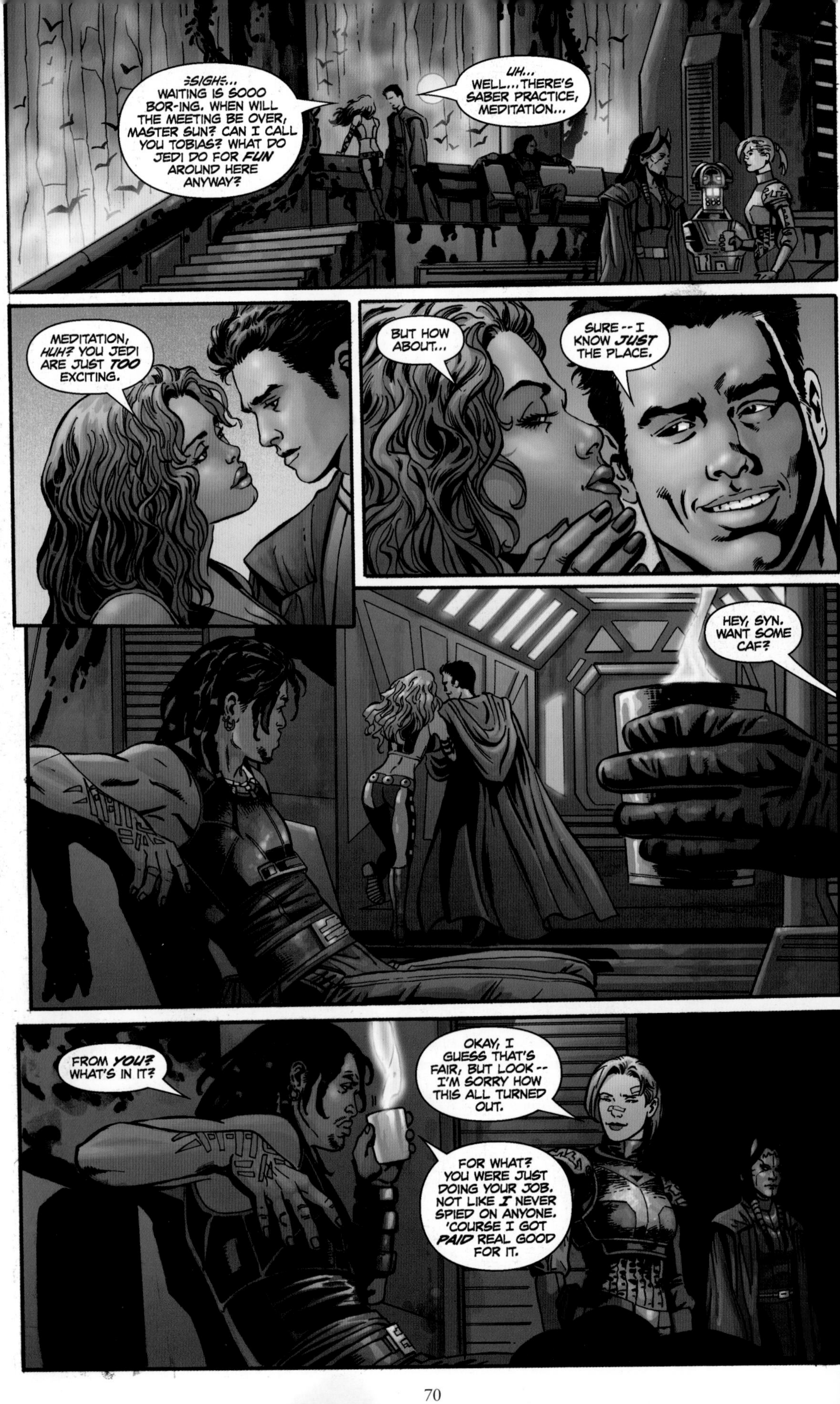
SIGH... WAITING IS SOOO BOR-ING. WHEN WILL THE MEETING BE OVER, MASTER SUN? CAN I CALL YOU TOBIAS? WHAT DO JEDI DO FOR FUN AROUND HERE ANYWAY?
UH... WELL... THERE'S SABER PRACTICE, MEDITATION...
MEDITATION, HUH? YOU JEDI ARE JUST TOO EXCITING.
BUT HOW ABOUT...
SURE -- I KNOW JUST THE PLACE.
HEY, SYN. WANT SOME CAF?
FROM YOU? WHAT'S IN IT?
OKAY, I GUESS THAT'S FAIR, BUT LOOK -- I'M SORRY HOW THIS ALL TURNED OUT.
FOR WHAT? YOU WERE JUST DOING YOUR JOB. NOT LIKE I NEVER SPIED ON ANYONE. 'COURSE I GOT PAID REAL GOOD FOR IT.

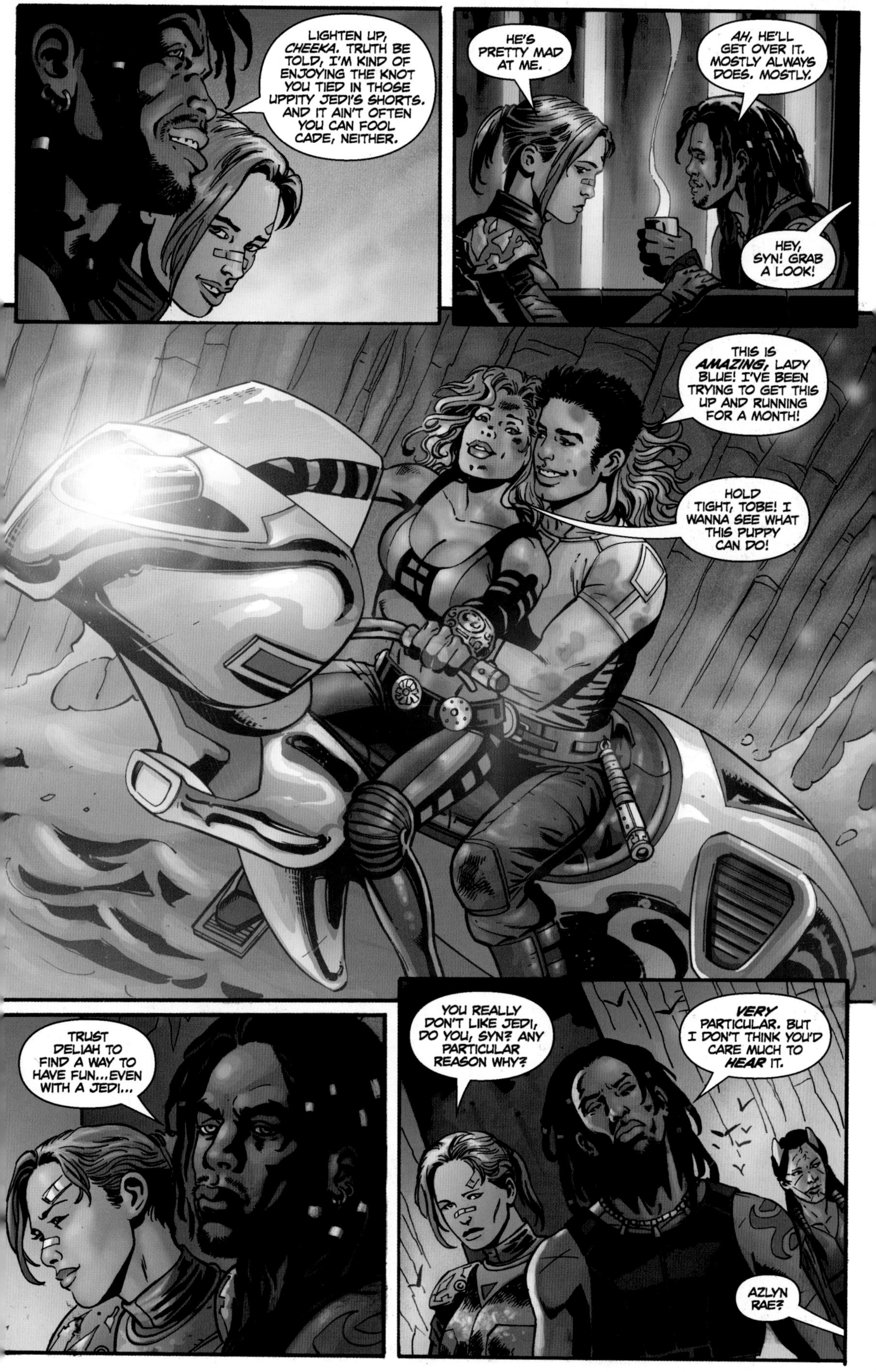
LIGHTEN UP, CHEEKA. TRUTH BE TOLD, I'M KIND OF ENJOYING THE KNOT YOU TIED IN THOSE UPPITY JEDI'S SHORTS. AND IT AIN'T OFTEN YOU CAN FOOL CADE, NEITHER.
HE'S PRETTY MAD AT ME.
AH, HE'LL GET OVER IT. MOSTLY ALWAYS DOES. MOSTLY.
HEY, SYN! GRAB A LOOK!
THIS IS AMAZING, LADY BLUE! I'VE BEEN TRYING TO GET THIS UP AND RUNNING FOR A MONTH!
HOLD TIGHT, TOBE! I WANNA SEE WHAT THIS PUPPY CAN DO!
TRUST DELIAH TO FIND A WAY TO HAVE FUN...EVEN WITH A JEDI...
YOU REALLY DON'T LIKE JEDI, DO YOU, SYN? ANY PARTICULAR REASON WHY?
VERY PARTICULAR. BUT I DON'T THINK YOU'D CARE MUCH TO HEAR IT.
AZLYN RAE?

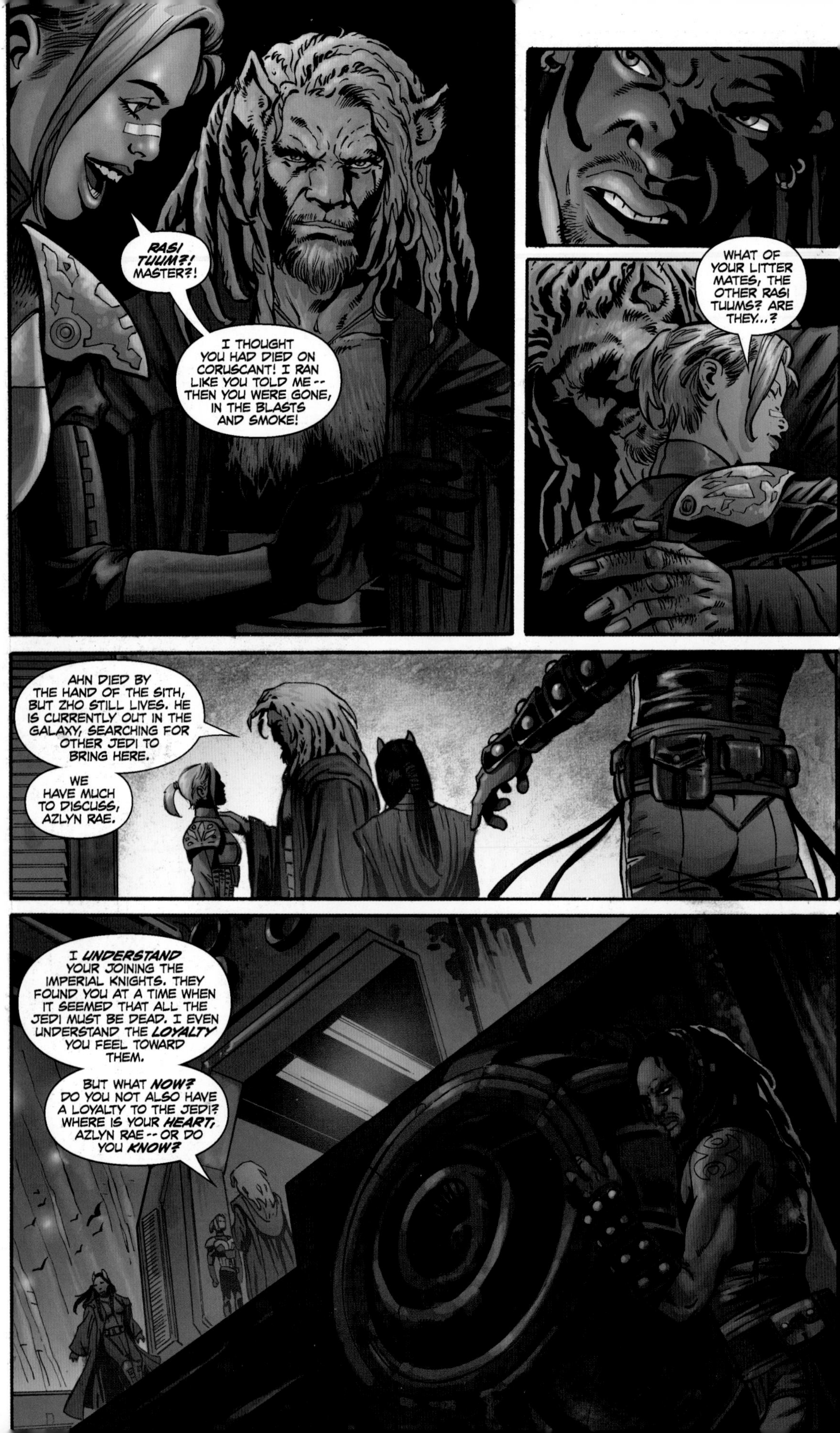
RASI TUUM?! MASTER?!
I THOUGHT YOU HAD DIED ON CORUSCANT! I RAN LIKE YOU TOLD ME -- THEN YOU WERE GONE, IN THE BLASTS AND SMOKE!
WHAT OF YOUR LITTER MATES, THE OTHER RASI TUUMS? ARE THEY...?
AHN DIED BY THE HAND OF THE SITH, BUT ZHO STILL LIVES. HE IS CURRENTLY OUT IN THE GALAXY, SEARCHING FOR OTHER JEDI TO BRING HERE.
WE HAVE MUCH TO DISCUSS, AZLYN RAE.
I *UNDERSTAND* YOUR JOINING THE IMPERIAL KNIGHTS. THEY FOUND YOU AT A TIME WHEN IT SEEMED THAT ALL THE JEDI MUST BE DEAD. I EVEN UNDERSTAND THE *LOYALTY* YOU FEEL TOWARD THEM.
BUT WHAT *NOW?* DO YOU NOT ALSO HAVE A LOYALTY TO THE JEDI? WHERE IS YOUR *HEART,* AZLYN RAE -- OR DO YOU *KNOW?*

IT'S THE JEDI...IT'S *HIM*...

NO GOOD MURGLIN' SON OF A--!

JARIAH SYN, ARE YOU ILL?

NO!

GET AWAY FROM ME!

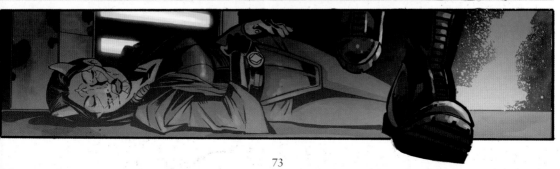

ASSASSINATION?!

IT'S THE *ONLY* WAY. KRAYT HAS NO HEIR. WITH HIM DEAD, HIS SITH ORDER WILL FALL IN UPON ITSELF.

JEDI RESPECT LIFE, YOUNG SKYWALKER -- *ALL* LIFE. THE FORCE CONNECTS *EVERYTHING* IN THE CYCLE OF DEATH AND RENEWAL -- EVEN THE *SITH*.

JEDI MAY TAKE LIVES IF THERE IS NO OTHER CHOICE, BUT TO *DELIBERATELY* SEARCH OUT ONE TO KILL? THIS IS *NOT* THE JEDI WAY.

NOT THE "JEDI WAY"? KRAYT WAS ONCE A JEDI, AND IT'S *HIS* WAY.

HOW MANY HAS HE ALREADY MURDERED SO HE CAN IMPOSE HIS VISION ON THE GALAXY? EVEN WAY OUT HERE YOU MUST HAVE HEARD WHAT HE'S DONE ON DAC!

I'M SURE MASTER SAZEN HAS TOLD YOU ABOUT THIS CRAZY HEALING THING I'VE GOT GOING ON. SAYS IT'S *DARK SIDE*, BUT IT WORKS. WANNA GIVE IT A TRY, MASTER K'KRUHK?

KRAYT DOES. WANTS ME TO *HEAL* HIM FROM WHATEVER VON PARASITES ARE CHEWIN' ON HIM. I DON'T EVEN KNOW I CAN, BUT IF KRAYT GETS HOLD OF ME AGAIN I'M NOT SURE I WON'T BE *FORCED* TO.

MAYBE IT'S THE WILL OF THE FORCE THAT THE JEDI DESTROY THIS MONSTER WHO WAS ONCE ONE OF THEIR *OWN* -- BEFORE *HE* DESTROYS *THEM*!

MAYBE IT'S TIME ASSASSINATION *WAS* THE JEDI WAY!

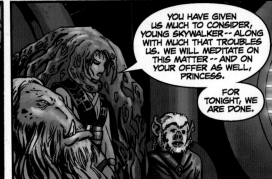

YOU HAVE GIVEN US MUCH TO CONSIDER, YOUNG SKYWALKER -- ALONG WITH MUCH THAT TROUBLES US. WE WILL MEDITATE ON THIS MATTER -- AND ON YOUR OFFER AS WELL, PRINCESS.

FOR TONIGHT, WE ARE DONE.

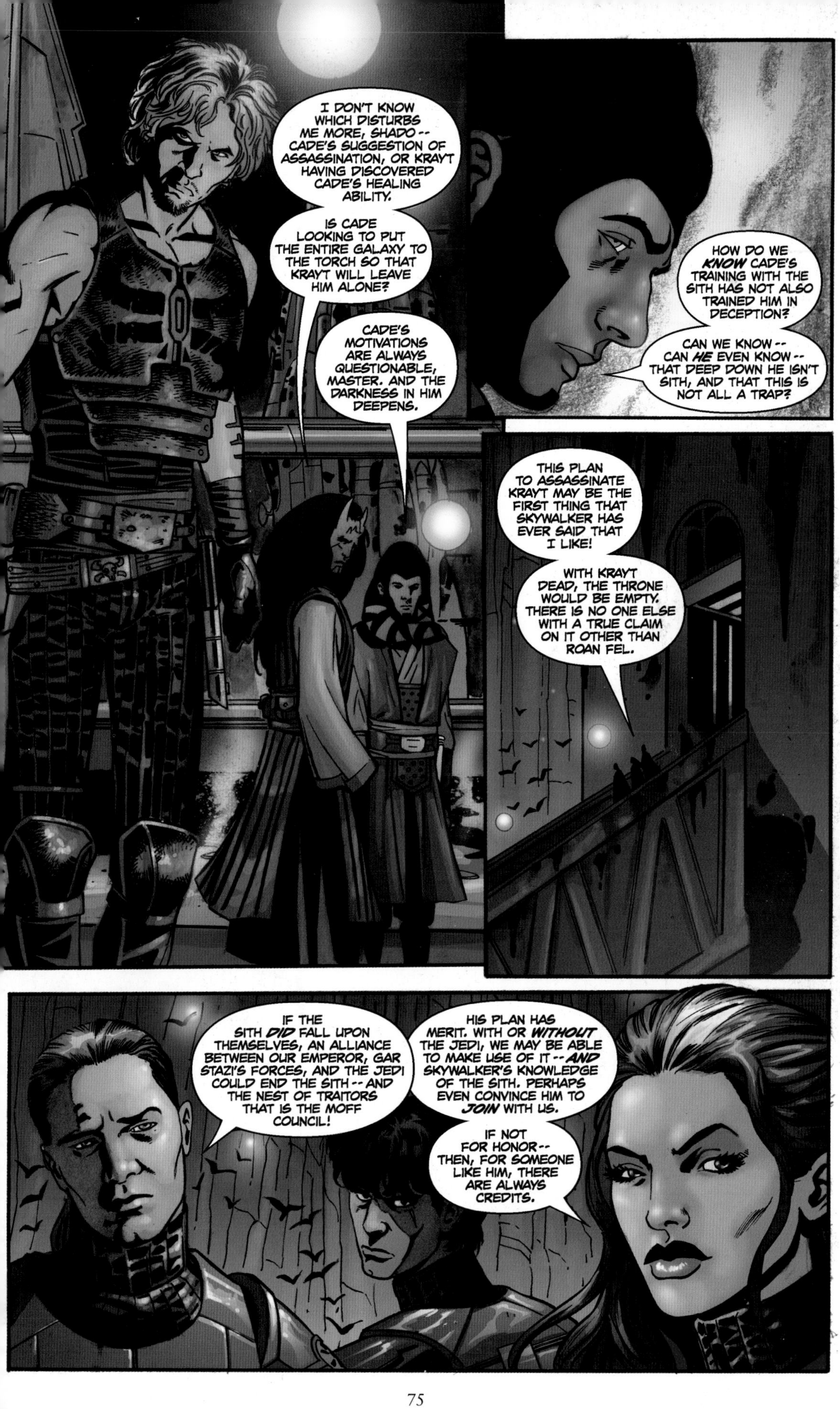
I DON'T KNOW WHICH DISTURBS ME MORE, SHADO -- CADE'S SUGGESTION OF ASSASSINATION, OR KRAYT HAVING DISCOVERED CADE'S HEALING ABILITY.
IS CADE LOOKING TO PUT THE ENTIRE GALAXY TO THE TORCH SO THAT KRAYT WILL LEAVE HIM ALONE?
CADE'S MOTIVATIONS ARE ALWAYS QUESTIONABLE, MASTER. AND THE DARKNESS IN HIM DEEPENS.
HOW DO WE KNOW CADE'S TRAINING WITH THE SITH HAS NOT ALSO TRAINED HIM IN DECEPTION?
CAN WE KNOW -- CAN HE EVEN KNOW -- THAT DEEP DOWN HE ISN'T SITH, AND THAT THIS IS NOT ALL A TRAP?
THIS PLAN TO ASSASSINATE KRAYT MAY BE THE FIRST THING THAT SKYWALKER HAS EVER SAID THAT I LIKE!
WITH KRAYT DEAD, THE THRONE WOULD BE EMPTY. THERE IS NO ONE ELSE WITH A TRUE CLAIM ON IT OTHER THAN ROAN FEL.
IF THE SITH DID FALL UPON THEMSELVES, AN ALLIANCE BETWEEN OUR EMPEROR, GAR STAZI'S FORCES, AND THE JEDI COULD END THE SITH -- AND THE NEST OF TRAITORS THAT IS THE MOFF COUNCIL!
HIS PLAN HAS MERIT. WITH OR WITHOUT THE JEDI, WE MAY BE ABLE TO MAKE USE OF IT -- AND SKYWALKER'S KNOWLEDGE OF THE SITH. PERHAPS EVEN CONVINCE HIM TO JOIN WITH US.
IF NOT FOR HONOR -- THEN, FOR SOMEONE LIKE HIM, THERE ARE ALWAYS CREDITS.

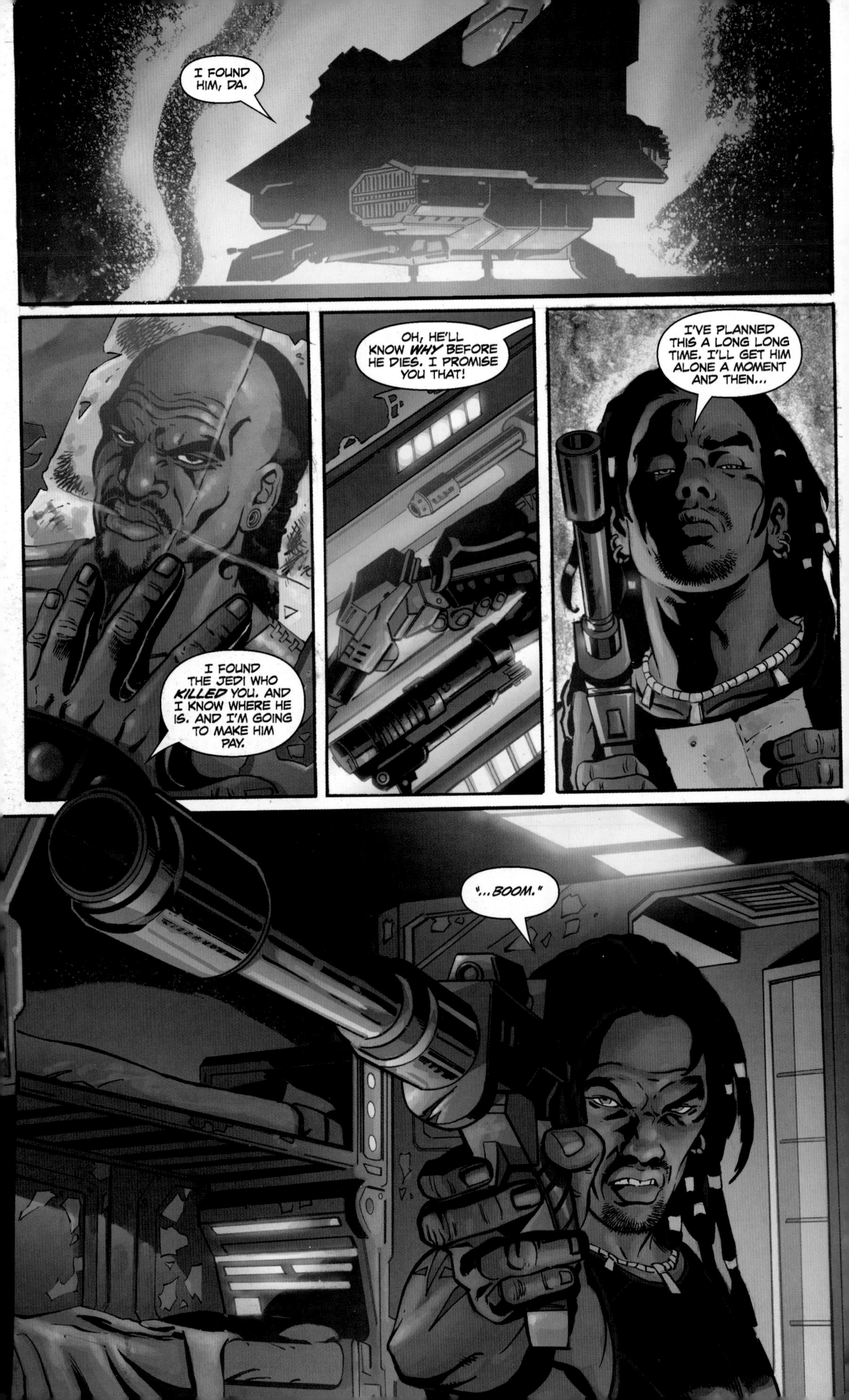
I FOUND HIM, DA.
I FOUND THE JEDI WHO *KILLED* YOU. AND I KNOW WHERE HE IS. AND I'M GOING TO MAKE HIM PAY.
OH, HE'LL KNOW *WHY* BEFORE HE DIES. I PROMISE YOU THAT!
I'VE PLANNED THIS A LONG LONG TIME. I'LL GET HIM ALONE A MOMENT AND THEN...
"...*BOOM*."

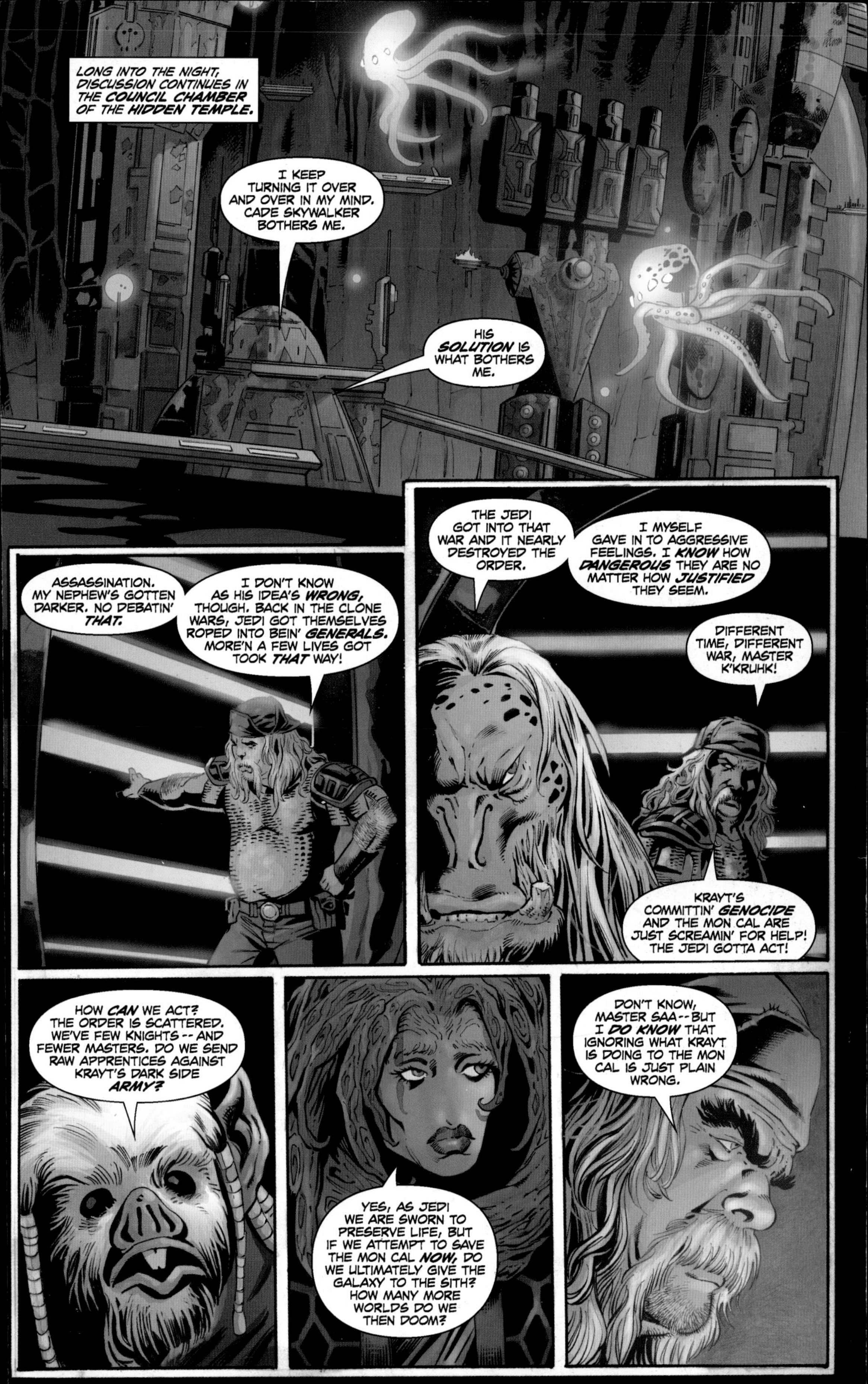
LONG INTO THE NIGHT, DISCUSSION CONTINUES IN THE COUNCIL CHAMBER OF THE HIDDEN TEMPLE.
I KEEP TURNING IT OVER AND OVER IN MY MIND. CADE SKYWALKER BOTHERS ME.
HIS SOLUTION IS WHAT BOTHERS ME.
ASSASSINATION. MY NEPHEW'S GOTTEN DARKER. NO DEBATIN' THAT.
I DON'T KNOW AS HIS IDEA'S WRONG, THOUGH. BACK IN THE CLONE WARS, JEDI GOT THEMSELVES ROPED INTO BEIN' GENERALS. MORE'N A FEW LIVES GOT TOOK THAT WAY!
THE JEDI GOT INTO THAT WAR AND IT NEARLY DESTROYED THE ORDER.
I MYSELF GAVE IN TO AGGRESSIVE FEELINGS. I KNOW HOW DANGEROUS THEY ARE NO MATTER HOW JUSTIFIED THEY SEEM.
DIFFERENT TIME, DIFFERENT WAR, MASTER K'KRUHK!
KRAYT'S COMMITTIN' GENOCIDE AND THE MON CAL ARE JUST SCREAMIN' FOR HELP! THE JEDI GOTTA ACT!
HOW CAN WE ACT? THE ORDER IS SCATTERED. WE'VE FEW KNIGHTS -- AND FEWER MASTERS. DO WE SEND RAW APPRENTICES AGAINST KRAYT'S DARK SIDE ARMY?
YES, AS JEDI WE ARE SWORN TO PRESERVE LIFE, BUT IF WE ATTEMPT TO SAVE THE MON CAL NOW, DO WE ULTIMATELY GIVE THE GALAXY TO THE SITH? HOW MANY MORE WORLDS DO WE THEN DOOM?
DON'T KNOW, MASTER SAA--BUT I DO KNOW THAT IGNORING WHAT KRAYT IS DOING TO THE MON CAL IS JUST PLAIN WRONG.

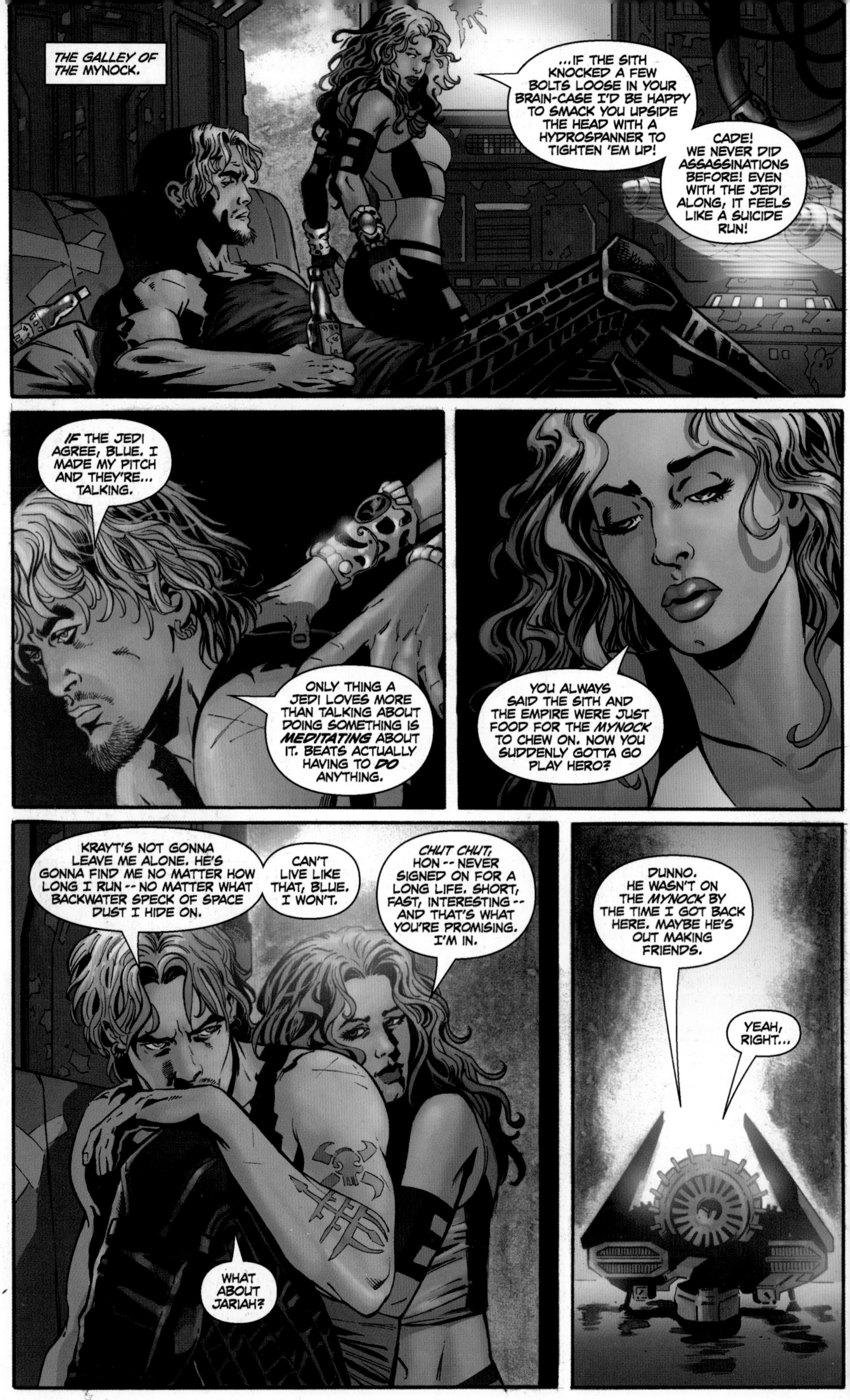
THE GALLEY OF THE MYNOCK.
...IF THE SITH KNOCKED A FEW BOLTS LOOSE IN YOUR BRAIN-CASE I'D BE HAPPY TO SMACK YOU UPSIDE THE HEAD WITH A HYDROSPANNER TO TIGHTEN 'EM UP!
CADE! WE NEVER DID ASSASSINATIONS BEFORE! EVEN WITH THE JEDI ALONG, IT FEELS LIKE A SUICIDE RUN!
IF THE JEDI AGREE, BLUE. I MADE MY PITCH AND THEY'RE... TALKING.
ONLY THING A JEDI LOVES MORE THAN TALKING ABOUT DOING SOMETHING IS MEDITATING ABOUT IT. BEATS ACTUALLY HAVING TO DO ANYTHING.
YOU ALWAYS SAID THE SITH AND THE EMPIRE WERE JUST FOOD FOR THE MYNOCK TO CHEW ON. NOW YOU SUDDENLY GOTTA GO PLAY HERO?
KRAYT'S NOT GONNA LEAVE ME ALONE. HE'S GONNA FIND ME NO MATTER HOW LONG I RUN -- NO MATTER WHAT BACKWATER SPECK OF SPACE DUST I HIDE ON.
CAN'T LIVE LIKE THAT, BLUE. I WON'T.
CHUT CHUT, HON -- NEVER SIGNED ON FOR A LONG LIFE. SHORT, FAST, INTERESTING -- AND THAT'S WHAT YOU'RE PROMISING. I'M IN.
WHAT ABOUT JARIAH?
DUNNO. HE WASN'T ON THE MYNOCK BY THE TIME I GOT BACK HERE. MAYBE HE'S OUT MAKING FRIENDS.
YEAH, RIGHT...

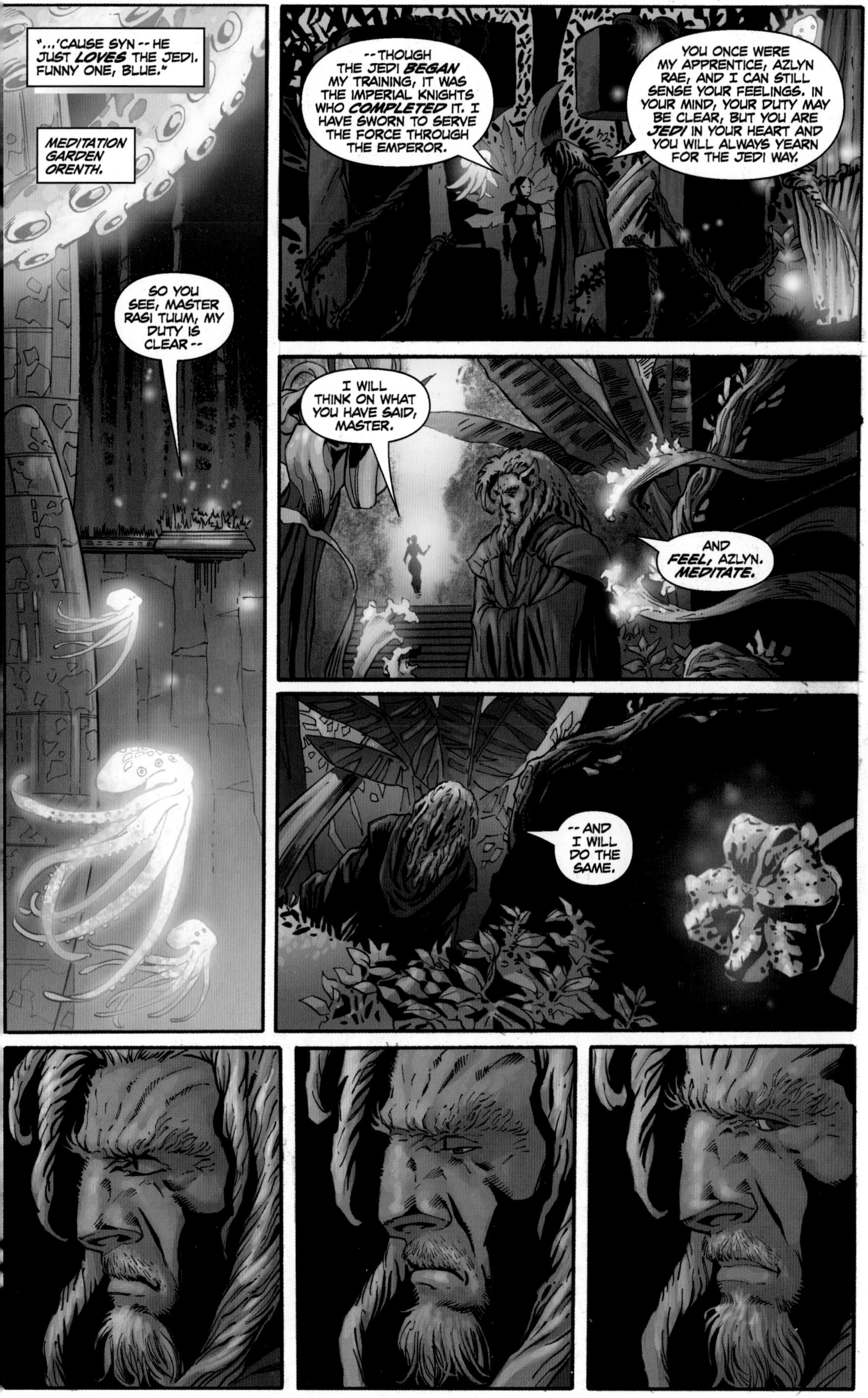

"...'CAUSE SYN -- HE JUST LOVES THE JEDI. FUNNY ONE, BLUE."
MEDITATION GARDEN ORENTH.
SO YOU SEE, MASTER RASI TUUM, MY DUTY IS CLEAR --
--THOUGH THE JEDI BEGAN MY TRAINING, IT WAS THE IMPERIAL KNIGHTS WHO COMPLETED IT. I HAVE SWORN TO SERVE THE FORCE THROUGH THE EMPEROR.
YOU ONCE WERE MY APPRENTICE, AZLYN RAE, AND I CAN STILL SENSE YOUR FEELINGS. IN YOUR MIND, YOUR DUTY MAY BE CLEAR, BUT YOU ARE JEDI IN YOUR HEART AND YOU WILL ALWAYS YEARN FOR THE JEDI WAY.
I WILL THINK ON WHAT YOU HAVE SAID, MASTER.
AND FEEL, AZLYN. MEDITATE.
-- AND I WILL DO THE SAME.

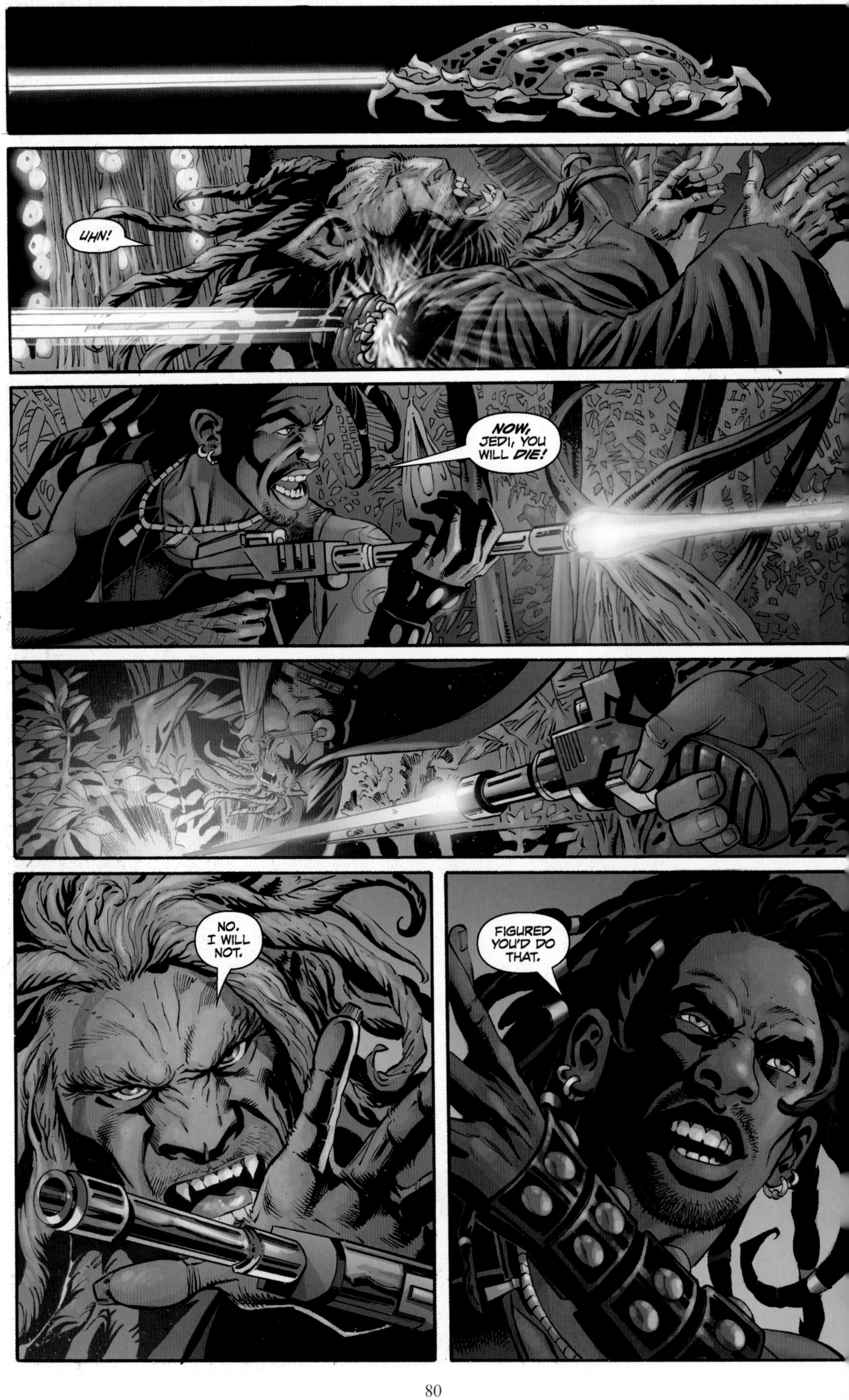
UHN!
NOW, JEDI, YOU WILL DIE!
NO. I WILL NOT.
FIGURED YOU'D DO THAT.

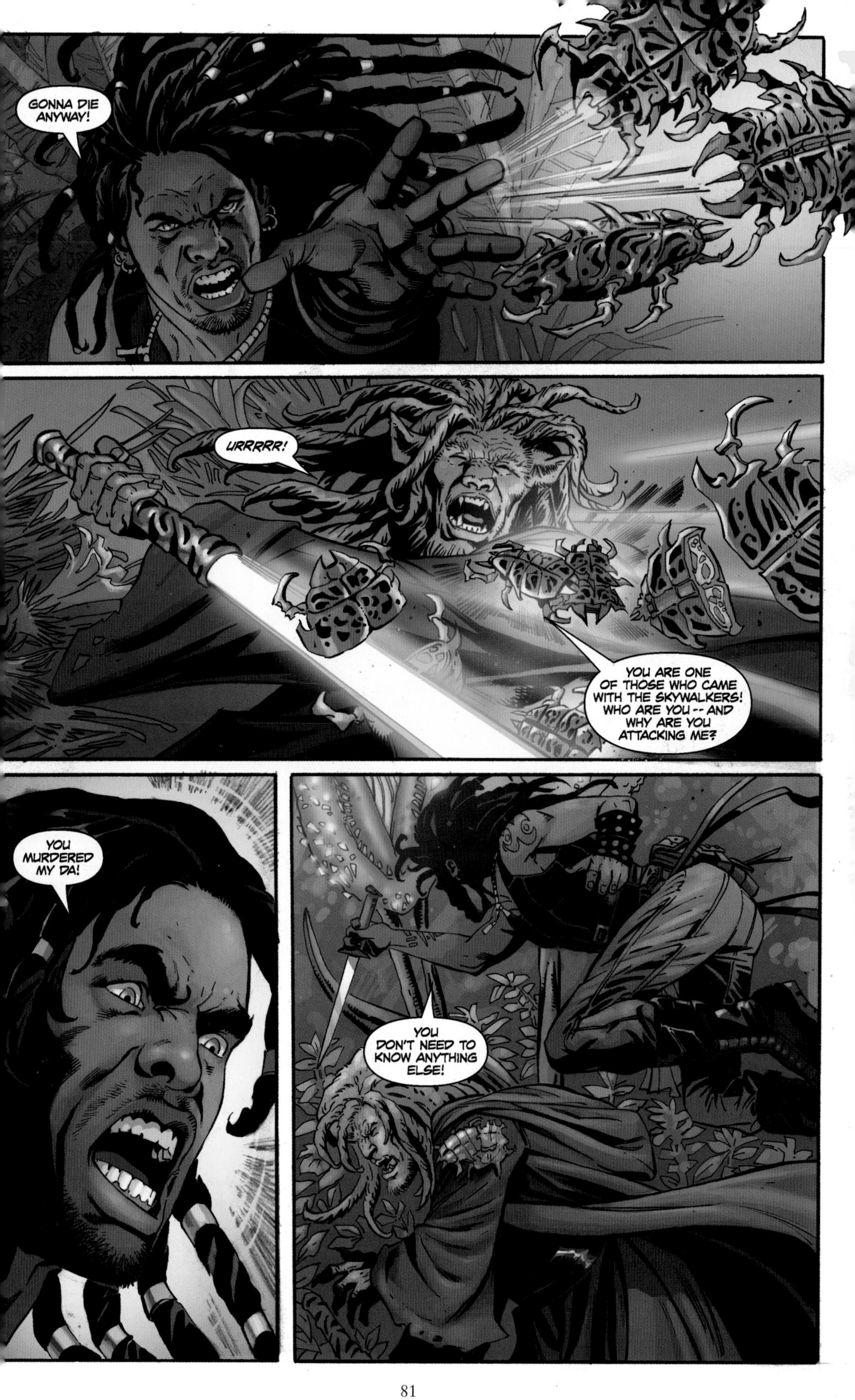
GONNA DIE ANYWAY!
URRRRR!
YOU ARE ONE OF THOSE WHO CAME WITH THE SKYWALKERS! WHO ARE YOU -- AND WHY ARE YOU ATTACKING ME?
YOU MURDERED MY DA!
YOU DON'T NEED TO KNOW ANYTHING ELSE!

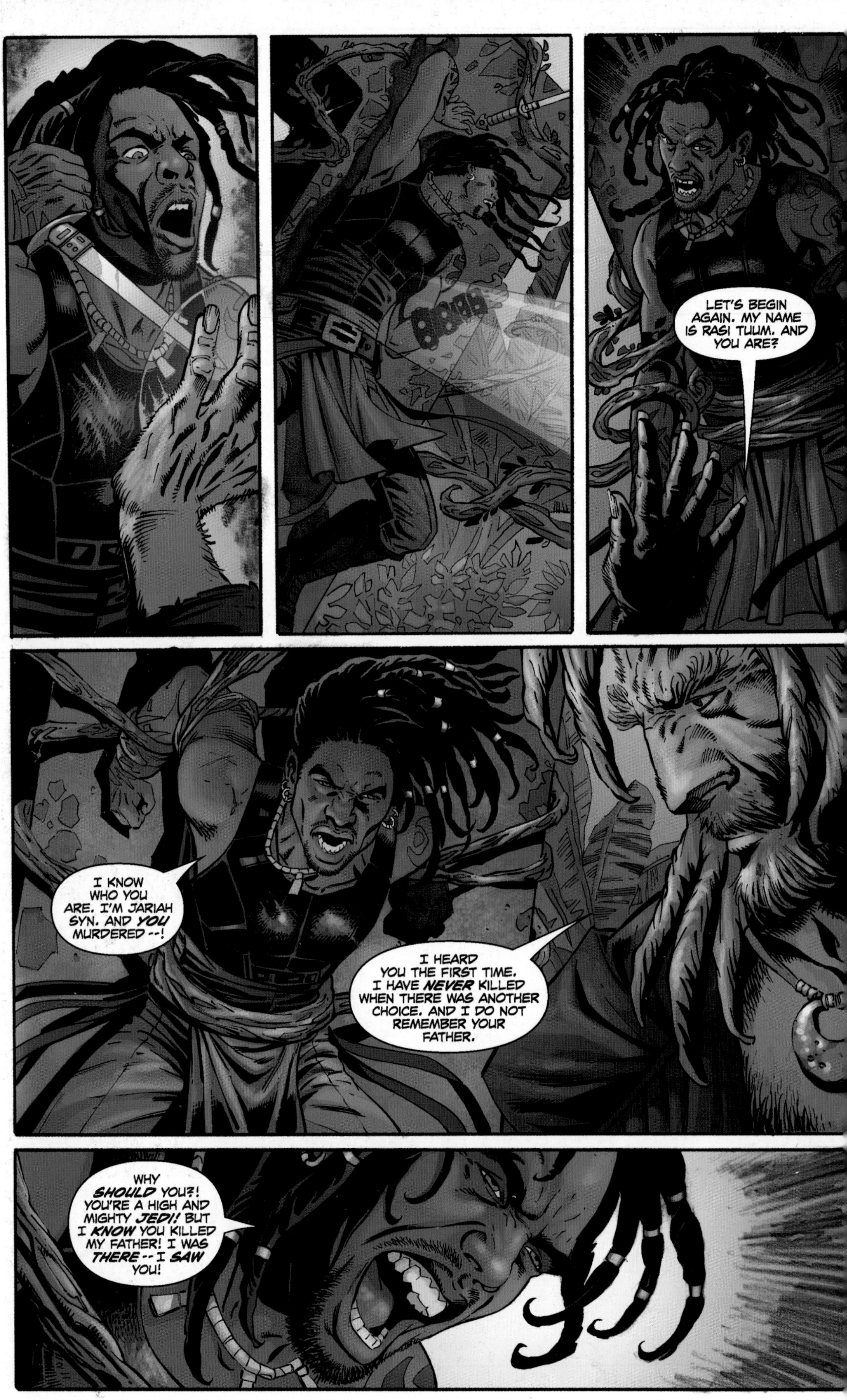
LET'S BEGIN AGAIN. MY NAME IS RASI TUUM. AND YOU ARE?
I KNOW WHO YOU ARE. I'M JARIAH SYN. AND YOU MURDERED --!
I HEARD YOU THE FIRST TIME. I HAVE NEVER KILLED WHEN THERE WAS ANOTHER CHOICE. AND I DO NOT REMEMBER YOUR FATHER.
WHY SHOULD YOU?! YOU'RE A HIGH AND MIGHTY JEDI! BUT I KNOW YOU KILLED MY FATHER! I WAS THERE -- I SAW YOU!

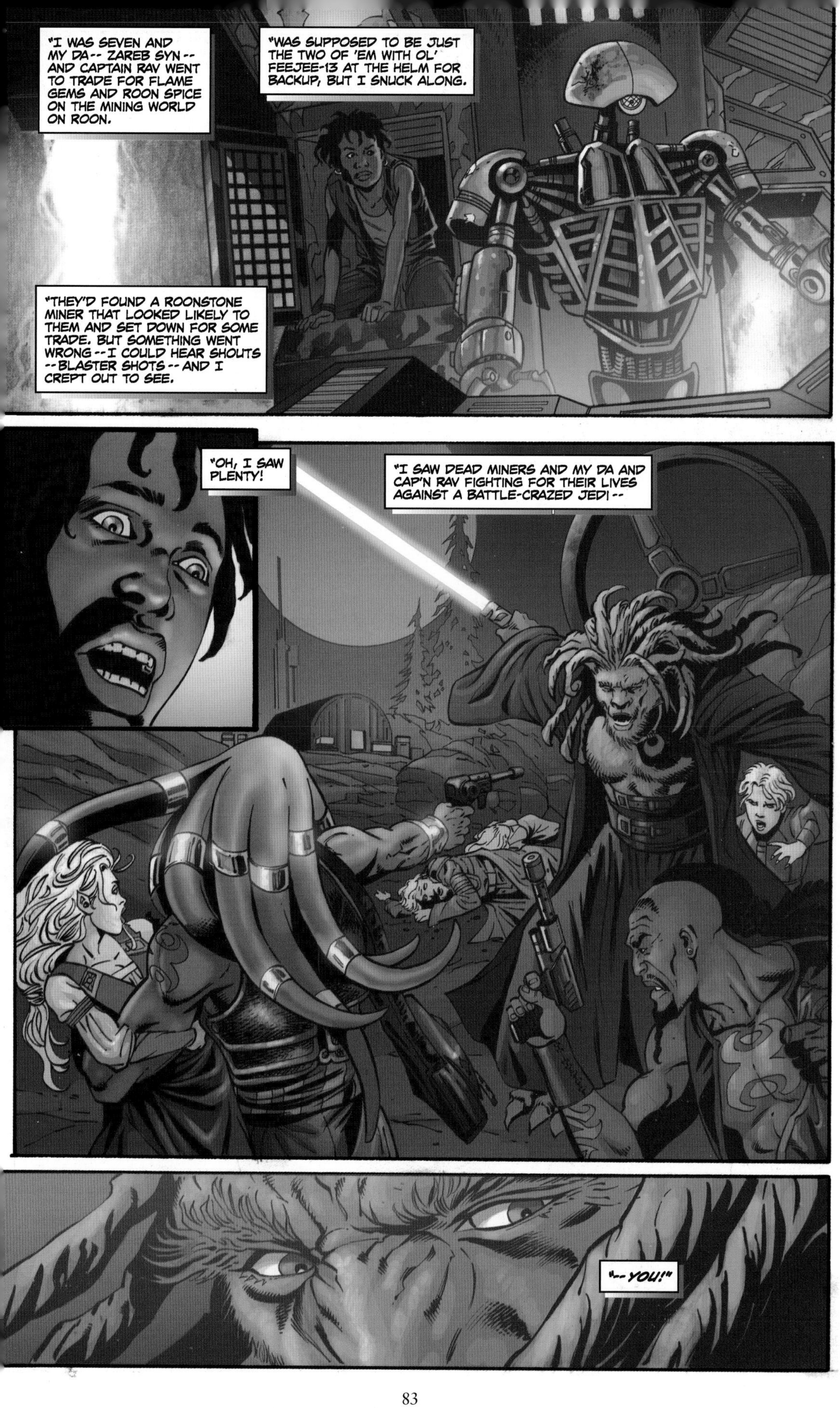
"I WAS SEVEN AND MY DA-- ZAREB SYN-- AND CAPTAIN RAV WENT TO TRADE FOR FLAME GEMS AND ROON SPICE ON THE MINING WORLD ON ROON.
"WAS SUPPOSED TO BE JUST THE TWO OF 'EM WITH OL' FEEJEE-13 AT THE HELM FOR BACKUP, BUT I SNUCK ALONG.
"THEY'D FOUND A ROONSTONE MINER THAT LOOKED LIKELY TO THEM AND SET DOWN FOR SOME TRADE. BUT SOMETHING WENT WRONG--I COULD HEAR SHOUTS --BLASTER SHOTS--AND I CREPT OUT TO SEE.
"OH, I SAW PLENTY!
"I SAW DEAD MINERS AND MY DA AND CAP'N RAV FIGHTING FOR THEIR LIVES AGAINST A BATTLE-CRAZED JEDI--
"--YOU!"

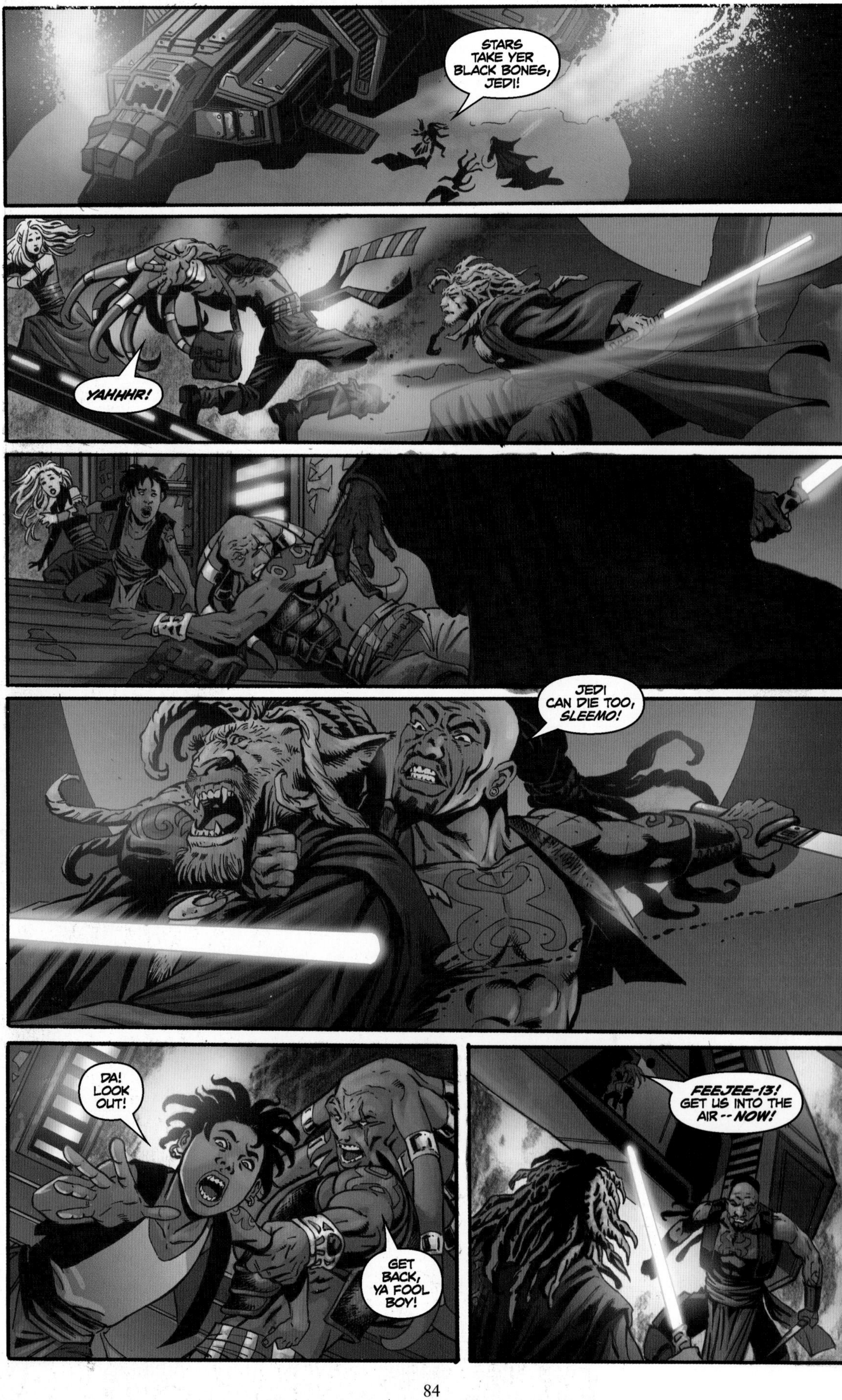
STARS TAKE YER BLACK BONES, JEDI!
YAHHHR!
JEDI CAN DIE TOO, SLEEMO!
DA! LOOK OUT!
GET BACK, YA FOOL BOY!
FEEJEE-13! GET US INTO THE AIR -- NOW!

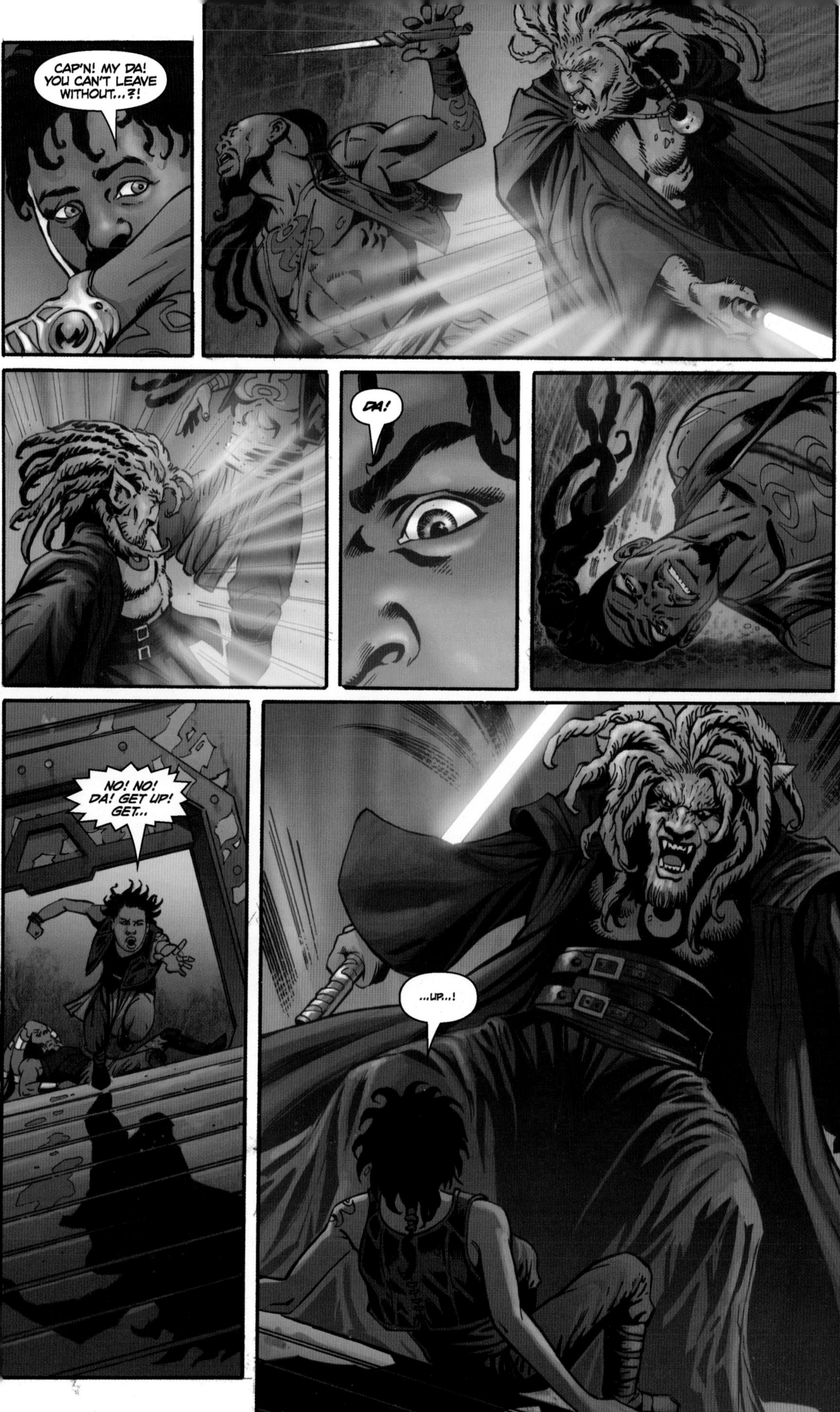
CAP'N! MY DA! YOU CAN'T LEAVE WITHOUT...?!
DA!
NO! NO! DA! GET UP! GET...
...UP...!

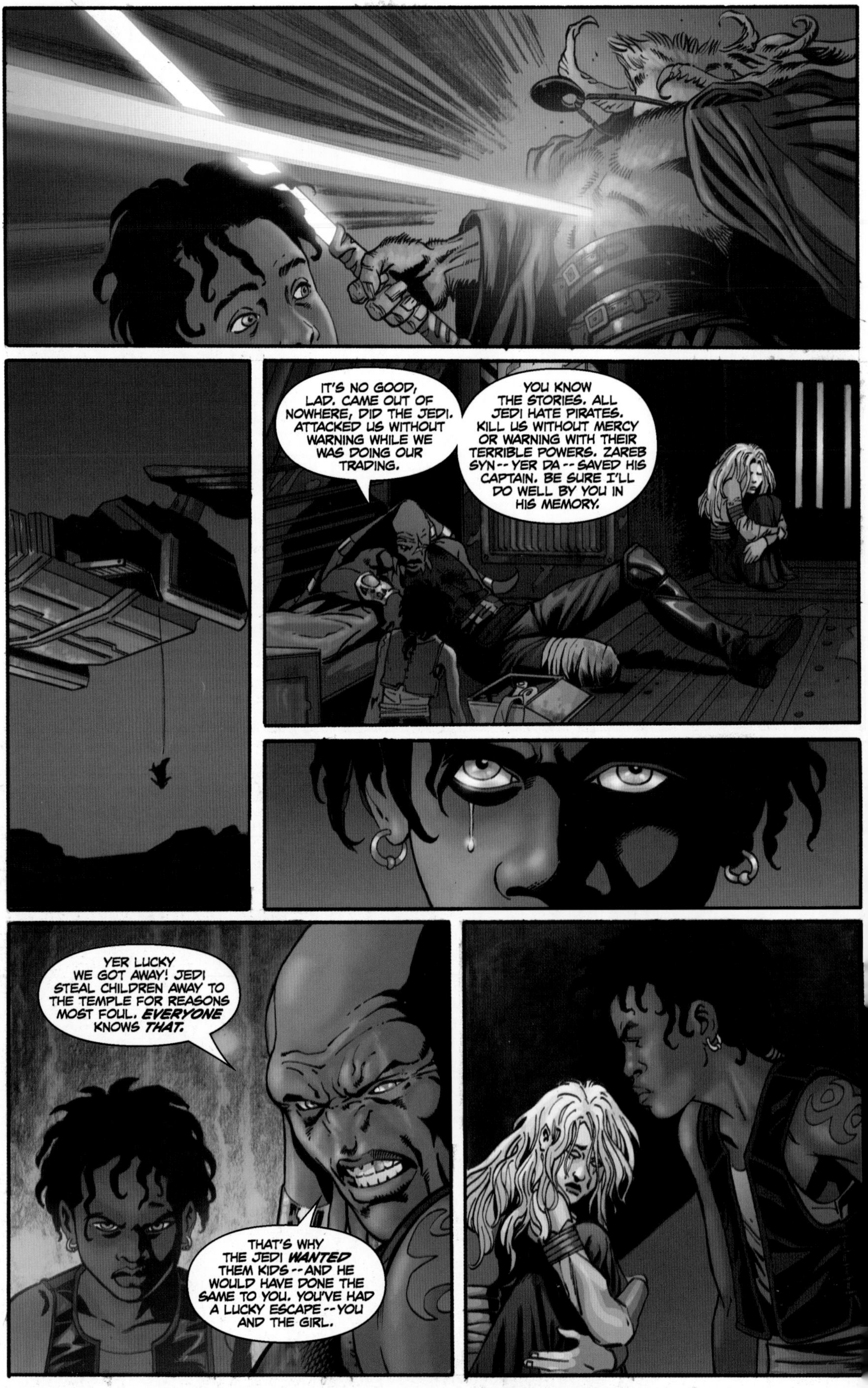
IT'S NO GOOD, LAD. CAME OUT OF NOWHERE, DID THE JEDI. ATTACKED US WITHOUT WARNING WHILE WE WAS DOING OUR TRADING.
YOU KNOW THE STORIES. ALL JEDI HATE PIRATES. KILL US WITHOUT MERCY OR WARNING WITH THEIR TERRIBLE POWERS. ZAREB SYN--YER DA--SAVED HIS CAPTAIN. BE SURE I'LL DO WELL BY YOU IN HIS MEMORY.
YER LUCKY WE GOT AWAY! JEDI STEAL CHILDREN AWAY TO THE TEMPLE FOR REASONS MOST FOUL. ***EVERYONE*** KNOWS ***THAT.***
THAT'S WHY THE JEDI ***WANTED*** THEM KIDS--AND HE WOULD HAVE DONE THE SAME TO YOU. YOU'VE HAD A LUCKY ESCAPE--YOU AND THE GIRL.

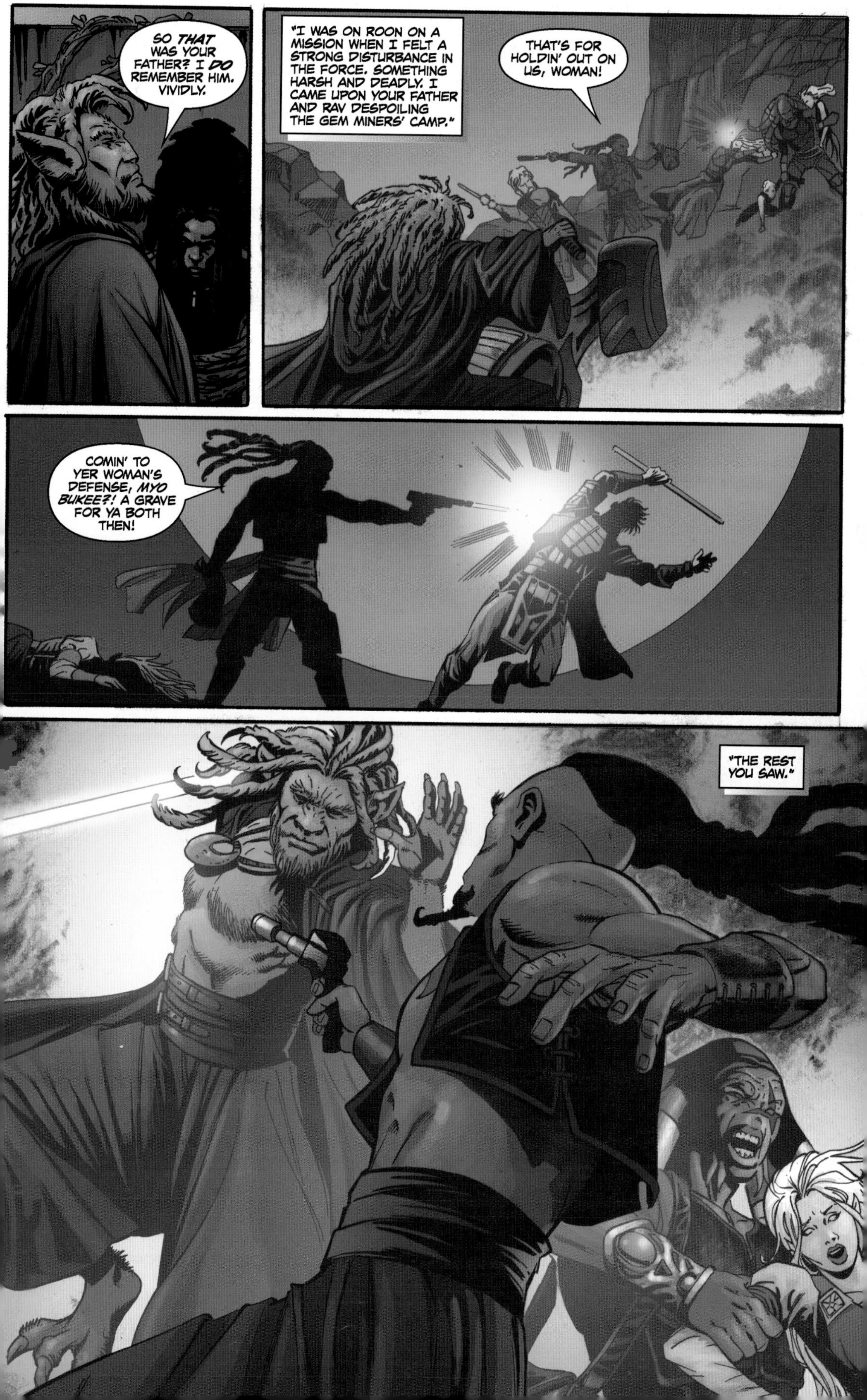
SO THAT WAS YOUR FATHER? I DO REMEMBER HIM. VIVIDLY.
"I WAS ON ROON ON A MISSION WHEN I FELT A STRONG DISTURBANCE IN THE FORCE. SOMETHING HARSH AND DEADLY. I CAME UPON YOUR FATHER AND RAV DESPOILING THE GEM MINERS' CAMP."
THAT'S FOR HOLDIN' OUT ON US, WOMAN!
COMIN' TO YER WOMAN'S DEFENSE, MYO BUKEE?! A GRAVE FOR YA BOTH THEN!
"THE REST YOU SAW."

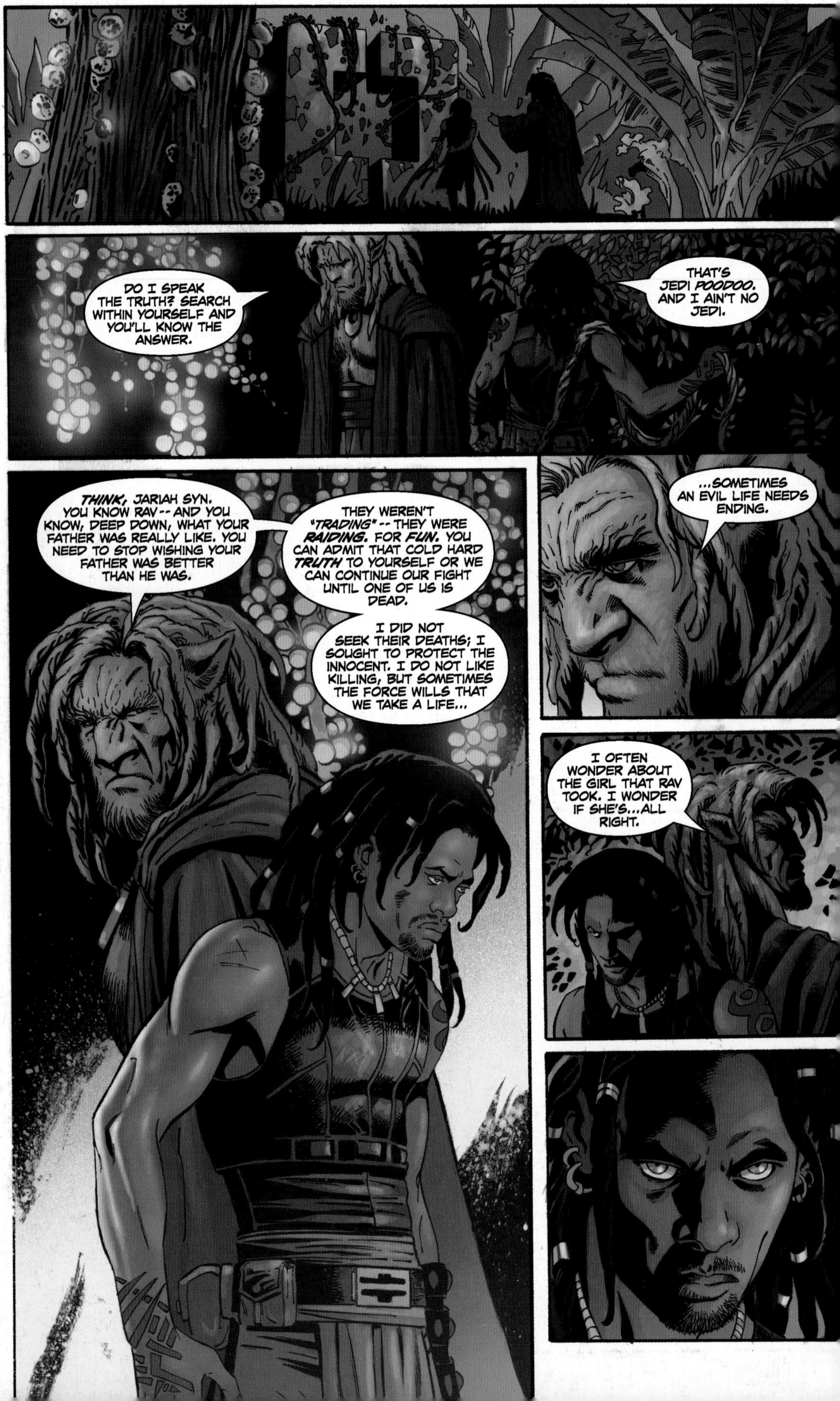
DO I SPEAK THE TRUTH? SEARCH WITHIN YOURSELF AND YOU'LL KNOW THE ANSWER.
THAT'S JEDI *POODOO*. AND I AIN'T NO JEDI.
THINK, JARIAH SYN. YOU KNOW RAV-- AND YOU KNOW, DEEP DOWN, WHAT YOUR FATHER WAS REALLY LIKE. YOU NEED TO STOP WISHING YOUR FATHER WAS BETTER THAN HE WAS.
THEY WEREN'T *"TRADING"* -- THEY WERE ***RAIDING.*** FOR ***FUN.*** YOU CAN ADMIT THAT COLD HARD ***TRUTH*** TO YOURSELF OR WE CAN CONTINUE OUR FIGHT UNTIL ONE OF US IS DEAD.
I DID NOT SEEK THEIR DEATHS; I SOUGHT TO PROTECT THE INNOCENT. I DO NOT LIKE KILLING, BUT SOMETIMES THE FORCE WILLS THAT WE TAKE A LIFE...
...SOMETIMES AN EVIL LIFE NEEDS ENDING.
I OFTEN WONDER ABOUT THE GIRL THAT RAV TOOK. I WONDER IF SHE'S...ALL RIGHT.

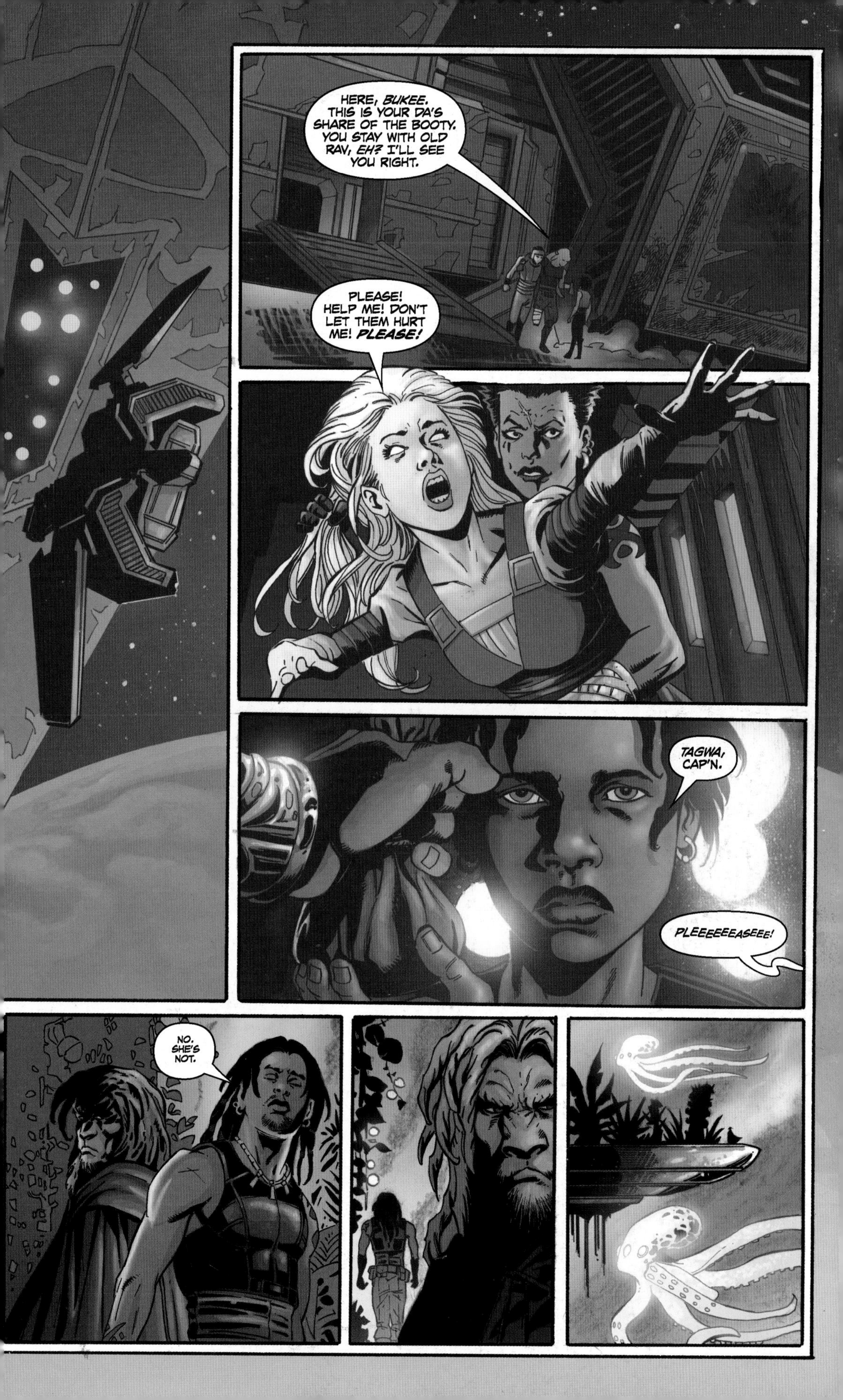
HERE, *BUKEE.* THIS IS YOUR DA'S SHARE OF THE BOOTY. YOU STAY WITH OLD RAV, *EH?* I'LL SEE YOU RIGHT.
PLEASE! HELP ME! DON'T LET THEM HURT ME! ***PLEASE!***
TAGWA, CAP'N.
PLEEEEEEASEEE!
NO. SHE'S NOT.

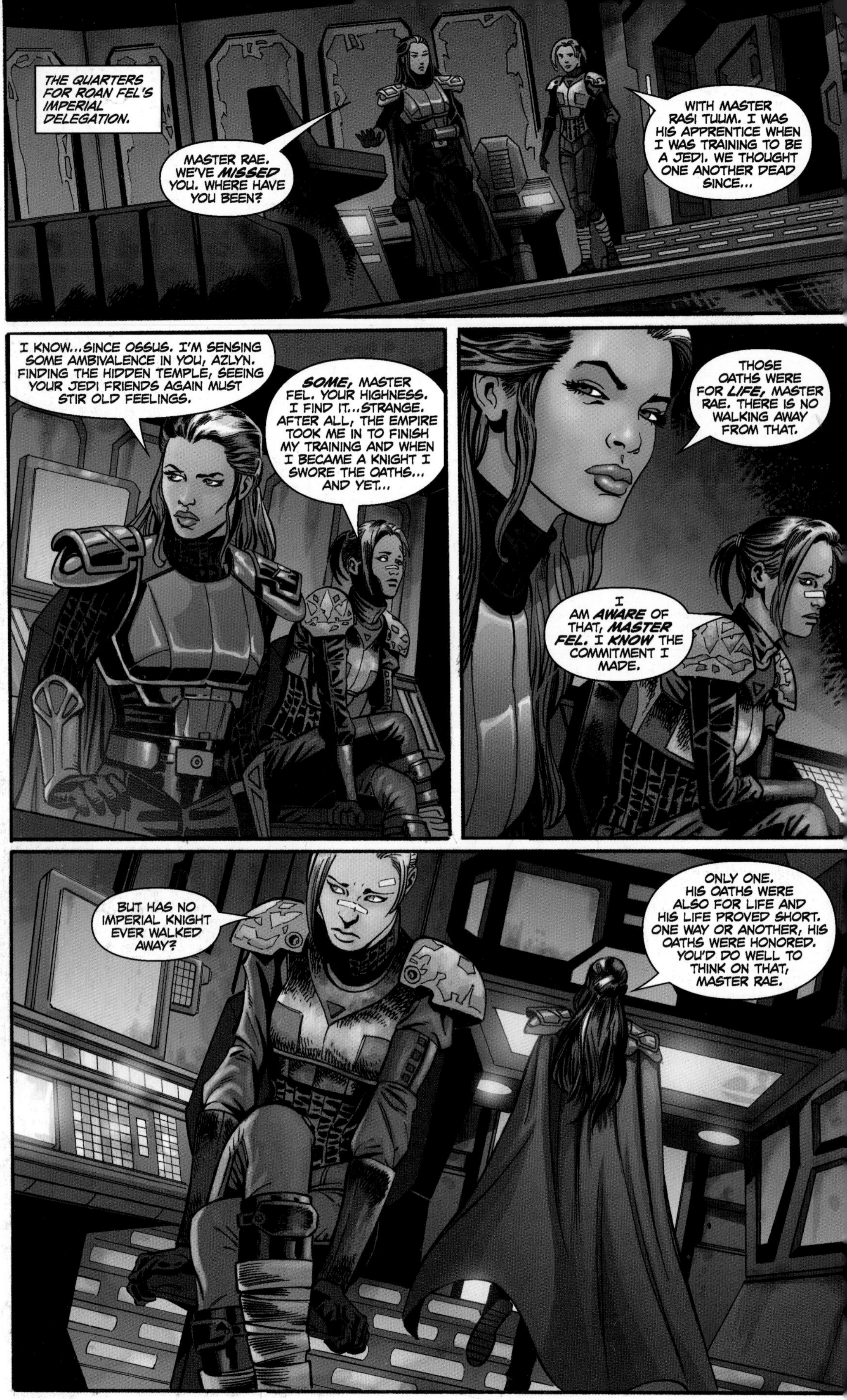
THE QUARTERS FOR ROAN FEL'S IMPERIAL DELEGATION.
MASTER RAE. WE'VE MISSED YOU. WHERE HAVE YOU BEEN?
WITH MASTER RASI TUUM. I WAS HIS APPRENTICE WHEN I WAS TRAINING TO BE A JEDI. WE THOUGHT ONE ANOTHER DEAD SINCE...
I KNOW...SINCE OSSUS. I'M SENSING SOME AMBIVALENCE IN YOU, AZLYN. FINDING THE HIDDEN TEMPLE, SEEING YOUR JEDI FRIENDS AGAIN MUST STIR OLD FEELINGS.
SOME, MASTER FEL. YOUR HIGHNESS. I FIND IT...STRANGE. AFTER ALL, THE EMPIRE TOOK ME IN TO FINISH MY TRAINING AND WHEN I BECAME A KNIGHT I SWORE THE OATHS... AND YET...
THOSE OATHS WERE FOR LIFE, MASTER RAE. THERE IS NO WALKING AWAY FROM THAT.
I AM AWARE OF THAT, MASTER FEL. I KNOW THE COMMITMENT I MADE.
BUT HAS NO IMPERIAL KNIGHT EVER WALKED AWAY?
ONLY ONE. HIS OATHS WERE ALSO FOR LIFE AND HIS LIFE PROVED SHORT. ONE WAY OR ANOTHER, HIS OATHS WERE HONORED. YOU'D DO WELL TO THINK ON THAT, MASTER RAE.

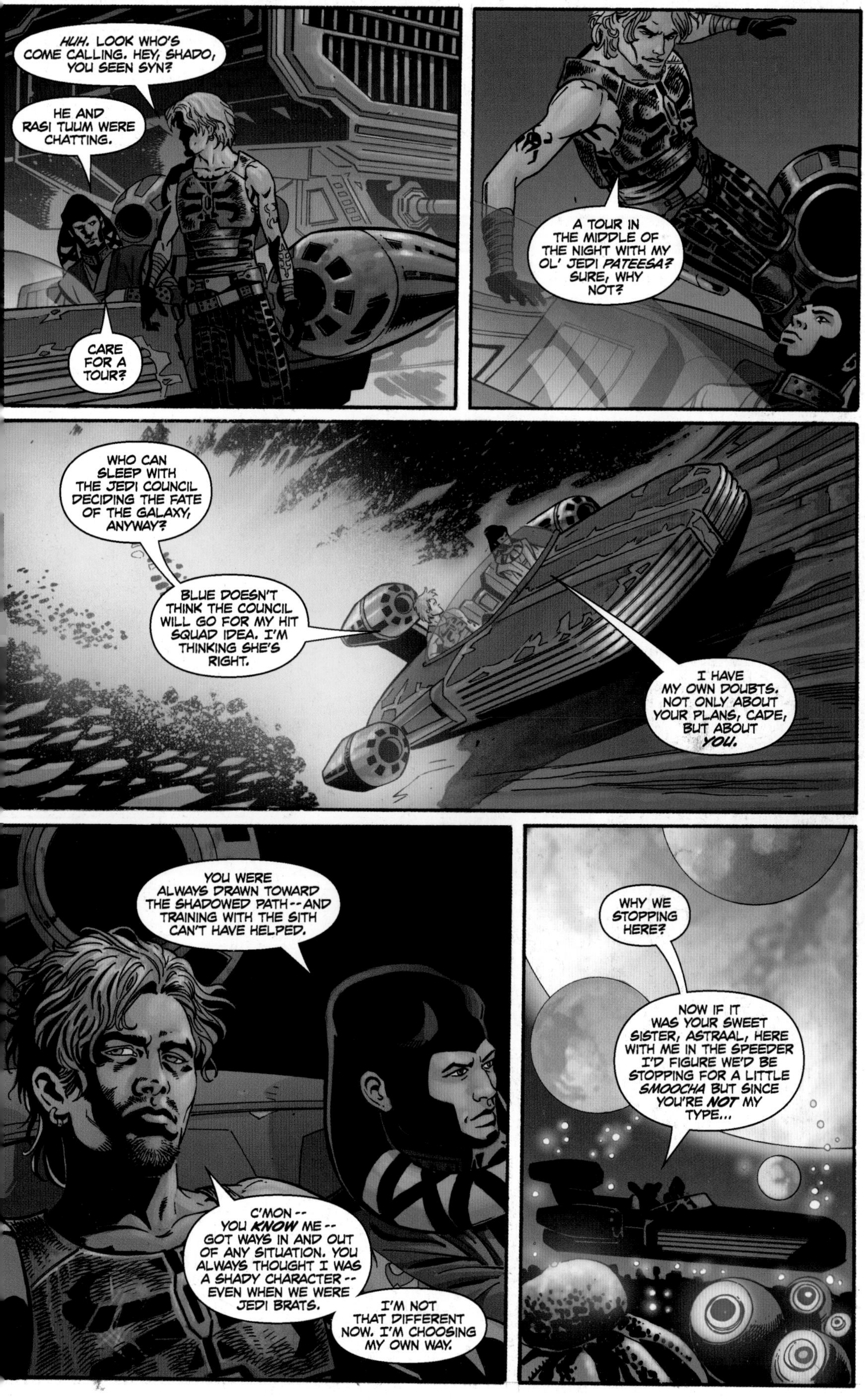
HUH. LOOK WHO'S COME CALLING. HEY, SHADO, YOU SEEN SYN?
HE AND RASI TUUM WERE CHATTING.
CARE FOR A TOUR?
A TOUR IN THE MIDDLE OF THE NIGHT WITH MY OL' JEDI PATEESA? SURE, WHY NOT?
WHO CAN SLEEP WITH THE JEDI COUNCIL DECIDING THE FATE OF THE GALAXY, ANYWAY?
BLUE DOESN'T THINK THE COUNCIL WILL GO FOR MY HIT SQUAD IDEA. I'M THINKING SHE'S RIGHT.
I HAVE MY OWN DOUBTS. NOT ONLY ABOUT YOUR PLANS, CADE, BUT ABOUT YOU.
YOU WERE ALWAYS DRAWN TOWARD THE SHADOWED PATH--AND TRAINING WITH THE SITH CAN'T HAVE HELPED.
C'MON -- YOU KNOW ME -- GOT WAYS IN AND OUT OF ANY SITUATION. YOU ALWAYS THOUGHT I WAS A SHADY CHARACTER -- EVEN WHEN WE WERE JEDI BRATS.
I'M NOT THAT DIFFERENT NOW. I'M CHOOSING MY OWN WAY.
WHY WE STOPPING HERE?
NOW IF IT WAS YOUR SWEET SISTER, ASTRAAL, HERE WITH ME IN THE SPEEDER I'D FIGURE WE'D BE STOPPING FOR A LITTLE SMOOCHA BUT SINCE YOU'RE NOT MY TYPE...

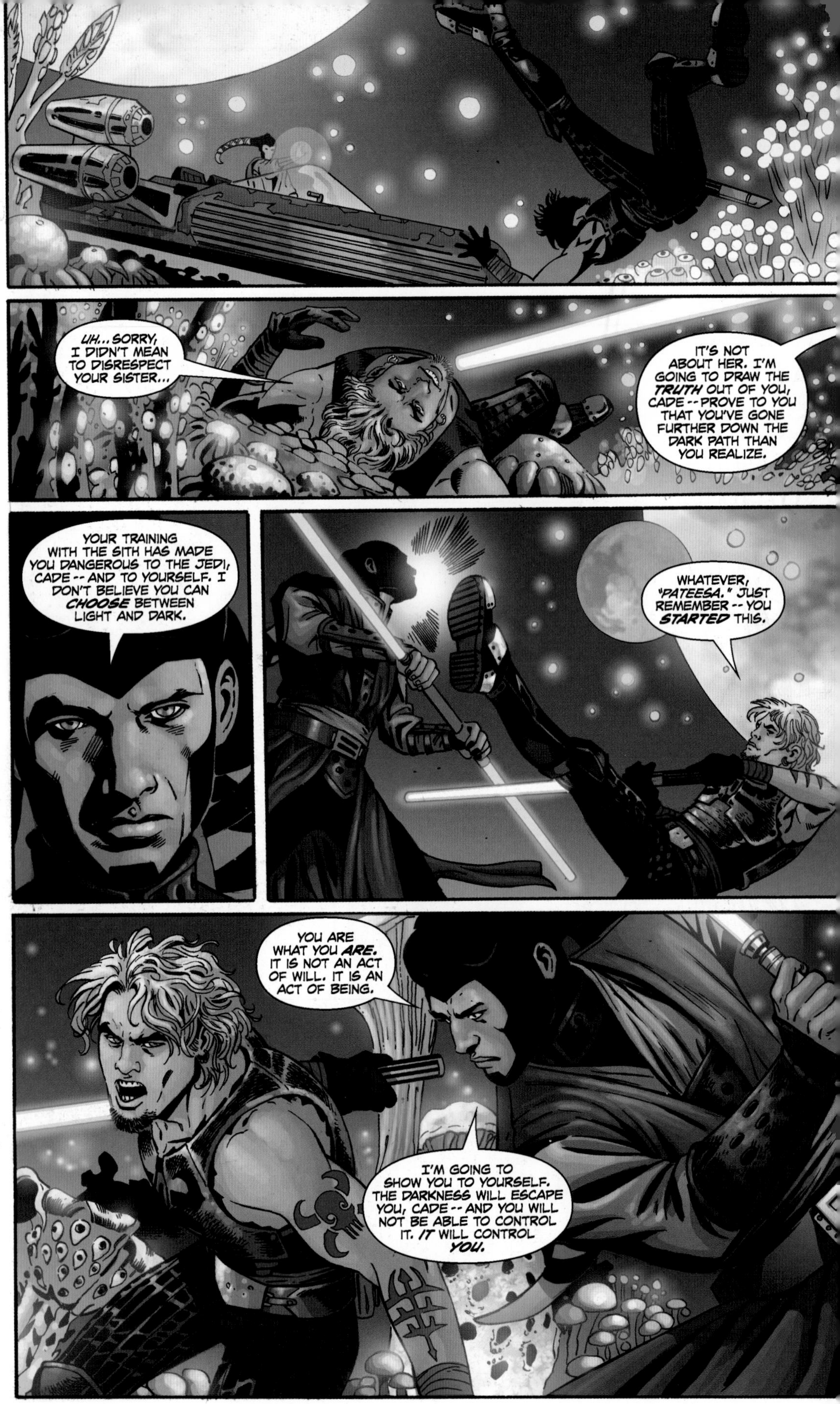
UH... SORRY, I DIDN'T MEAN TO DISRESPECT YOUR SISTER...
IT'S NOT ABOUT HER. I'M GOING TO DRAW THE TRUTH OUT OF YOU, CADE--PROVE TO YOU THAT YOU'VE GONE FURTHER DOWN THE DARK PATH THAN YOU REALIZE.
YOUR TRAINING WITH THE SITH HAS MADE YOU DANGEROUS TO THE JEDI, CADE--AND TO YOURSELF. I DON'T BELIEVE YOU CAN CHOOSE BETWEEN LIGHT AND DARK.
WHATEVER, "PATEESA." JUST REMEMBER--YOU STARTED THIS.
YOU ARE WHAT YOU ARE. IT IS NOT AN ACT OF WILL. IT IS AN ACT OF BEING.
I'M GOING TO SHOW YOU TO YOURSELF. THE DARKNESS WILL ESCAPE YOU, CADE--AND YOU WILL NOT BE ABLE TO CONTROL IT. IT WILL CONTROL YOU.

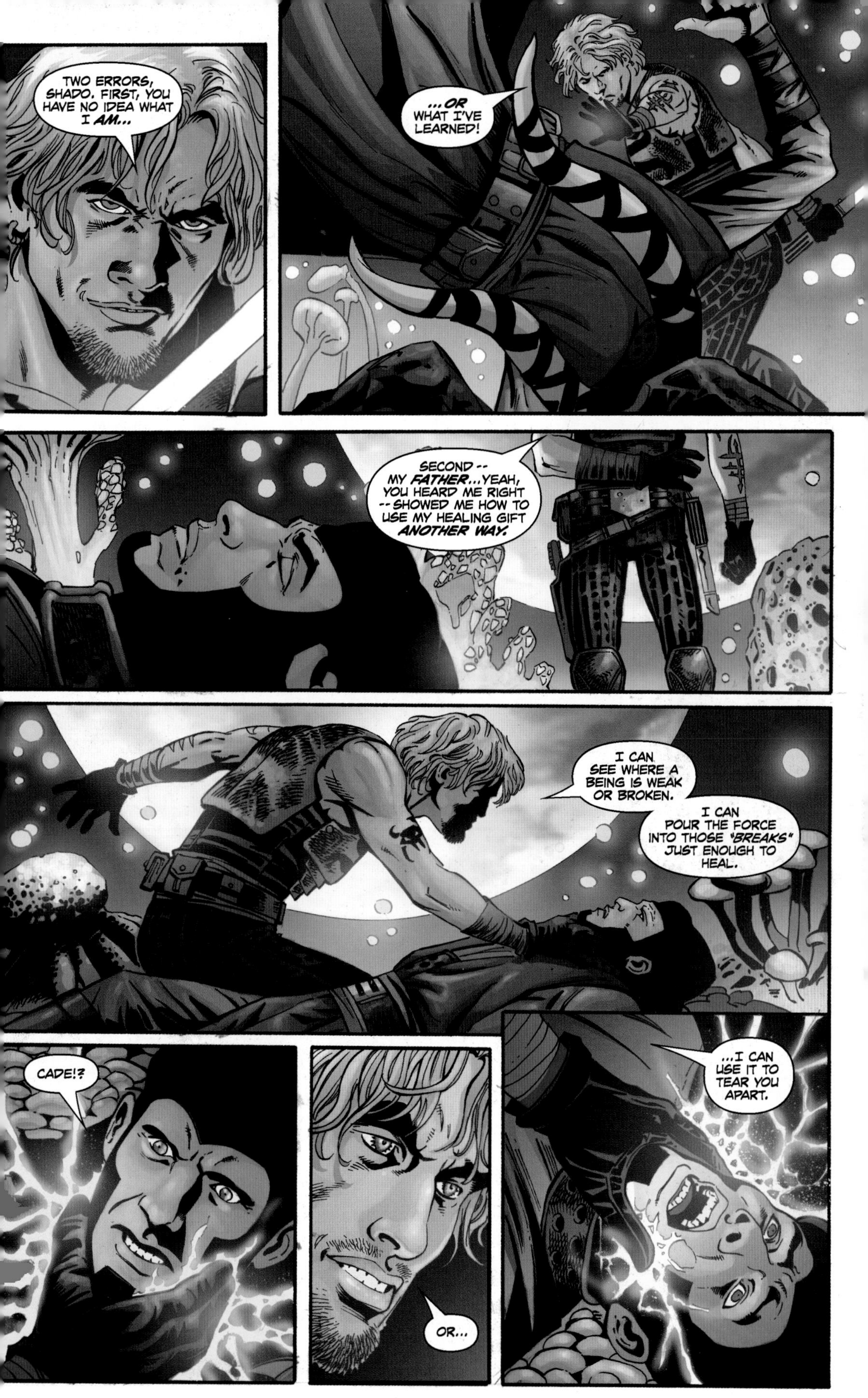
TWO ERRORS, SHADO. FIRST, YOU HAVE NO IDEA WHAT I AM...
...OR WHAT I'VE LEARNED!
SECOND -- MY FATHER...YEAH, YOU HEARD ME RIGHT -- SHOWED ME HOW TO USE MY HEALING GIFT ANOTHER WAY.
I CAN SEE WHERE A BEING IS WEAK OR BROKEN.
I CAN POUR THE FORCE INTO THOSE "BREAKS" JUST ENOUGH TO HEAL.
CADE!?
OR...
...I CAN USE IT TO TEAR YOU APART.

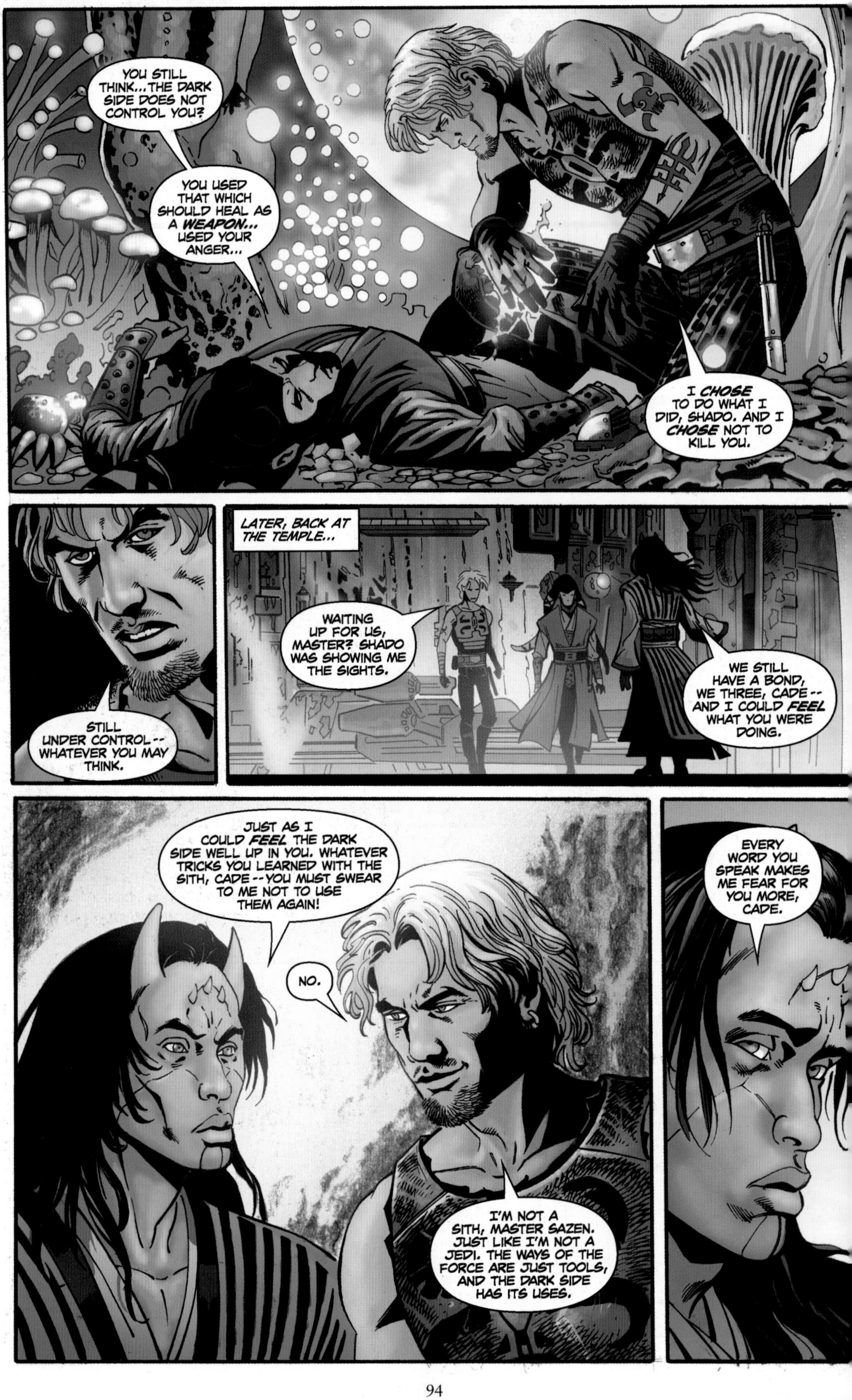
YOU STILL THINK... THE DARK SIDE DOES NOT CONTROL YOU?
YOU USED THAT WHICH SHOULD HEAL AS A *WEAPON...* USED YOUR ANGER...
I *CHOSE* TO DO WHAT I DID, SHADO. AND I *CHOSE* NOT TO KILL YOU.
STILL UNDER CONTROL -- WHATEVER YOU MAY THINK.
LATER, BACK AT THE TEMPLE...
WAITING UP FOR US, MASTER? SHADO WAS SHOWING ME THE SIGHTS.
WE STILL HAVE A BOND, WE THREE, CADE -- AND I COULD *FEEL* WHAT YOU WERE DOING.
JUST AS I COULD *FEEL* THE DARK SIDE WELL UP IN YOU. WHATEVER TRICKS YOU LEARNED WITH THE SITH, CADE -- YOU MUST SWEAR TO ME NOT TO USE THEM AGAIN!
NO.
I'M NOT A SITH, MASTER SAZEN. JUST LIKE I'M NOT A JEDI. THE WAYS OF THE FORCE ARE JUST TOOLS, AND THE DARK SIDE HAS ITS USES.
EVERY WORD YOU SPEAK MAKES ME FEAR FOR YOU MORE, CADE.

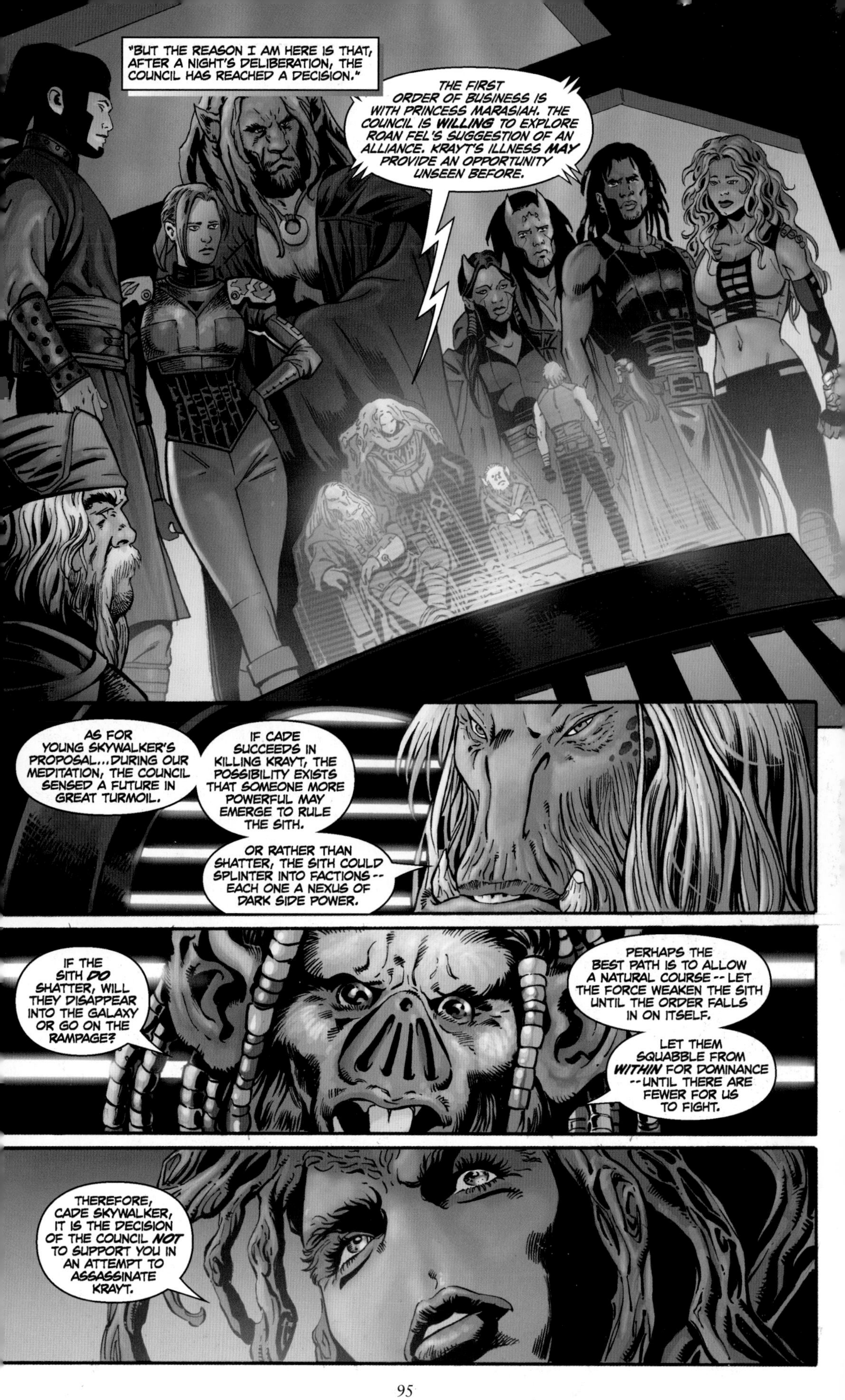
"BUT THE REASON I AM HERE IS THAT, AFTER A NIGHT'S DELIBERATION, THE COUNCIL HAS REACHED A DECISION."
THE FIRST ORDER OF BUSINESS IS WITH PRINCESS MARASIAH. THE COUNCIL IS WILLING TO EXPLORE ROAN FEL'S SUGGESTION OF AN ALLIANCE. KRAYT'S ILLNESS MAY PROVIDE AN OPPORTUNITY UNSEEN BEFORE.
AS FOR YOUNG SKYWALKER'S PROPOSAL... DURING OUR MEDITATION, THE COUNCIL SENSED A FUTURE IN GREAT TURMOIL.
IF CADE SUCCEEDS IN KILLING KRAYT, THE POSSIBILITY EXISTS THAT SOMEONE MORE POWERFUL MAY EMERGE TO RULE THE SITH.
OR RATHER THAN SHATTER, THE SITH COULD SPLINTER INTO FACTIONS -- EACH ONE A NEXUS OF DARK SIDE POWER.
IF THE SITH DO SHATTER, WILL THEY DISAPPEAR INTO THE GALAXY OR GO ON THE RAMPAGE?
PERHAPS THE BEST PATH IS TO ALLOW A NATURAL COURSE -- LET THE FORCE WEAKEN THE SITH UNTIL THE ORDER FALLS IN ON ITSELF.
LET THEM SQUABBLE FROM WITHIN FOR DOMINANCE -- UNTIL THERE ARE FEWER FOR US TO FIGHT.
THEREFORE, CADE SKYWALKER, IT IS THE DECISION OF THE COUNCIL NOT TO SUPPORT YOU IN AN ATTEMPT TO ASSASSINATE KRAYT.

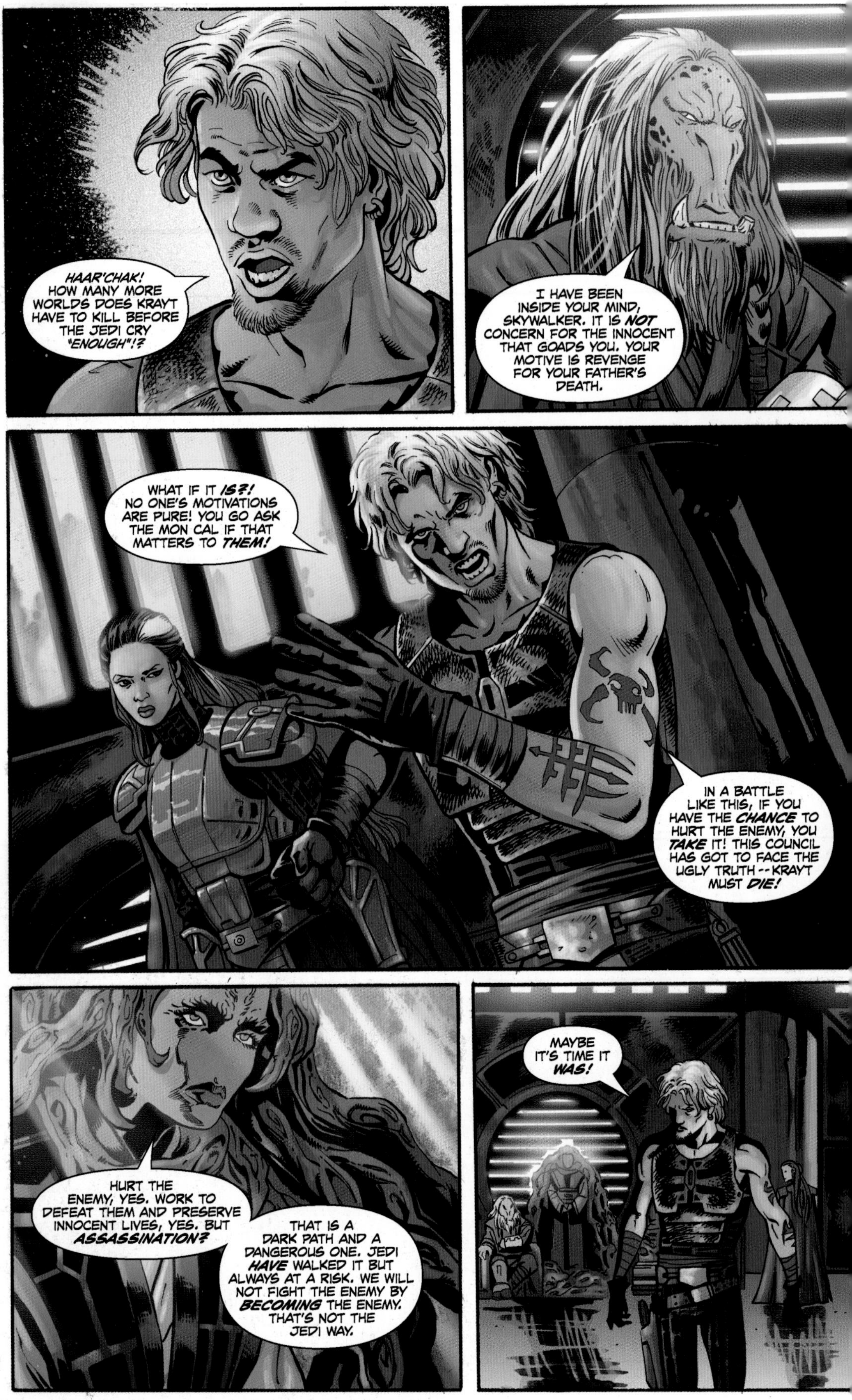
HAAR'CHAK! HOW MANY MORE WORLDS DOES KRAYT HAVE TO KILL BEFORE THE JEDI CRY "ENOUGH"!?
I HAVE BEEN INSIDE YOUR MIND, SKYWALKER. IT IS NOT CONCERN FOR THE INNOCENT THAT GOADS YOU. YOUR MOTIVE IS REVENGE FOR YOUR FATHER'S DEATH.
WHAT IF IT IS?! NO ONE'S MOTIVATIONS ARE PURE! YOU GO ASK THE MON CAL IF THAT MATTERS TO THEM!
IN A BATTLE LIKE THIS, IF YOU HAVE THE CHANCE TO HURT THE ENEMY, YOU TAKE IT! THIS COUNCIL HAS GOT TO FACE THE UGLY TRUTH--KRAYT MUST DIE!
HURT THE ENEMY, YES. WORK TO DEFEAT THEM AND PRESERVE INNOCENT LIVES, YES. BUT ASSASSINATION?
THAT IS A DARK PATH AND A DANGEROUS ONE. JEDI HAVE WALKED IT BUT ALWAYS AT A RISK. WE WILL NOT FIGHT THE ENEMY BY BECOMING THE ENEMY. THAT'S NOT THE JEDI WAY.
MAYBE IT'S TIME IT WAS!

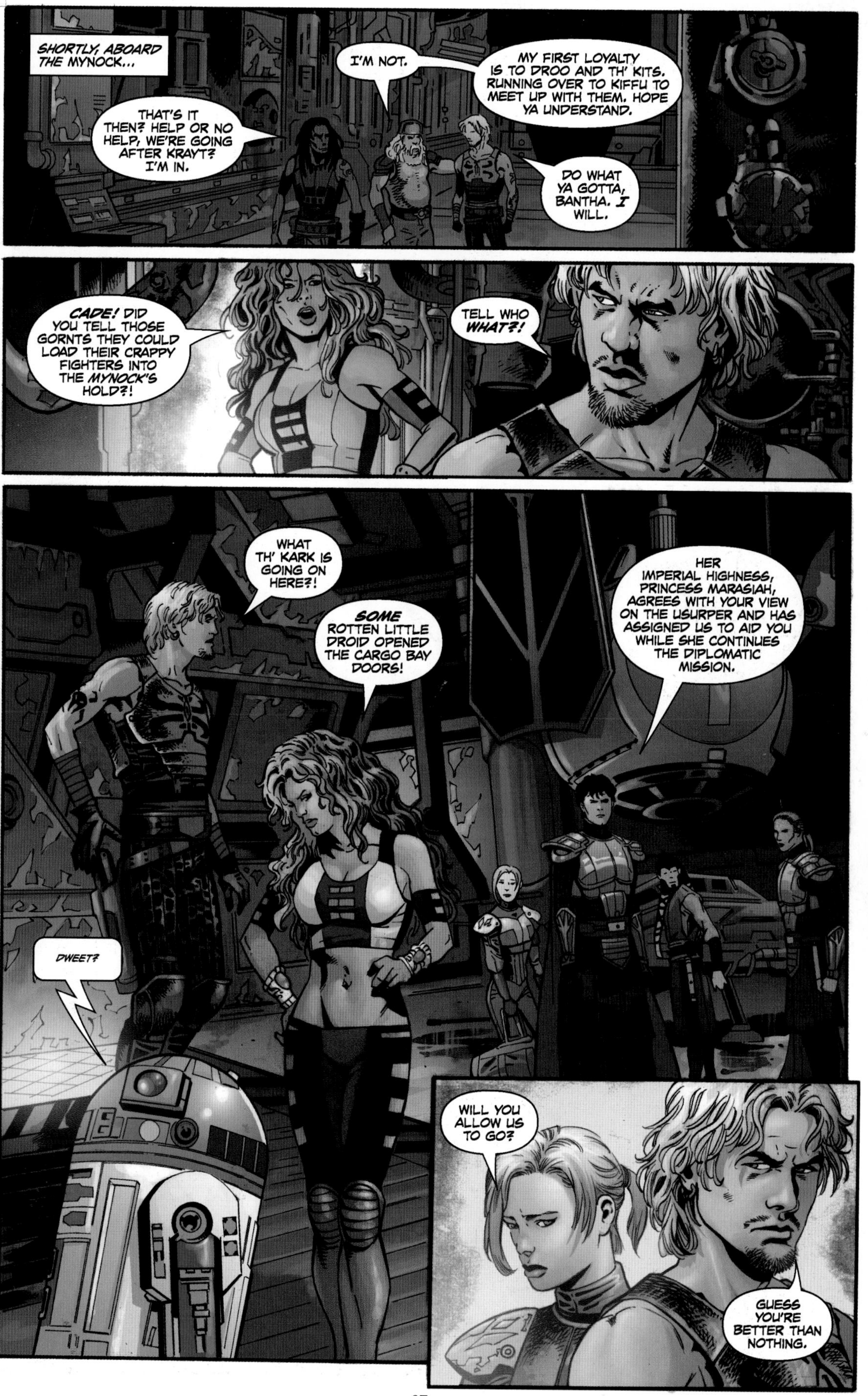
SHORTLY, ABOARD THE MYNOCK...
THAT'S IT THEN? HELP OR NO HELP, WE'RE GOING AFTER KRAYT? I'M IN.
I'M NOT.
MY FIRST LOYALTY IS TO DROO AND TH' KITS. RUNNING OVER TO KIFFU TO MEET UP WITH THEM. HOPE YA UNDERSTAND.
DO WHAT YA GOTTA, BANTHA. I WILL.
CADE! DID YOU TELL THOSE GORNTS THEY COULD LOAD THEIR CRAPPY FIGHTERS INTO THE MYNOCK'S HOLD?!
TELL WHO WHAT?!
WHAT TH' KARK IS GOING ON HERE?!
SOME ROTTEN LITTLE DROID OPENED THE CARGO BAY DOORS!
HER IMPERIAL HIGHNESS, PRINCESS MARASIAH, AGREES WITH YOUR VIEW ON THE USURPER AND HAS ASSIGNED US TO AID YOU WHILE SHE CONTINUES THE DIPLOMATIC MISSION.
DWEET?
WILL YOU ALLOW US TO GO?
GUESS YOU'RE BETTER THAN NOTHING.

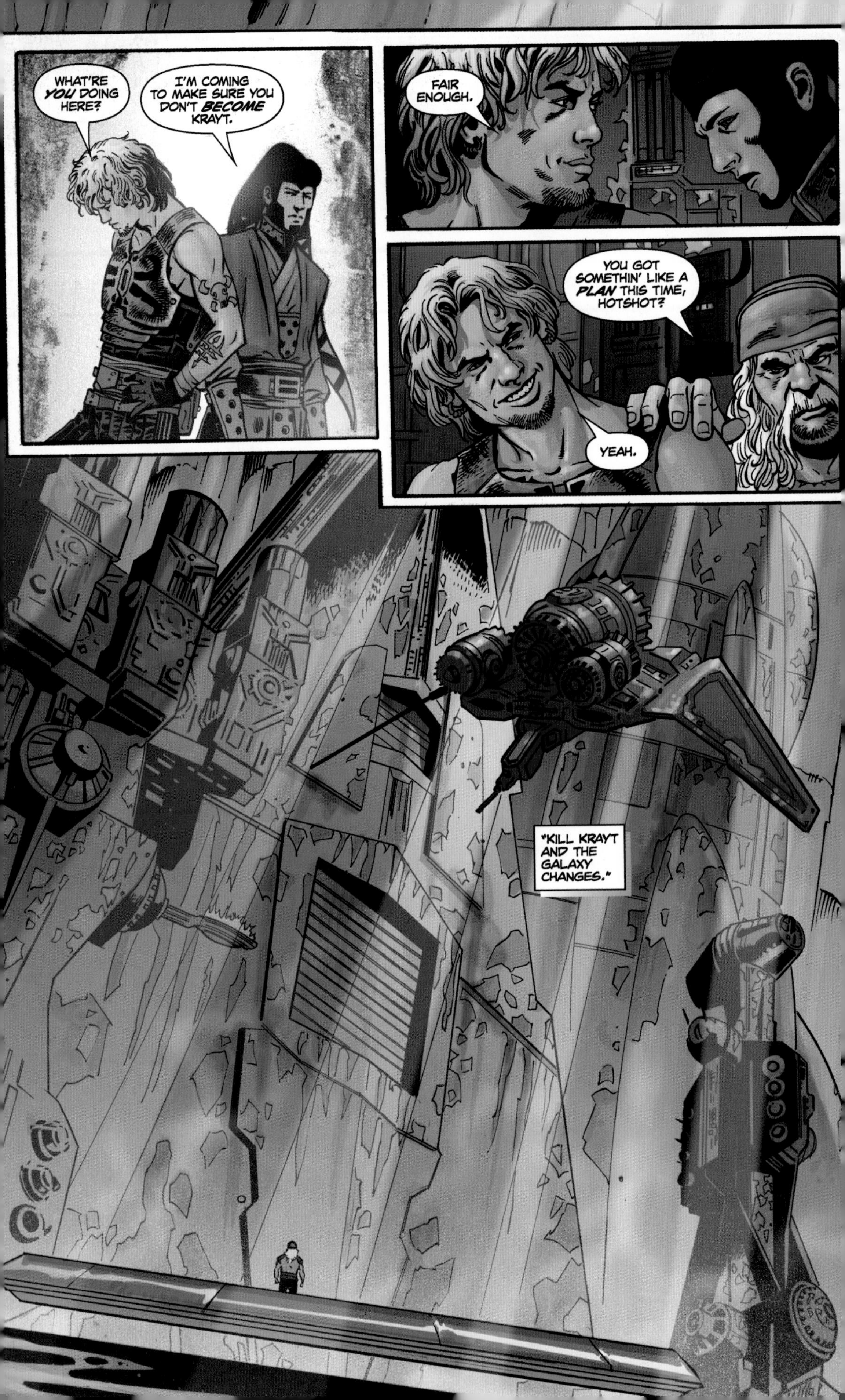
WHAT'RE YOU DOING HERE?
I'M COMING TO MAKE SURE YOU DON'T BECOME KRAYT.
FAIR ENOUGH.
YOU GOT SOMETHIN' LIKE A PLAN THIS TIME, HOTSHOT?
YEAH.
"KILL KRAYT AND THE GALAXY CHANGES."

HUTTESE
GLOSSARY

bukee: boy

cheeka: woman

dopa-meekie: double-crossing

gornt: domesticated omnivorous creature, raised for meat

haar'chak: Mando'a expletive

kark: derogatory expletive

karking: derogatory modifier

keepuna: (exclamation) shoot; darn

murglak: derogatory spacer term

pateesa: friend; sweetie; darling

patogga: pie

sleemo: slimeball

tagwa: yes

wermo: stupid person; idiot; worm; slang: boy

"**Cha skrunee da pat, sleemo.**": Don't count on it, slimeball.

"**Me yarga! Me chuga!**": I'm hungry! I'm thirsty!

"**Uma ji muna.**": I love you.

STAR WARS GRAPHIC NOVEL TIMELINE (IN YEARS)

Tales of the Jedi—5,000–3,986 BSW4
Knights of the Old Republic—3,964–3,963 BSW4
Jedi vs. Sith—1,000 BSW4
Jedi Council: Acts of War—33 BSW4
Prelude to Rebellion—33 BSW4
Darth Maul—33 BSW4
Episode I: The Phantom Menace—32 BSW4
Outlander—32 BSW4
Emissaries to Malastare—32 BSW4
Jango Fett: Open Seasons—32 BSW4
Twilight—31 BSW4
Bounty Hunters—31 BSW4
The Hunt for Aurra Sing—30 BSW4
Darkness—30 BSW4
The Stark Hyperspace War—30 BSW4
Rite of Passage—28 BSW4
Jango Fett—27 BSW4
Zam Wesell—27 BSW4
Honor and Duty—24 BSW4
Episode II: Attack of the Clones—22 BSW4
Clone Wars—22–19 BSW4
Clone Wars Adventures—22–19 BSW4
General Grievous—22–19 BSW4
Episode III: Revenge of the Sith—19 BSW4
Dark Times—19 BSW4
Droids—5.5 BSW4
Boba Fett: Enemy of the Empire—3 BSW4
Underworld—1 BSW4
Episode IV: A New Hope—SW4
Classic Star Wars—0–3 ASW4
A Long Time Ago . . . —0–4 ASW4
Empire—0 ASW4
Rebellion—0 ASW4
Vader's Quest—0 ASW4
Boba Fett: Man with a Mission—0 ASW4
Jabba the Hutt: The Art of the Deal—1 ASW4
The Force Unleashed—2 ASW4
Splinter of the Mind's Eye—2 ASW4
Episode V: The Empire Strikes Back—3 ASW4
Shadows of the Empire—3.5 ASW4
Episode VI: Return of the Jedi—4 ASW4
X-Wing Rogue Squadron—4–5 ASW4
Mara Jade: By the Emperor's Hand—4 ASW4
Heir to the Empire—9 ASW4
Dark Force Rising—9 ASW4
The Last Command—9 ASW4
Dark Empire—10 ASW4
Boba Fett: Death, Lies, and Treachery—10 ASW4
Crimson Empire—11 ASW4
Jedi Academy: Leviathan—12 ASW4
Union—19 ASW4
Chewbacca—25 ASW4
Legacy—130–137 ASW4

Old Republic Era
25,000 – 1000 years before
Star Wars: A New Hope

Rise of the Empire Era
1000 – 0 years before
Star Wars: A New Hope

Rebellion Era
0 – 5 years after
Star Wars: A New Hope

New Republic Era
5 – 25 years after
Star Wars: A New Hope

New Jedi Order Era
25+ years after
Star Wars: A New Hope

Legacy Era
130+ years after
Star Wars: A New Hope

Infinities
Does not apply to timeline

Sergio Aragonés Stomps Star Wars
Star Wars Tales
Star Wars Infinities
Tag and Bink
Star Wars Visionaries

BSW4 = before *Episode IV: A New Hope*. ASW4 = after *Episode IV: A New Hope*.

STAR WARS® VECTOR

An event with repercussions for every era and every hero in the *Star Wars* galaxy begins here! For anyone who never knew where to start with *Star Wars* comics, *Vector* is the perfect introduction to the entire *Star Wars* line! For any serious *Star Wars* fan, *Vector* is a must-see event with major happenings throughout the most important moments of the galaxy's history!

VOLUME ONE
(*Knights of the Old Republic* Vol. 5; *Dark Times* Vol. 3)
ISBN 978-1-59582-226-0 | $17.95

VOLUME TWO
(*Rebellion* Vol. 4; *Legacy* Vol. 6)
ISBN 978-1-59582-227-7 | $17.95

KNIGHTS OF THE OLD REPUBLIC

Volume One: Commencement
ISBN 978-1-59307-640-5 | $18.95

Volume Two: Flashpoint
ISBN 978-1-59307-761-7 | $18.95

Volume Three: Days of Fear, Nights of Anger
ISBN 978-1-59307-867-6 | $18.95

Volume Four: Daze of Hate, Knights of Suffering
ISBN 978-1-59582-208-6 | $18.95

REBELLION

Volume One: My Brother, My Enemy
ISBN 978-1-59307-711-2 | $14.95

Volume Two: The Ahakista Gambit
ISBN 978-1-59307-890-4 | $17.95

Volume Three: Small Victories
ISBN 978-1-59582-166-9 | $12.95

LEGACY

Volume One: Broken
ISBN 978-1-59307-716-7 | $17.95

Volume Two: Shards
ISBN 978-1-59307-879-9 | $19.95

Volume Three: Claws of the Dragon
ISBN 978-1-59307-946-8 | $17.95

Volume Four: Alliance
ISBN 978-1-59582-223-9 | $15.95

Volume Five: The Hidden Temple
ISBN 978-1-59582-224-6 | $15.95

DARK TIMES

Volume One: The Path to Nowhere
ISBN 978-1-59307-792-1 | $17.95

Volume Two: Parallels
ISBN 978-1-59307-945-1 | $17.95

www.darkhorse.com

AVAILABLE AT YOUR LOCAL COMICS SHOP OR BOOKSTORE.
TO FIND A COMICS SHOP IN YOUR AREA, CALL 1-888-266-4226
For more information or to order direct: On the web: darkhorse.com
E-mail: mailorder@darkhorse.com • Phone: 1-800-862-0052 Mon.–Fri.
9 A.M. to 5 P.M. Pacific Time. STAR WARS © 2004–2008 Lucasfilm Ltd. & ™ (BL8005)

DARK HORSE BOOKS